Ethics and Public Policy

METHOD AND CASES

William T. Bluhm
The University of Rochester

Robert A. Heineman
Alfred University

Upper Saddle River, New Jersey 07458

Library of Congress Cataloging-in-Publication Data
Bluhm, William Theodore
Ethics and public policy: method and cases / by William T. Bluhm
  and Robert A. Heineman.
p. cm.
Includes index.
ISBN-13: 978-0-13-189343-6 (pbk.)
ISBN-10: 0-13-189343-2 (pbk.)
1. Public administration—Moral and ethical aspects.   2. Public administration—
United States.   3. Political ethics—United States.
I. Heineman, Robert A.   II. Title.
JF1525.E8B58 2007
172´.2—dc22   2006016907

Editorial Director: Charlyce Jones Owen
Executive Editor: Dickson Musslewhite
Associate Editor: Rob DeGeorge
Editorial Assistant: Jennifer Murphy
Director of Marketing: Brandy Dawson
Marketing Manager: Emily Cleary
Marketing Assistant: Jennifer Lang
Senior Managing Editor: Lisa Iarkowski
Production Liaison: Fran Russello
Manufacturing Buyer: Mary Ann Gloriande
Cover Design: Kiwi Design
Composition/Full-Service Project Management: Babitha Balan/GGS Book Services
Printer/Binder: RR Donnelley & Sons Company

Credits and acknowledgments borrowed from other sources and reproduced, with
permission, in this textbook appear on appropriate page within text.

Pearson Prentice Hall™ is a trademark of Pearson Education, Inc.
Pearson® is a registered trademark of Pearson plc
Prentice Hall® is a registered trademark of Pearson Education, Inc.

Pearson Education LTD. London   Pearson Education North Asia Ltd
Pearson Education Singapore, Pte. Ltd   Pearson Educación de Mexico, S.A. de C.V.
Pearson Education, Canada, Ltd   Pearson Education Malaysia, Pte. Ltd
Pearson Education–Japan   Pearson Education, Upper Saddle River,
Pearson Education Australia PTY,   New Jersey
  Limited

10 9 8 7 6 5 4 3 2 1
ISBN: 0-13-189343-2

For Elly and Alice

CONTENTS

PREFACE

Democratic policymaking moves on an endless belt. Representatives formulate proposals in response to sensed public need and to the demands of citizens and pressure groups. Analysts refine these proposals into detailed legislative and administrative drafts. The bargaining processes of our many-faceted political system swirl and tumble about society's myriad special pleadings until they produce something that can be taken for a general will. The generality of that will (the extent of its acceptance) depends on the adequate working of our arrangements for circulating information, judgments, and feelings about proposals from grass roots to officials and back again, for the duration of the legislative process. After legislation has been implemented and has had its impact on the world, the process begins all over again. Policy analysis thus involves citizens, professional analysts, and elected and administrative officials in an elaborate and endless process of deliberation.

As politicians declare what it is that The People need and want, individual citizens who comprise that People need to be self-consciously involved in the public scrutiny of political pronouncements. Reason requires the establishment of a just proportion between ends and means. Ethical choice requires measuring both ends and means by a public code of good and right. This book is intended as an aid to reasoned and ethical public choice and to policy evaluation. It is addressed to citizens, to students of public policy, to policy analysts, and to elected officials. We hope that our work will show that ethical reasoning and public policymaking can and must come together in effective democratic decisions.

ACKNOWLEDGMENTS

We would like to thank David L. Weimer, Hank Jenkins-Smith, and Tim Madigan for their advice, guidance, and encouragement in the development and publication of this book. We are also grateful to James Johnson for bibliographical suggestions for chapter 5. Thanks are also due to the Department of Community and Preventive Medicine and the Department of Humanities in Medicine of the Medical School of the University of Rochester, and to the Department of Political Science of the University of Rochester for the opportunity to develop a course in ethics and public policy, from which grew the idea of this book. We are also grateful to the reference librarians of Rush Rhees Library, especially Alan Unsworth, and to Francis R. McBride of the Herrick Memorial Library, for their patient help in running down references. We thank also all the editors at Prentice-Hall and at GGS Book Services for their expert work in the production of the book. Thanks also to the readers who recommended the book for publication, and for their many useful suggestions for its improvement.

WTB & RAH

PART ONE

AMERICAN VALUES, ETHICAL ANALYSIS, AND DEMOCRATIC PROCESS

CHAPTER 1

Introduction

The words *moral* and *ethical* are used interchangeably in everyday parlance to refer to the goodness and badness of human actions. *Moral* also has a second meaning—to be *free*. Unless our wills are mechanically determined (in which case they are not really *wills*), every human choice is a moral choice. Moral freedom makes it possible for us to make ethical (or unethical) choices when we have a public standard of *good* or *right* in view.

Most of our actions affect others as well as ourselves, because we live in society, not as isolated individuals. We are *social*, if not always *sociable*. Even deciding whether to brush one's teeth when in a hurry to keep an appointment can affect others. Individual choices almost always have social consequences. John Stuart Mill set up a false dichotomy when he defined individual liberty in terms of self-regarding and other-regarding acts. In more modern parlance, whether preferences are self-interested or altruistic, their expression has a social impact.

Some of our choices are for groups as well as for ourselves as individuals, and by definition these choices have social consequences. This is so whenever we participate in an election—be it for the officers of a condominium association, of a labor union, or for congressional representatives. We also choose for a group when we vote a school budget up or down, or if we take part in a referendum on state policy.

ETHICS AND POLICYMAKING

Policy analysts usually take values as given, as quantifiable, and as capable of being served by calculations of costs and benefits. Research shows, however, that values and norms are in fact variable, situation dependent, and often in conflict. Specific goal values are, in fact, an output rather than an input of analysis. Moral discourse and deliberation that lead to value choice are, therefore, at the heart of policymaking.

Our purpose in this book is to help citizens, policy analysts, and public officials carry on an ethical deliberation about policy issues in a systematic way. The book also presents a method for exercising ethical judgment in specific issue areas. We recognize, of course, that no analytical method is sufficient for any ethical decision if the policymaker is not a prudent person. Only good character can profit from technical advice. Our focus, however, will not be on such matters as lying, whistle-blowing, leaking, resigning, or other such matters of personal integrity. These things have received careful scholarly treatment elsewhere. (See, e.g., Tong 1986; Bok 1979; French 1983; Hirschman 1970; Weimer and Vining 1999.)

Our chief focus will be on the ethical substance of alternative policies when dealing with the pressing issues of our time. There can be dilemmas enough when a problem is familiar and the norms to be applied are clear. But in a period of rapid technological change, we are faced with ethical quandaries that are entirely new. What ethical resources does our culture have for dealing with questions that arise from our new ability, for example, to manipulate genes, both human and animal? How do we extend established principles and maxims to wholly new situations? How do we decide whether cloning human beings is ethical, since the capability of doing this is entirely new? To what, for example, in the realm of traditional ethical discourse is cloning analogous? In a time when medicine has made it almost possible to extend life indefinitely, how do we distinguish between killing and letting die? Now that a large number of human organs can successfully be transferred from person to person, is it ethical to permit a market in body parts? Can there be a just war in an era when nuclear weapons are available? In a time of globalization, what is an ethical approach to dealing with global terrorism? These are the kinds of dilemmas that *must* be systematically and conscientiously pondered. Whether we do this or not, the wheels of policy will grind on, and decisions will be made. Society will have to live with the consequences.

OVERVIEW

In Part One we present a look at the American political culture—its core values, value conflicts, and the manner in which values alter in weight with changing circumstances. (September 11, for example, marks a point of dramatic change in the hierarchy of American values and norms.) We follow this examination with a critique of the typical methods of ethical analysis—Kantianism (deontology), utilitarianism (consequentialism), and prudent pragmatism, each of which has played an important role in American political thinking. We then give reasons for our view that prudent pragmatism, a systematic case method, is superior to the others in the ethical formulation of public policy. Next we consider how prudent pragmatism, as casuistry, arose in a monist society, the role it played there, and how it has been adapted to our pluralist world. We then canvass the nature of a participatory and deliberative democracy, the character of policy analysis in such a society, and the roles played by citizen, expert, and legislator.

Part Two contains a collection of cases in leading policy areas: public health, criminal justice, medical technology, environmental conservation, and others. We introduce each issue area and each case with a historical background statement. There follows a thick description of the case in hand. (For example, in dealing with public healthcare as a policy area, we present a brief history of the federal and state public health systems. Turning then to the issue of controlling tobacco as a hazardous substance, we discuss the history of federal legislation in this field, followed by a contemporary case about corporate and individual responsibility in the production and use of cigarettes.) In each case study we ask the reader to compare the strengths and weaknesses of three schools of ethical analysis—utilitarianism, deontological (contractual) ethics, and prudent pragmatism—in dealing with the moral issues at hand.

In the conclusion we summarize the characteristics of American values and the special problems of ethical policy choice for our times. We ask whether there are any universal values available, and if so, how they can be related to the American value consensus.

REFERENCES

Bok, Sissela. *Lying: Moral Choice in Public and Private Life*. New York: Vintage Books, 1979.

French, Peter A. *Ethics in Government*. Englewood Cliffs, NJ: Prentice Hall, Inc., 1983.

Hirschman, Albert. *Exit, Voice, and Loyalty: Responses to Decline in Firms, Organizations, and States*. Cambridge, MA: Harvard University Press, 1970.

Tong, Rosemarie. *Ethics in Policy Analysis*. Englewood Cliffs, NJ: Prentice Hall, Inc., 1986.

Weimer, David L., and Aidan R. Vining. *Policy Analysis: Concepts and Practice*, 3rd ed., Upper Saddle River, NJ: Prentice Hall, 1999.

CHAPTER 2

American Political Culture: Core Values

I n order to do policy analysis from an ethical perspective, we need to understand our shared public values. These values are the raw material of the enterprise of public policy; they are the things that give American political culture its special flavor.

FIVE VALUE CLUSTERS

The contemporary stream of American political culture has been fed by many and diverse currents. The major tributary was, of course, English, especially the constitutionalist thought of the seventeenth century as well as the long tradition of English common law and English liberties. Puritan theology and political theory also put a stamp on American culture that is clearly noticeable today. French Enlightenment thought, along with aspects of French Revolutionary ideas, played a role in shaping the American mind. In the first part of the nineteenth century, German idealism, a school of philosophy opposed to Enlightenment rationalism and materialism, made an important contribution. The thoughts of Immanuel Kant and Georg Friedrich Hegel have been especially influential. The circumstances of American life and political events determined both how particular elements were selected out of these various intellectual currents and how they blended with one another to form a new, specifically American, liberal democratic culture.

The Individual: The Politics of Interest

Individuals endowed with rights stand at the center of the American value system. In the Declaration of Independence these rights appear as the rights to life, liberty, and the pursuit of happiness. (In an early draft Jefferson wrote, "life, liberty, and property," a more Lockean formula.) All persons are understood to enjoy these rights equally as the gift of a benevolent God in a precivil state. But the state of nature is a vulnerable one, and it exists without a judge to settle disputes or an armed force to restrain the violent. Such a state must, therefore, be abandoned in favor of civil society, which comes into being by contract among free and independent persons. This was a powerful and attractive myth, because the divinely given rights of Locke and Jefferson corresponded perfectly to the fundamental desires of the colonists. (See Goldwin in Caplan and Callahan 1981, 117ff.)

There are no natural obligations according to this theory. By nature, persons have only rights. (See Goldwin in Caplan and Callahan.) Obligations are defined by laws that natural persons agree to after having signed the social contract. The purpose of these laws is to protect rights, especially the rights to life, liberty, and property, and to provide for the common defense. The contractors acquire property by mixing their labor with wild nature, and by law all citizens are bound to respect this private property. Obligations can be altered only by the consent of the governed, either by constitutional amendment or by legislation within the parameters of the original contract, the constitution.

Lockean language about natural rights, the state of nature, and the social contract was common currency among the American colonists who adopted the Declaration of Independence and the federal Constitution. (See Brown 2001, 1–14.) It was a language that seemed to fit the conditions of their life in the new world, which appeared as a true state of nature. A vast wilderness, inhabited only by small bands of Indians who lived principally by hunting, trapping, and fishing—and who practiced only a subsistence agriculture—it was ready to be marked off in tracts and appropriated as private property by the white settlers. Land was sometimes purchased from Indian communities whose inhabitants had no understanding of English concepts of property, and sometimes it was simply appropriated. Colonial property rights thus came into being, and with them contracts of government to protect them. In the background, as a surrogate divine benefactor, was the British government, with its awards of colonial charters and grants of land that it did not possess. These concepts make up the sum and substance of the American "politics of interest," one of five strands of thought that constitute American political culture. (See Heineman et al. 2002, ch. 3.)

Alexis de Tocqueville writes of American individualism in the Jacksonian period, and he distinguishes it from selfishness. He describes it rather as a kind of mature sense of independence, of self-reliance, which *can*, however, sap public spirit and eventuate in socially destructive selfishness. In America, however, he thought this result was avoided by "the principle of self-interest rightly understood" (de Tocqueville, I 1945, 123). He believed that

> ... the inhabitants of the United States almost always manage to combine their own advantage with that of their fellow citizens ... [T]hey maintain that [civic] virtue is useful and prove it every day. The American moralists do not profess that men ought to sacrifice themselves for their fellow creatures

because it is noble to make such sacrifices, but they boldly aver that such sacrifices are as necessary to him who imposes them upon himself as to him for whose sake they were made. (ibid., 121–22)

De Tocqueville explains this behavior as the result of the absence in America of an aristocracy and a paternal government, which in Europe would have been looked to for assistance in accomplishing social goals. Forced back on their own resources in a wilderness environment, Americans found it necessary to combine with other individuals in order to secure the necessities of human life. This produced a spirit of associationism, which we will discuss later in this chapter, and attitudes of enlightened self-interest. From this flows a concept of citizenship and political cooperation with other individuals, who possess similar rights and interests; a concept of common good.

The politics of interest also incorporates the work ethic as the chief means for acquiring the good things of this world. This idea originated in the Puritan theology of election. The Calvinist doctrine that God's will is inscrutable—and that He arbitrarily saves and damns human souls as He pleases—led to deep anxiety. Supposing that there might be some outward signs of "election," Puritans judged that those who worked hard, lived comfortably (though not luxuriously), and supported their families well were more likely to be among the saved than wastrels who let their children go hungry. One result of this way of thinking today is to celebrate a middling way of life as best: Middle class values are authoritative in today's world. When Americans are asked in polls to what class they belong, they invariably respond, "middle class." This is also the class that politicians claim they wish to serve.

The secularized version of this idea developed into the Horatio Alger myth, and it is still with us today as an aspect of our politics of interest. In an opinion survey of 1976, one that dealt with American values, Jennifer Hochschild found that even quite needy respondents believed that anyone in America could make his or her way if only he or she worked hard enough. One respondent in particular, someone who earned $6,000.00 a year, saw herself as an achiever, and she expressed an ambition to rise on the social scale (Hochschild 1981, 29). She was an enthusiastic capitalist and subscribed to Adam Smith's "Unseen Hand" doctrine, which converts self-interest into social utility. Liberty, as the right to accumulate without limit, runs sharply contrary to the ideal of equality, which is also authoritative in American culture. When compelled to choose between these values, Americans at all levels of society choose liberty over equality.

The Individual: The Politics of Conscience

American individualism also involves a politics of conscience, which derives from the Puritan origins of the New England colonists. The starting point of Puritan theory, like that of Lockean natural right doctrine, is a state of nature.

But the Puritans saw this as a wild condition, in which unregenerate persons have a liberty (rather than right) to do whatever they wish—even engage in mayhem and murder. Those who receive the spirit of God in this ill condition will choose to leave it and form civil societies. As with the Lockean formula, legitimate government comes into being by free consent, by contract. But the Puritan contract, in the first instance, is not to protect rights but mutually to oblige the contractors to live by God's law. The Mayflower Compact is an example of this idea—a freely undertaken obligation to do what the Christian conscience demands. Thus John Winthrop writes that though government comes into being only by an act of a free people and must be responsible to those who set it up, its obligation is not to protect natural rights, but to maintain a state of liberty that permits individuals to do only that "which is good, just, and honest" (quoted in Miller and Johnson 1938, 190). Nevertheless, since in this Puritan view all human beings tend to radical self-seeking and to mutual depredation, limits must be placed on government, since rulers are also sinful by nature.

Egalitarian and democratic accents in American political culture derive from a different brand of the politics of conscience, one that has its roots in another part of the colonial experience. This is the political thought of Thomas Hooker, Anne Hutchinson, and Roger Williams, three Congregationalists who rejected the theocratic authoritarianism of churchmen like John Winthrop. Inspired by a spirit of mysticism, all three believed in a divine inner light rather than in a public teaching authority as the guide of conscience. For them freedom of conscience was sovereign in the political order, which demanded a separation of church and state, an equality of consciences, a tolerance of all religious opinions, and ultimately the sovereignty of the people, by which they meant the majority. One might also argue that these thinkers were the founders of American pluralism, since they conceived the church as analogous to a trading corporation, one with a right to legal autonomy in its public life within a democratic society.

American populism and, much later, the expansion of the idea of equality to encompass such positive rights as freedom from want and freedom from fear also have their origins here. The underlying concept of this variety of colonial thought is the dignity of the individual as a child of God rather than as an acquisitive entrepreneur. A secularized version of this idea is Jefferson's faith in the goodness of human nature, as exemplified in the American common man. This was the ground of his faith in democracy, in contrast to the skepticism of Federalists such as John Adams, a skepticism that flowed from a pessimistic view of human nature, which was grounded in the Calvinism of churchmen like Winthrop.

Middle-of-the-road and left-leaning Democrats may be the chief inheritors of Jeffersonian optimism about the common man. But Republicans and conservatives also celebrate him. Witness President George W. Bush's remark of December 2001 that other Americans like him, who had low college grades, can aspire to the presidency. It is Republicans and libertarians, however, who chiefly embrace Jefferson's minimalist theory, his belief in small and decentralized government.

The ideal of democracy in America today joins majoritarianism with minority rights, including (and perhaps especially) the right of property. Survey research shows that today's common man, like his forebears, rejects a leveling conception of equality. Robert Lane, in a 1962 study, found that blue-collar workers were actually afraid of economic equality. They liked the idea of a superintending economic elite, which made them feel secure. They had no sympathy for people below them on the socio-economic scale, nor did they want government aid themselves in order to achieve. They believed it important to safeguard individual incentive. A generation later, Jennifer Hochschild found the same attitudes prevalent among her respondents. The rich, these respondents believed, had worked hard to achieve their wealth—and they deserved it. "Soak the rich" proposals had no appeal to them. Their individualism trumped their egalitarianism. (See Lane 1962; Hochschild 1981.)

The idea of the supremacy of conscience and the egalitarian democracy implicit in it received a new infusion of life from the transcendentalism of Emerson and Thoreau in the second third of the nineteenth century. This idea brought into American intellectual life the thought of Immanuel Kant, which remains today a significant influence in the political and social concepts of American philosophers such as John Rawls, who was an influential Harvard professor. Kantianism is also an extremely important worldview among professional applied ethicists today, as we shall see in Chapter 3. Its influence can also be seen in the welfare state ideas of Roosevelt's New Deal. This form of the politics of conscience is especially authoritative today in the liberal left and center of the Democratic party. It is in some cases a thoroughly secularized version of conscientious individualism, one that has entirely shed its origins in Puritan religion and in transcendental philosophy.

Concepts of the politics of interest and of the politics of conscience are deeply intermingled in American political culture today, but they receive different emphases from segment to segment of the spectrum of American political life. All Americans agree that the Bill of Rights is a specification of the rights of nature. But in contrast to conservatives and conservative Republicans, libertarians, liberal Republicans, and Democrats view political society as a secular affair. The second group read the First Amendment very liberally on free speech and very strictly on the separation of church and state.

Libertarians stand strongly against school prayer and against religious displays in public places. Liberal Republicans, Democrats, and libertarians support the freedom of the media to publish material with sexual content with few restrictions. Cultural conservatives and conservative Republicans hold for a much stricter standard of public morality. They accept the Puritan assumption that there is a God-given moral law that should be legally binding. Conservatives such as the evangelist Pat Robertson still think of America as a Christian society that should publicly acknowledge God's presence in public life. A continuing public debate on sex in the media, on school prayer, and on the mention of God in the Pledge of Allegiance shows that the present state of the law on these questions remains subject to peaceful contest. The issue of abortion rights divides adherents of the politics of interest from those who stand with the politics of conscience, and this clash of views continues to occasion violent behavior.

The Community: Populism

The counterpart to the individual in political thought is, of course, the community. In American political culture, as we have already noted, the individual holds the center stage. Americans have very clear and definite—though often diverse—ideas about the individual's rights and interests, but they have a hazy view of what the community is or what it may legitimately require of them. Elizabeth Frazer writes that " '[c]ommunity' is a concept with open frontiers and vague contours, which seems to extend across a very heterogeneous class of things, which contains a wealth of meaning—it appeals to people's emotions, it is shot through with value judgments, it conjures up associations and images from a wide range of discourses and contexts" (Frazer 1999, 60).

There is always an outcry about the sacredness of property rights when a town or state attempts to exercise eminent domain for some public purpose. Of late, threats to the environment have produced groups that organize themselves around campaigns to save an animal species about to go extinct or to save a primeval stand of redwoods from destruction. But their claims on behalf of the community are always met by counterclaims of unlawful "taking" by the defenders of private property. In American political culture, individual and community do not have a clearly defined and agreed-upon relationship.

In recent years American academia has spawned an entire literature of communitarian thought, in which attempts have been made to clarify and enrich the concept of community in our national life, and to instill ideas of natural obligations parallel to our concept of natural rights. The literature arises from the belief that our individualism has become atomistic. Its authors are worried that the social bond has become badly frayed in America. But the literature has been met with vigorous opposition by liberal and libertarian thinkers, who charge both that it contains a hidden organicism and that it harbors totalitarian tendencies. It is argued that communitarian thought is in conflict with the contractarian assumption that political society comprises only independent individuals who predate its existence in imagined time and have moral priority at all times. (See Etzioni, ed. 1998; Lawler and McConkey, eds. 1998.) The truth of the matter is that contemporary communitarianism probably represents an attempt to embody a new politics of conscience in a revived but secularized Puritan organicism.

Individualist politics of conscience celebrates the freedom and equality of all persons. Communitarian politics of conscience warns that the celebration has gotten out of control and threatens to destroy the social matrix.

Paradoxically, the idea of *The People*, a synonym for *The Community*, has been honored in America since the beginning of the Republic. De Tocqueville, writing in the Jacksonian period, announced that "the people reign in the American political world as the Deity does in the universe. They are the cause and the aim of all things; everything comes from them and everything is absorbed in them" (de Tocqueville, I 1945, 58).

The People is a sovereign authority. Political leaders of all ideological persuasions, from left to right, today regularly invoke *The People* as the source of their authority and the sole object of their concern. Typically, *The People* is contrasted with and opposed to *The Interests*, who are understood to be selfish groups and individuals who would govern in the private rather than the public interest. *The People* is a holy and mystical entity, in which all individuals are in some sense summed up, and in which all individual goods are included. This is obviously a very different sort of community from the legal jurisdiction that demands the sacrifice of some individual claim of right.

The paradoxical coexistence of individualism and populism in American political culture is partly to be explained by the fact that the idea of *The People* did not arise in opposition to the principle of individual right, but as a democratic rejection of the aristocratic institutions of Europe. American egalitarianism—the idea that all individuals are of equal worth before God—was a root idea of the congregationalism we discussed earlier under the heading "The Politics of Conscience."

Authoritative concepts of popular sovereignty and of majority rule thus live side by side in the American psyche with our individualism as expressed in the notion of *minority rights*. There is certainly not a perfectly logical compatibility between these ideas, and they are sometimes invoked against one another. Their conflict is softened, however, by the fact that whether Americans are majoritarians or believers in minority rights depends wholly on the circumstances of the moment and not on where one might be ranged along a deep social cleavage. Since we are a society of groups characterized by cross-cutting cleavages, and because our majorities are shifting coalitions of minorities, not permanent majorities, the apparent conflict between the concepts does not mark a serious fault in our political culture.

Partisan populist concepts historically have been associated with periods of major political and social reform in America. The first great wave of democratization took place during the Revolution as a function of the popularization of republicanism and the discrediting of monarchy and its associated aristocratic institutions. As colonies turned into states, agrarian populists seized the moment to establish democratic state governments in the name of *The People* and the common man. Their objects were broadly based electorates, majority rule, and decentralized, minimal government. As a party, they became known as Jeffersonian Republicans. Alarmed by images of European rabbles bent on the expropriation of the wealth of the rich, urban commercial interests were quick to support the Federalist party, with its program of centralized federal government that was elaborately constructed with a system of separated and balanced powers designed to thwart any such populist attempt.

But the "Revolution of 1800," when Jefferson won the presidency, proved to be no revolution at all. Unlike European democrats, Americans were broadly propertied, with no intention of using political power to expropriate anyone. Their only desire was to live in freedom, to have the opportunity to make their way in the world, and to attain riches themselves. Vernon Parrington describes the culture of Jefferson's day in these terms: It was a simple world, with a

> simple domestic economy. More than ninety per cent were plain country folk, farmers and villagers, largely freeholders, managing their local affairs in the traditional way. There were no great extremes of poverty or wealth, no closely organized class groups. (Parrington, I 1930, 355)

Two more periods of populist reform brought a further democratization of the political system. The Jacksonian Revolution that followed the panic and depression of 1819 pitted a coalition of southwest farmers and a growing eastern seaboard working class against eastern moneyed interests. It was during this period that mass parties arose to mobilize the strength of the aspiring many and to sweep away the last vestiges of property qualifications for public office. Presidential nominations would thereafter take place in large representative conventions, no longer in the cronydom of congressional caucuses. At the end of the century another agrarian movement, one that was based once more in the south and west, briefly formed a third party to carry on the battle with eastern banking and industrial interests. The aims of this short-lived Populist Party were then adopted by the Progressives, who extended the tradition of grass-roots democracy by establishing the referendum and recall in a number of states. The Progressives also worked for the direct election of U.S. senators and for women's suffrage through constitutional amendment.

The Progressives turned populism into an ideology espousing positive rather than negative government. Humanitarian demands for social and economic reform produced wages-and-hours legislation at the state level, along with factory legislation to protect the lives and limbs of workers, as well as calls for government social insurance programs. Progressivism also brought concern for the environment, which has culminated in today's environmental movement. All of these changes were accomplished in a meliorist rather than in a revolutionary frame of mind, with emphasis on incremental and gradual change.

Populism had yet another rebirth during the Great Depression of the 1930s. Franklin Roosevelt's New Deal brought Progressivist social and economic reforms to the national level with a panoply of laws that produced relief for the poor, the abolition of child labor, wages-and-hours measures, factory regulations to protect workers, a comprehensive program of social security, a comprehensive program for the protection of organized labor, a Federal Deposit Insurance Commission, an Agricultural Adjustment Administration, a Homeowners' Loan Administration, a Civilian Conservation Corps, a Works Progress Administration, a Public Works Administration, and much more, thus signaling that the era of Big Government had arrived.

The most recent populist reform movements have aimed at the protection of identifiable minorities from discrimination in the political, economic, and social spheres—the civil rights movements of the 1960s and later. Blacks, women, gays, and the handicapped have sought the help of government in acquiring a more equal place in American society. These efforts have all been viewed as attempts to produce a broader range of freedom for all individuals in American society. Populism and individualism thus have come to live in a symbiotic relationship within the national creed.

The Community: Associationism

If the ideal of community, understood as *The People*, has been somewhat amorphous, even mystical at the national level, American associationism has been crystal clear as a name for the American penchant for joining voluntary associations. It is a communitarian spirit that forms the cement of our civil society, the vital foundation of our political and economic order. De Tocqueville wrote in the 1830s that

> in no country in the world has the principle of association been more successfully used or applied to a greater multitude of objects than in America. Besides the permanent associations which are established by law under the names of townships, cities, and counties, a vast number of others are formed and maintained by the agency of private individuals.
> . . . . In the United States associations are established to promote the public safety, commerce, industry, morality, and religion. There is no end which the human will despairs of attaining through the combined power of individuals united into a society. (de Tocqueville, I 1945, 191, 192)

He explains this phenomenon as a function of the self-reliant individualism and democratic spirit of Americans. Typically, Americans are suspicious of established authority and prefer to accomplish their ends in ad hoc association with their fellows rather than to petition a government official. De Tocqueville found this attitude to be distinctively American and very different from the European approach to social action through established authority. Voluntary associations in America take the place of a hereditary aristocracy in the performance of vital social functions. This remains as true today as in de Tocqueville's time.

It is out of our associationism that our peculiarly American pluralism has grown. Americans have banded together to found hospitals, firefighting companies, charitable associations, architectural preservation societies, land conservation organizations, and a myriad of religious groups. In the face of great religious diversity, it early became impossible to establish official churches, even at the state level, though this was for a short time a practice (e.g., in Virginia and Massachusetts). Thus, religion became an entirely private affair, regulated minimally by law, but separate from the institutions of the state. Linguistic pluralism has also been a standard feature of American life from the very beginning. Benjamin Franklin thought that German, rather than English, might come to be the language used in the Pennsylvania state legislature, since the balance between those early dominant groups was very close. Italians, Irish, Poles, Lithuanians, Ukrainians, and other nationalities have typically formed associations for mutual aid and support shortly after their arrival. While religious and ethnic conflicts have certainly not been unknown in America, by comparison with societies abroad, they have been remarkably mild, and with American diversity has grown up a spirit of toleration and of live-and-let-live. Also, the ethnic groups have remained open to intermarriage—and thus to ethnic mixing.

The structure of the American national electoral system is also affected by pluralism and joinerism. Though the United States operates a two-party system for nominating and electing members of Congress and president, American parties are not monoliths, but loose collections of groups, whose members cross over party lines to produce varying majorities from election to election. Madison writes of this early on in the Tenth *Federalist*, in which he notes that the size of the country and the vast number of interest groups that comprise it make it impossible for any single-minded interest to dominate the whole in a tyrannous way. Thus associationism, by building a strong civil society as the sociological basis of the political system, serves as an important guarantee of everyone's freedom. Once again, the way in which Americans express the need for community dovetails well with our individualism and passion for the security of individual rights. This may explain why the recent research of Robert Putnam, which finds a marked decline in American volunteerism and in the strength of the associationist spirit, has occasioned concern about the future health of our political culture (Putnam 2000).

Putting It All Together: American Pragmatism

We have seen in the foregoing discussion of American political culture that our core values do not form a logical structure within a general philosophical system. We may compare them to a piece of music with many themes, which appear over and over with variations, and which are sometimes blended, sometimes set in discordant opposition. Or we may see them as a poem, made up of words with many definitions, some of which overlap and some of which clash. In this poetic metaphor, however, we are presented with an entity whose parts form a coherent whole. In this way, our logically untidy political culture functions coherently to underpin a stable and functioning liberal democratic system.

In his *Democracy in America* de Tocqueville remarked that American political life did not contain "grand parties." By this he meant that our two parties did not put forward highly abstract and opposed programs that are based on fundamentally different principles, such as those that plagued France in his time. American parties rested on interests rather than on general principles. And they "agreed upon the most essential points"—that is, on basic values. "Neither of them had to destroy an old constitution or to overthrow the structure of society in order to triumph" (de Tocqueville, I 1945, 176). It is significant that in the hotly contested election of 2004, John Kerry, the Democratic candidate for president, delivered an acceptance speech upon his nomination that even conservatives remarked could have been given by a Republican.

At the beginning of the republic, there had been grand parties for a while—Federalists versus Jeffersonians—but by de Tocqueville's time Jeffersonian democracy had triumphed and the Federalists had disappeared. Their Whig successors accepted the victory of democracy and decided that they could live with the Jeffersonian legacy. Similarly, the Jeffersonians did not attempt to undo the complex structure of separated powers and checks and balances that the Federalists had built to limit the thrust of democracy. In fact, "a considerable number of Federalist principles . . . were embodied at last in the political creed of their opponents" (ibid., 177). The result of this development was that in the absence of any deep ideological division, political opponents were divided more on questions of means rather than on general ends.

The reality of a functioning, though unarticulated, value consensus remains with us today. Differences between our major parties tend to be differences in degree rather than in kind, and on means rather than on ends. This is true despite the alleged profound differences between the so-called Republican red states and the Democratic blue states of the 2004 presidential election. Professor Morris Fiorina and his colleagues, in a volume entitled *Culture War? The Myth of a Polarized America* (2004), argue that differences between Republicans and Democrats are badly overblown in the media. They argue, for example, that six of ten voters, no matter what region of the country they live in, agree that corporate America is too powerful, and majorities in both red and blue states support stricter gun control and the death penalty. Former President Clinton attributed the Democratic loss in 2004 not to a cultural war, but to the party's failure to combat how its program was portrayed by Republicans to rural and small-town America. "If we let people believe that our party doesn't believe in faith and family, doesn't believe in work and freedom, that's our fault," he said (Dolnick, *Rochester Democrat and Chronicle*, 2004, 7A).

One can argue that behind Republican and Democratic proposals on a variety of issues, especially economic ones, there hide somewhat veiled aristocratic versus democratic "passions," as de Tocqueville put it. But a central truth of the matter is that both parties must appeal for support to the same citizenry, which is not divided into hostile classes but is rather a mosaic of cross-cutting interest groups that are arranged in ever-shifting coalitions. There are, of course, fringe groups on both right and left of the political spectrum whose principles place them outside the consensus, but they are small and do not affect the stability of the political system.

The absence of deep conflicts about first principles in our political culture has resulted in a condition that Daniel J. Boorstin has called "givenness." This is the belief that "values in America are in some way or other automatically defined." We assume that " 'the American Way of Life' harbors an 'American Way of Thought' which can do us for a political theory" (Boorstin 1953, 9). This does not mean that we do not *have* principles, but rather that we do not theorize about them. Our job is to put them into practice, continuously to test them as we apply them to specific problems at hand. Our approach to political decision making is, therefore, experimental and incremental. Large innovative programs, such as Hillary Clinton's proposal for overhauling the American healthcare system in the 1990s, are rejected out of hand. (See ch. 6.)

The experimental attitude has been central to our political practice since the early days of the Republic. Madison wrote in *The Federalist* of the newly drafted Constitution as an experiment. And in his farewell address to the nation, Andrew Jackson many years later pronounced the experiment a successful one. Even so innovative a program as Franklin Roosevelt's New Deal was characterized by its author as an experiment.

An important result of the givenness of American political values is the pragmatic character of the American mind. Pragmatism as a school of philosophy is a native growth, and it is generally agreed that our most important philosopher is the pragmatist John Dewey. William James, an early proponent of the pragmatic method, stated its essential characteristics as follows:

> A pragmatist . . . turns away from abstraction . . . towards concreteness and adequacy, towards facts, towards action and towards power.
> . . . You must bring out of each [abstract] word its practical cash-value, set it at work within the stream of your experience. It appears less as a solution . . . than as a program for more work, and more particularly as an indication of the ways in which existing realities may be *changed*.
> *Theories thus become instruments, not answers to enigmas in which we can rest . . .* Pragmatism unstiffens all our theories, limbers them up and sets each one at work. (William James in Konvitz and Kennedy, eds. 1960, 31, 32)

In politics, the adoption of a pragmatic method produces a problem-solving approach to policymaking. For Dewey, this meant both solving the problem of making our democracy work better than it had in the past and also reforming it in such a way as to embody more fully the meaning of our abstract values of liberty, equality, and community. In his most important political work, Dewey writes of this enterprise as a problem of converting a Great Society of clashing and short-sighted interests into a

Great Community, one in which these interests would be harmonized in the form of a nationwide, self-conscious Public that administered its affairs through an agreed-upon comprehensive policy agenda. The Interests and the People would become one. Dewey's pragmatism was in some part utopian. Rather than the rationalization of interests, American pragmatism at work has relied on compromise as the engine of policy agreement. Indeed, it is precisely through the continuing compromise of interests that our common values have been realized.

VALUES AND GENERATIONAL CHANGE

The elements of the value system we have described do not have constant weights over time. Emphasis and focus alter as historical situations change. Also, the pushing and tugging that are part and parcel of public deliberation produce new meanings, new understandings of what the core values signify. For example, in the seventeenth and eighteenth centuries, individual liberties were conceived negatively—as the right to be free of governmental interference with one's property, or the right to speak freely and worship freely. Equality meant the right to the equal protection of the laws and to equal rights before the law. By the 1830s equality embraced the idea of the equal right of all male citizens to participate in the choice of public servants. The trauma of the Civil War, by bringing about the abolition of slavery, broadened these meanings to include the black as well as the white population. In the last century *liberty* and *equality* developed positive meanings— freedom from want, freedom from fear, the right to equality of opportunity to strive for wealth and status. Civil rights legislation makes the federal government the guarantor of individual rights against discrimination at the ballot box, in obtaining housing, in the use of public facilities, in job placement, and so on. Blacks and women have been this legislation's principal beneficiaries. Public deliberation at present focuses on such questions as the right of gay partners to marry and raise families with the protection of the law. The consensus to which we referred in earlier sections, therefore, is a rolling one that develops out of the processes of public deliberation and legislation. The attribution of ever-new meanings to our basic value notions of liberty and equality is a developmental process that moves from year to year through ever-changing equilibria.

Situations of prosperity and of want, of peace and of war, bring different emphases in the value system. During the long period of growing affluence after World War II (despite periodic economic setbacks), individual expectations increased enormously, and with this development we have seen new conceptions of individual rights in what we earlier called the politics of interest. The public opinion polls of Daniel Yankelovich, for example, have found a long-term decline in the importance attached to obligations to others . . . The positive good of pleasure, including bodily pleasures, has increased. Censoriousness toward "incorrect" sexual behavior has diminished. The importance of self-fulfillment and the expression of one's individualism has increased, especially among women. The value of sacrifice as a moral good has diminished. (Reported by David Popenoe in Aaron et al. 1994, 5)

In public policy these cultural changes have been reflected in a relaxation of censorship in all the media as well as in a variety of changes in the welfare program—for example, the institution of workfare. At the same time, new emphases have appeared in the politics of conscience—a new concern for the equality and dignity of women, blacks, Hispanics, homosexuals, and other minorities. If libertarian individualism, in the context of expanding affluence, makes us "revel in expanding . . . life choices," our egalitarianism produces public policies that expand those choices for all (Popenoe in ibid., 5).

Some scholars are concerned that in the postwar period of heightened individualism and expanded expectations, a dangerous imbalance may have developed between individual and community:

> Because affluent individuals and families need not directly rely so much on others for economic support, their personal and social autonomy concomitantly increases. Through relying on market goods and on state-provided welfare, individuals in affluent societies are able to distance themselves from those intimate social structures and community groupings that have long been the basis for personal security. As these structures of "civil society" weaken, so does the social order. (Popenoe in ibid., 84)

In Popenoe's view, public policies are needed to offset this imbalance, policies that will shore up the nuclear family and other local communities while protecting individual rights. We need to "promote community identity and solidarity through local, social, educational, cultural, and religious organizations, and deeply respect the wishes and concerns of each subcultural grouping" (Popenoe in ibid., 93). Popenoe calls the cultural result he hopes for "communitarian individualism."

Wartime typically brings a shift in cultural focus from individual to community values. During World War II there were numerous examples of a marked increase in public willingness to sacrifice individual values for the national community. The crisis of 9-11 may be producing a similar change. A harbinger in the private sector was the extraordinary outpouring of sympathy, dollars, and blood from all over the country for the victims of the World Trade Center attack. Presidential rhetoric declared the value shift fully accomplished when Bush stated that the attacks of September 11 revived the American sense of unity and purpose. He said,

> We've been living through a unique moment in American history . . . This is a time of rediscovery, of heroism and sacrifice and duty and patriotism.

These are the core values of our country and they're being renewed. We found them waiting for us just when we needed them. (*Rochester Democrat and Chronicle*, 2001, 7A)

Whether this "unique moment" will result in a fundamental shift in American values and a consequent reorientation of American views on domestic policy priorities remains to be seen.

The war on terrorism has also, at least in one significant instance, produced a willingness to suspend our penchant for incrementalism in favor of sweeping change. The Homeland Security Act, signed into law in November 2002, has brought under one administrative roof dozens of agencies that were formerly either independent or parts of other federal departments. (See ch. 7.) For example, the functions of the Coast Guard, the Customs Service, the Immigration and Naturalization Service, the Border Patrol, the plant inspection service of the Department of Agriculture, and the new Transportation Security Administration have been lodged within the new department. Homeland Security will also fuse and analyze intelligence pertaining to homeland threats from the CIA, NSA, FBI, INS, and several other intelligence gathering agencies.

REFERENCES

Aaron, Henry J. et al. *Values and Public Policy*. Washington, DC: Brookings, 1994.

Boorstin, Daniel J. *The Genius of American Politics*. Chicago: University of Chicago Press, 1953.

Brown, Gillian. *The Consent of the Governed: The Lockean Legacy in Early American Culture*. Cambridge, MA: Harvard University Press, 2001.

Caplan, Arthur L., and Daniel Callahan. *Ethics in Hard Times*. New York: Plenum Press, 1981.

Chicago Tribune. "Bush Wants World Trade as Weapon." *Rochester Democrat and Chronicle*. October 18, 2001, 7A.

De Tocqueville, Alexis. *Democracy in America*. Edited by P. Bradley. 2 vols. New York: Knopf, 1945.

Dolnick, Sam. "Clinton: Bush Win Is Not That Bad." *Rochester Democrat and Chronicle*. November 6, 2004, 7A.

Etzioni, Amitai, ed. *The Essential Communitarian Reader*. Lanham, MD: Rowman and Littlefield, 1998.

Fiorina, Morris et al. *Culture War? The Myth of a Polarized America*. New York: Pearson Longman, 2004.

Frazer, Elizabeth. *The Problems of Communitarian Politics*. New York: Oxford University Press, 1999.

Heineman, Robert A. et al. *The World of the Policy Analyst*, 3rd ed. Chatham, NJ: Chatham House, 2002.

Hochschild, Jennifer. *What's Fair? American Beliefs about Distributive Justice*. Cambridge, MA: Harvard University Press, 1981.

Konvitz, Milton R., and Gail Kennedy, eds. *The American Pragmatists*. New York: Meridian Books, Inc., 1960.

Lane, Robert. *Political Ideology: Why the American Common Man Believes What He Does*. New York: Free Press of Glencoe, 1962.

Lawler, P.A., and D. McConkey, eds. *Community and Political Thought Today*. Westport, CT: Praeger, 1998.

Miller, Perry, and Thomas H. Johnson. *The Puritans*. New York: The American Book Co., 1938.

Parrington, Vernon. *Main Currents in American Thought*. 3 vols. New York: Harcourt Brace, 1930.

Putnam, Robert. *Bowling Alone: The Collapse and Revival of American Society*. New York: Simon and Schuster, 2000.

CHAPTER 3

A Framework for Ethical Public Policy Analysis

How do we go from a review of American values, in all their complexity and multiformity, to a systematic method of ethical analysis? Perhaps the most appropriate way would be to canvass the methods that are used by ethicists today and to try them on "for fit." There are three that are especially popular, and all of them have variations. One is utilitarianism (or consequentialism), another is Kantianism. (This is also known by the cumbersome expression *deontological ethics*.) A third is a case-by-case approach that is variously called *casuistry*, *case method*, *situationism*, and *the method of moral descriptions*. We prefer a version of this approach that we call *prudent pragmatism*.

Each of these methods has its origin in European philosophy, as have many American concepts of value. In the manner of its employment, each also highlights specific and different aspects of American political culture. Our majoritarian populism and self-interested individualism are both, paradoxically, mirrored in utilitarian method as well as in our concern for efficiency in the use of resources. The Kantian approach stresses the primacy of transcendent right as well as the equal moral worth of every individual. Prudent pragmatism reflects both American disdain for disembodied abstractions (de Tocqueville's "grand ideas") and our recognition that the world of values is multifaceted and untidy. This method can also deal with conflicts among our foremost notions of liberty and equality. Those who use it also believe that prudent compromise is virtuous activity.

UTILITARIANISM

The leading ideas of utilitarian thought were first formulated by the English philosopher Jeremy Bentham (1748–1833). His starting point was equating "good" with "desire," with whatever people happen to want. A famous saying of Bentham's was that "push-pin [a child's game] is as good as poetry."

His conclusion followed upon more than 200 years of religious strife about the content of God's will as the source of all norms as well as centuries of ideological and social conflict about the meaning of the expression *the law of nature*. Bentham's conclusions reflected the fact that traditional moral words had been hollowed out by their exploitation by those seeking to justify conflicting group interests. The goodness of an act, according to Bentham, must be measured not by intentions but by its consequences for society, which were calculated as pleasures and pains. At one point he was ready to say that social good should be equated with the greatest good of the greatest number. But he usually embraced the idea of the greatest quantity of pleasure overall as the object of social policy.

In a time of increasing democratization, both social and political, another of Bentham's fundamental assumptions was that everyone's good should count equally with everyone else's, and that the quantitative social good should be arrived at by somehow adding up individual goods. To accomplish this end, he devised a "felicific calculus," which took account of such things as the intensity, certainty, duration, fecundity, and propinquity of pleasurable and painful events. But it proved very difficult to quantify subjective pleasure using his method. Also, people take pleasure in different things. Are these pleasures all to be treated as qualitatively equal in value? John Stuart Mill, in a rejoinder to Bentham's proposal, asked whether it was not better to be Socrates dissatisfied than a pig satisfied. In the history of utilitarian thought, this difficulty has come to be known as the problem of interpersonal comparisons of utility, a problem that remains debated and unresolved today.

Utilitarianism had almost immediate fruits in British social policy. Liberal reformers of the time had been arguing for moderating the severe and cruel penalties traditionally exacted for crimes. It was Bentham who came up with the idea of "letting the punishment fit the crime" by proportioning the pain that ought to be visited upon a malefactor to the pain experienced by society as a result of that individual's delict. Extensive changes in the penal law resulted from legislation enacted by parliaments influenced by Benthamite philosophy, and these changes eliminated such barbarous practices as maiming and disemboweling, and they shortened prison sentences.

Benthamite utilitarianism figures very greatly today in cost-benefit and cost-risk analyses, which are widely used by government agencies in the evaluation of alternative public policies, ranging from the placement of a municipal airport facility to the purchase of automatic weapons by the military forces. Needless to say, few of these choices can be reduced to purely technical calculations, as Bentham had hoped, because of the problem of varying individual perceptions of "good" as well as by inherent conflicts of interest. The method works well when analysts employ restricted and uncontested assumptions about the values to be maximized in a given choice—for example, in choosing materials for the construction of a new system of shelters in a national park.

If pleasure and pain were the wellsprings of human moral behavior, it is clear that the individual would then attempt to maximize his or her own well-being. But why should an individual want to maximize society's? Utilitarian theory cannot readily adduce a motive for such efforts, because the theory does not allow for one objective to be judged better than another. Philosophers such as J.J. Rousseau and the utilitarian John Stuart Mill have argued that there are benevolent sentiments innate in human nature, which prompt people to desire the social good. But what if an individual does not, in fact, display such sentiments? The theory contains no grounds for dubbing that person unethical or depraved. A sentiment is, after all, just a sentiment, and it is without ethical value.

Perhaps the best that can be done is to refer to the idea of enlightened self-interest and to argue that if society is better off as a result of a particular policy, the individual will probably be so as well. For example, a policy that increases the overall social product may raise everyone's level of satisfaction (the "trickle-down theory"). But then again, it might not. Another difficulty with the utilitarian approach is that, on the assumptions specified, it cannot supply a principle or rule for distributing goods justly. How do we know what share of social value any particular individual should receive?

There is yet another aspect of utilitarian method that requires comment. In some cases cost-benefit analysis can produce an opposition between individual and social good. For example, a study done in 2000 by the Harvard Center for Risk Analysis concluded that despite evidence that using a cellular phone while driving creates risks both for drivers and others it might have been premature to legislate substantial restrictions at that time. This was because the study found the risk that someone might be killed by a driver using a cellular phone was very small—merely one chance in a million per year. This was smaller than the risk of being struck by a drunk driver. Additionally, economic studies had suggested that the dollar value of using a cellular phone while driving exceeds the costs, even when those costs include safety risk costs. Thus restrictions on cellular phone use while driving would be inefficient. One might ask, however, whether risk to human life can adequately be expressed in dollar terms. Also, it is accepted public policy to remove drunk drivers from the road. But it would appear that no one supposes that drunk driving contributes to economic efficiency. A study done two years later by the Risk Analysis Center showed that due to a sharp increase in cell phone use on the road, social costs had risen to equal economic benefits. The Center concluded that in light of the new statistics, legislation (such as that passed by the State of New York) that banned calling while driving, might have become appropriate. (See Lissy 2000.)

"Act utilitarianism" is the simplest form of this philosophy. It holds that every moral act requires that we calculate the quantity of social benefit to be derived from alternative policies under consideration. For example, should federal money be employed to expand and improve highways, or should we develop a better system of mass transportation? The concern is entirely with present benefits, and policymakers have to use whatever evidence is available about the comparative productivity of the two approaches as their basis of judgment. But how useful will our calculations be if we do not take long-term effects into account? What of the costs of pollution to future generations if the United States adopts the highways-versus-mass-transportation approach, as the government has? What of the future availability of fossil fuel, the risks of dependence on sources abroad, and a host of other questions? Act utilitarianism cannot help us answer these questions.

Rule utilitarianism is a more long-term approach. It assumes that if policymakers limit their choices by employing certain general rules, social value will be maximized in the long run. For example, consider these traditional maxims: "Do not lie" and "Abide by what you have promised to do." They are not viewed as principles of absolute right, but simply as standards of utility, which if employed over the long run will produce a greater quantity of social value than if they are not. The various recent accounting frauds committed by major American corporations, such as Enron, and their adverse effect on the stock market would seem to provide ample evidence of the wisdom of the rule utilitarian approach. Certainly, capital markets cannot operate efficiently if the actors in the system are not able to trust one another. But this may not be true in all areas of public life. Take treaty-making, for example. It is probably true in a general sense that "treaties are made to be kept" (*Pacta sunt servanda*). And treaties are a form of promise. This is a venerable rule of international law and comity. But in international law, the rule is not given as one that is to obtain always and everywhere. It is qualified by the phrase *providing that circumstances remain the same (Rebus sic stantibus)*. If circumstances alter in the long run, an exception may be made. For example, the Antiballistic Missile Treaty between the United States and Russia was agreed to during the cold war as a means of reducing tensions between the two great competing powers. But today, with the cold war over, it may not be a wise policy for the United States to follow. The new nuclear threat comes not from Russia but from a number of small rogue states that have recently acquired nuclear capabilities, that harbor deep animosities toward the sole remaining superpower, and that have no regard for the principles of international law. It might, therefore, be prudent for the United States to denounce the Antiballistic Missile Treaty, as the Bush administration has done, for the sake of security. There might be a better approach to the rogue state problem, one that would allow the treaty to stand, however. But on the face of it, the policy chosen appears reasonable. A case can be made for it, though such unilateral actions certainly lead to problems of international comity. Whether it is the right decision depends on the prudence and foresight of Mr. Bush and the wisdom of his advisers. The point is that such an exception to the promises rule is allowable in cases like this, and such exceptions may be called for in the name of prudence. Thus, the rule falls to the ground. We are back to act utilitarianism. (See Rosemarie Tong's succinct discussion of utilitarianism in 1986, 82–84. Also see Richard B. Brandt 1983, 37–43.)

DEONTOLOGICAL ETHICS (KANTIANISM)

We call an ethical system *deontological* if its rules do not allow us to specify what is good independently from what is right. Deontology holds that some acts are inherently right or wrong, quite apart from their consequences. In this view, telling the truth and fidelity to promises, for example, are two principles that must be observed independently of consequences.

Immanuel Kant (1724–1804), the chief apostle of deontology, grounded his ethics in the idea of law. His starting point was the observation that the natural world is governed by laws. This idea underlay the work of the natural sciences that in his time had begun to unfold an understanding of the natural principles upon which the increasingly more powerful technology of our time is grounded. Since the world all around us is governed by laws, Kant concluded that human nature must also be so governed. But moral laws are different from physical ones, because human beings sense that they act freely. To date, no one has shown that behavior is determined by our heredity or by our genes—nor that it is necessitated by things in the environment—though all these factors may condition what we do. People are free agents, not automata. Reason requires that we be governed by law and not behave randomly or arbitrarily. But the law we observe must be self-given.

Kant's problem, therefore, was to find a law that is compatible with free agency. In solving this problem, his point of departure was his judgment that human beings are capable of exercising good will—that is, of willing that the right be done. And what can we all agree is right? According to Kant, the ultimate principle of right must be the idea of what it is to be a law. And this is universality. What we mean by *law* is that which obtains universally or unexceptionally. For free agents this is the *categorical imperative.*

The categorical imperative can be stated in two ways. The first formulation is: "So act that the maxim of your will may be made a universal principle of nature." In other words we cannot act according to maxims which would be self-frustrating. An example used by Kant is this maxim: "Borrow money, making the mental reservation that you do not intend to repay it." If we imagine that everyone in the world acts according to this principle and if we make it a universal principle of nature, the maxim is self-frustrating. For no money would be lent, and no borrowing could occur. (See Kant 1981.) Lying, according to Kant, is another behavior that cannot be universalized without contradiction. As universal behavior, it would destroy the distinction between truth and falsehood.

Kant also presents us with a second formulation of his categorical imperative, which is a corollary of the first: "So act as to treat others always as ends in themselves, never only as means." This follows from the realization that persons are free agents, not objects in the physical world that are moved only by external forces. This is moral freedom, the quality that gives us a special dignity as human beings, and it is the ground of our claim to political freedom and to equality of treatment before the law. Kantianism is therefore a rights-oriented ethical philosophy, and it gives individual autonomy a special place in the American system of values. It insists on the equal moral right and moral worth of all individuals.

Ethicists in the Kantian tradition played a central role in the last two decades in the movement to give patient autonomy a special place in medical decision making. Before they undergo medical procedures in hospitals, patients must now read and understand the Patient Bill of Rights, and they must give their informed consent in writing to the treatment they are to undergo. A new individualist and democratic element has been added to what had been a strictly hierarchical and authoritarian medical culture. Another version of Kantian autonomy has entered the vociferous debate between the proponents of life and the defenders of choice regarding the legitimacy of abortion. The autonomy of the woman, her right to freedom of choice, is here pitted against the right to life of the fetus.

In recent years ethicists have attempted to produce hybrid systems in which utilitarian and deontological principles are brought together. John Harsanyi, Richard Brandt, and R.M. Hare have been foremost among these scholars. All of these approaches, however, represent efforts to reduce the problem of ethics to finding an adequate system of general rules. They proceed from a few asserted supreme and general principles of morality, by linear reasoning (i.e., deductively) to conclusions. In so doing, in procrustean fashion they exclude the relevance of circumstance to moral choice. They both narrow and prejudge the values to be realized. Utilitarians and deontologists often plug in the facts of a dilemmatic situation to document a conclusion already deductively arrived at. (See French 1983, 31.) By contrast, case ethicists emphasize the idea that it is the *circumstances* that determine what are *seen* as governing norms or values. These ethicists work from the choice situation out to the ethical principles rather than from principles inward to the situation. They claim that only in this way can one adequately deal with value conflicts inherent in a case as well as bring into play all the values implicit in a choice situation. We turn now to the case approach to ethical choice.

PRUDENT PRAGMATISM

The beginnings of the case method in ethics go much farther back than do those of the other two approaches we have discussed. We find them in the sixth book of Aristotle's *Ethics*. Aristotle there distinguishes between pure reason, with which we understand the world of universals as they unfold themselves as possibilities within the material world, and practical reason, which tells us how to act in our choices. To be a person of practical reason requires the development of the virtues, especially moderation—that is, acting according to the mean. (For example, in warfare, courage is a mean between recklessness and cowardice.) But action according to the mean is the only general rule that Aristotle presents. And employing it is a matter of cultivating our character in all our activity, not simply following a rule in particular choices. Practical reason also requires the virtue of prudence, which is displayed in fitting particulars to universals. To be able to do this demands much experience as well as acting with moderation and restraint in all our choices. Only through experience does a person become acquainted with the variety of circumstances that significantly color ethical choice. A novice has too little relevant material at hand to inform his or her choices.

Becoming a person of prudence and knowing how to act with practical reason mean for Aristotle constant activity, immersion in the world of particulars. We must be doers who have a feel for the facts, for varying circumstances. It is not by knowing a lot of universal rules that we become good people, but by knowing what rules to apply to particular circumstances. Witness the following strange example that Aristotle gives us: The good physician is not one who knows abstractly that white meats are healthful but does not know what meats are light. He is rather the one who knows from his experience that chicken (a white meat) is good for the patient and prescribes it, even though he may not know the general rule about white meats (Aristotle 1941, 1029).

Aristotle does indeed hold that certain kinds of action are always in and of themselves evil—such things as lying, theft, murder, and adultery—most of the things that we find in the Judeo-Christian *Decalogue*. In such matters the principle of the mean does not apply. Aristotle tells us that "[w]e know by their names that they are wrong" (ibid., 959). In other words social agreement on their wickedness is evidenced in the very labels attached to the acts. But for Aristotle it is not sufficient to know these universals to act well. It is only through experience of making choices in varying circumstances that we know how to apply these universals. Not every killing is a murder.

Julius Kovesi, a modern ethicist, has done an especially useful job in fleshing out Aristotle's thought about moral universals and particulars in a volume entitled *Moral Notions* (1967). Like Aristotle, he tells us that universal moral ideas like murder, adultery, and lying signify acts that are in themselves recognized to be evil. The ethical problem does not consist in knowing what the universals are, but rather in deciding when to apply them to the situations in which we find ourselves. When we are following principles, Kovesi tells us, we simply note that the facts involved constitute a case or instance of a general idea (ibid., 101). For example, we don't need to specify that "lying is wrong." We know that. Rather, we need to understand what acts constitute a lie (ibid., 103). Facts are not divorced from values but are intimately tied to them (ibid., 28).

This intimate relationship demands that we look very carefully at the circumstances of a case to be sure we have in hand all the *relevant* facts. And these circumstances will usually take us beyond mere observations of events. We may observe two people being thrown off cliffs. In order to understand what is going on, we will need to inquire who the people involved are and what the act of throwing means. In one case we learn that the thrower is a thug who has just beaten up the person whom he has cast over the cliff. In the other case (having traveled back in our time machine), we learn that the thrower is a Roman official who is carrying out a sentence on a convicted felon at the edge of the Tarpeian Rock, a place of execution. Despite their empirical similarities, the two acts turn out to have profoundly different moral meanings. One signifies murder, the other legal execution. The important point to note is that description is not morally neutral; it includes evaluation. Of course, opponents of the death penalty argue that legal execution is never justified and *also* constitutes murder. But this idea demonstrates Kovesi's point as well. It is not the act that reveals moral significance, but rather its interpretation.

Kovesi calls moral concepts such as those we have just discussed "complete moral notions." But not all that we do and say that has ethical significance can be so readily identified. For example, if a terrorist were to burst into Camp David, looking for the president, it would be morally incumbent on the staff people he found there to convince him that the president was in Washington, even though he was standing in the next room. In light of the circumstances, we are not ready to call such an action a lie. We do not have a name for such an act, and Kovesi suggests that we might call it a "saving deceit," which would create a complete moral notion.

Other scholars of our time have developed Aristotelian practical reasoning under the name of *casuistry*, reviving a term that in early modern times had a certain amount of opprobrium attached to it because of its abuse by seventeenth-century confessors. (It became popular opinion that Jesuit priests in that early state-building period frequently manipulated moral principles in such a way as to accommodate the consciences of kings who used ruthless methods to acquire and hold their thrones . . . *Raison d'etat*.) Especially noteworthy is the work of Albert Jonsen and Stephen Toulmin in the field of medical ethics. These authors employ the expression *paradigm case* to serve in the place of Kovesi's *complete moral notion*. Classical paradigms are such things as "taking unfair advantage of others' misfortunes," "damaging the community through disloyalty," "being inconsiderate to others," "willful violence against innocent persons." These are clear and unambiguous ideas, with which one can readily associate many empirical events (Jonsen and Toulmin 1988, 307).

But the world changes, and general cultural change can alter moral judgments markedly. In precapitalist times, lending money at interest was considered usury, which meant out of greed, taking advantage of a person in difficulty. It was considered sinful and was also unlawful in western European countries. In the capitalist world, however, it is a normal practice, which is not considered oppressive, but rather it is the lifeblood of the good life. The paradigm of usury, with its evil connotations, has given way to the approved idea of a bank loan.

Today's world of rapid technological advance has created a similar need for new paradigms and maxims of action. It is by no means obvious how to fit certain new combinations of facts to a particular paradigm. For example, if we withhold care from a weak and badly deformed neonate, are we violating the maxim "Never commit willful violence against an innocent"? Or are we following the maxim "Mercifully refrain from prolonging a painful life"? The answer to this question is important, since under present federal law, withholding care from a newborn is equated with child abuse and neglect. We need to research questions both about the quality of life such a deformed child may expect and about the social cost of minimizing his or her suffering. We would also need to weigh and balance utilitarian cost concerns against a Kantian's devotion to the value of life as such. We need to ponder what the relevant considerations are and obtain adequate factual knowledge of the circumstances surrounding them if we are to judge that the law should be changed.

Technological change has produced even more dramatic questions. What moral and legal principles do we apply to relationships that derive from sex change? In a recent inheritance lawsuit by a son, the court was asked to disinherit his father's last wife, a person who had undergone a sex change. The son claimed that since she was not actually a woman, she had no right to inherit. New situations such as this demand new moral paradigms if we are to be able to make prudent moral judgments.

Jonsen and Toulmin have also contributed important ideas about how case reasoning can help us in circumstances in which we must deal with problems of conflicting values. Democratic politics is, of course, rife with such questions. Policy problems invariably involve bringing together the values of liberty and equality, and as a result, they lead to a search for a balance among opposed group interests. Neither utilitarianism nor deontological ethics is of much use in such cases. What we need to do in a particular case is to pick out specific values that we would like to realize, set up a series of maxims to follow in order to accomplish the result desired, and then rank-order them in the light of the circumstances, weighing and balancing the values as we go along. Determining what the relevant considerations are and amassing adequate empirical evidence about them are central.

Some Case Illustrations

Let us now illustrate the elements of prudent pragmatism as a method of ethical analysis with a few cases. Here is the first, which deals with the dilemmatic right to die question:

You are a citizen of New York who has been approached by a death with dignity organization, which is lobbying the state legislature. Its proponents want you to join the organization and write to state legislators urging the enactment of a law like that of the State of Oregon, which legalizes physician-assisted suicide. Here is the information with which you have been presented as a basis for your decision about whether to support the group's work.

By popular initiative the State of Oregon on November 8, 1994, adopted a "Death With Dignity" Act. The vote statewide was divided 51 percent in favor and 49 percent opposed. Legal maneuvers by opponents to enjoin implementation of the act on constitutional grounds held up the measure until 1997. The U.S. Supreme Court settled the matter by indicating that it would view laws such as the one in question as presenting political rather than constitutional issues. It did hold, however, that there is no constitutional right to assisted suicide under the Due Process Clause. State courts have held that there is no state interest in prolonging the life of terminally ill patients. An attempt to overturn the act was defeated in 1997 by a popular vote of 60 percent to 40 percent. Measures like the Oregon act were defeated in Washington State and California in 1991 and 1992, respectively.

Proponents of the Oregon Death With Dignity Act argued that it would reduce the enormous costs involved in keeping the terminally ill alive. Those opposed countered by saying that aged and poor people would take their lives in order to save their families from a financial burden. The head of the Coalition for Compassionate Care argued that terminally ill patients are vulnerable to pressure. The Roman Catholic Archbishop of Portland called the measure "murder in the name of mercy." The wife of one backer of the measure had committed suicide with the aid of Dr. Jack Kevorkian when she learned she was suffering from Alzheimer's disease. This husband, a Portland financial analyst, was quoted by the AP as saying that he thought "the medical profession and hospitals [had] found a very positive correlation between cash flow and blood flow."

The Oregon law provides that a patient may obtain a prescription for a lethal medicine if two doctors agree the patient is suffering from a terminal disease (i.e., one from which he or she will die within six months). The attending physician must verify that the patient is mentally competent and has made an informed decision. The patient must make the request both orally and in writing, with a fifteen-day waiting period between the two requests. An additional waiting period of forty-eight hours is required between the second request and the writing of the prescription. Only residents of Oregon are eligible to request such a prescription. No healthcare provider is obliged to participate in the program. Persons who coerce or unduly influence a patient's decision shall be guilty of a Class A felony.

What do you think of the ethicality of the Oregon statute? In the eyes of the U.S. Supreme Court, as we have seen, this remains an open question. It is a matter for political debate and electoral action, not one of constitutional rights or obligations. Should other states in which there is discussion of the issue follow Oregon's lead, or not? Is the statute a good ethical precedent?

A useful starting place for analysis of this case is the matter of what to call the act of seeking the aid of a physician in hastening one's death. The Oregon Death With Dignity Act specifically states that actions taken in accordance with it "shall not, for any purpose, constitute suicide, assisted suicide, mercy killing, or homicide, under the law" (Haley and Lee 1998, 59). The act seems to be suggesting that a cluster of facts new in our time has created a new ethical reality for which there is as yet no adequate name. Is it appropriate to call the actions made legal by the act by a name which, in America, has always meant something evil and wrong—suicide? The act refuses the use of that name in law. Modern medical technology now makes it possible to prolong life far beyond what used to be its natural limits. Are there situations in which even withdrawal of this technology may leave patients with terminal illnesses in excruciating pain but still alive, sentient, and with a feeling of desperation? Medical science now makes possible better predictions of a patient's remaining time than was formerly possible. We also live in a time in which the value of patient autonomy has received a new prominence. Does a terminal patient always have comfort care adequate to alleviate suffering? Is this important to insure a truly autonomous decision? In a time of cultural pluralism and in view of the separation-of-state-and-church tradition in our political culture, should a person who does not believe that taking his or her own life in these special circumstances is wrong be prevented from doing so? In short, following Kovesi, are we faced with a new moral and ethical reality here that requires a name . . . a new moral notion parallel to the idea of *saving deceit* in our earlier discussion? Perhaps we might call it *physician-aided-dying*, a name which is, in fact, used by some, rather than the opprobrious term *suicide*? The answers to these questions are by no means clear and settled, but they require much deliberation and searching for relevant facts.

What are the values that must be weighed and balanced in deciding on the ethicality of the Oregon statute? The utilitarian value of saving money in medical situations in which someone will shortly die is one. What weight should be given to this factor? The deontological concern for the equal distribution of scarce resources is another. Respect for patient autonomy, understood as the right to control the timing of one's death in a terminal situation, is yet another. This idea derives from our culture's stress on individual freedom, both within the politics of interest and the politics of conscience. Another is our pluralism, which is both a fact and a value in American life. Still another value, a corollary of human autonomy, is merciful treatment of all individuals and the alleviation of unnecessary pain. Again, this value can be referred both to the politics of conscience and the politics of interest. Respect for life must also be recognized as a central concern in our decision making as well as (for the physician) the duty to preserve life (the politics of conscience).

Are there any more facts that we should collect before beginning our "weighing and balancing" and then rank-ordering the values we have enumerated? A task force convened by the Ethics in Health Care Center of the Oregon Health Sciences University, in a guidebook for healthcare providers that was issued after the enactment of the statute, urged policymakers to enact universal access to hospice care in Oregon and otherwise to improve the supply of adequate comfort care for the terminally ill. It also recommended mental health consultation for persons desiring a lethal prescription. In addition the task force advised mental health professionals with strong biases, either for or against medical assistance in dying, to consider declining such consultation. These and a host of other task force recommendations suggest that the ethical analyst must assess slippery slope problems in the administration of a statute such as the Oregon Death With Dignity Act. (In a gradual progression of excuses and exceptions, could interpretation of the act lead by small degrees from morally acceptable to morally unacceptable acts?) In a society whose health system operates within a market framework, might the ethos of economic efficiency add to the slipperiness of the slope?

These problems plainly require the broad canvassing of additional safeguards to insure the ethical implementation of the act.

Here is another case to illustrate the use of our analytical method.

As a citizen of the United States, you are trying to make up your mind about the ethicality of an administrative action by which the Department of Justice extended the surveillance powers of the FBI.

In May 2002, the U.S. Department of Justice extended the investigative powers of the FBI, allowing it to conduct surveillance on Americans without any evidence of intended or committed crime. Agents may now surf the Internet to search for bomb-making sites and other potential terrorist materials. These agents will also be permitted both to attend public rallies where suspects might be present and to monitor chatrooms where conspiratorial activity might be taking place. In addition, they may launch preliminary investigations for as long as a year without higher level approval.

Earlier administrative prohibition of these kinds of activities derived from abuses of the 1960s and 1970s, when FBI Director J. Edgar

Hoover had used them to conduct surveillance of the civil rights and antiwar movements, including spying on such people as Martin Luther King Jr. At the time the Supreme Court refused to forbid such monitoring, but by a very narrow margin. The majority opinion held that there was a clear analogy between such activities and what any good newspaper reporter would do to obtain material for a story.

Civil libertarians, though recognizing that the Justice Department is free to revise its guidelines for FBI activities, argue that monitoring of this kind will tend to put a damper on the unhampered public discussion that is the lifeblood of a functioning democracy. David D. Cole, a Georgetown law professor, has been quoted as saying that "there are significant First Amendment concerns. There is a real cost to the openness of a free political society if every discussion group needs to be concerned that the FBI is listening in on its public discussions or attending its public meetings." A representative of the Council on American-Islamic Relations has expressed the fear that surveillance of discussions in mosques and other religious settings might "erode some of the trust and good will that exists in these institutions, [particularly] if you are afraid they have been infiltrated by an undercover agent." A law professor at Hofstra University thinks that the new investigative methods will be used improperly and produce more damage to First Amendment values than advances in law enforcement.

On the other side of the argument, Mary Jo White, former U.S. Attorney in Manhattan, who has overseen a number of major terrorism prosecutions, points out that the country is now at war. "The public safety concern has to come first." Steven Lubet, a law professor at Northwestern University, who has been active in civil liberties cases, argues that the circumstances of today are not analogous to those of the 1960s and 1970s. "They're not conducting surveillance of a peace movement. J. Edgar Hoover has been dead for thirty years, and there is no reason the abuses of the 1960s should prevent the FBI from taking prudent measures today." (See Liptak article, *New York Times*, 2002, 1.)

In this case the fundamental American values of individual free expression, of equality of treatment before the law, and of privacy must be weighed and balanced against the physical security of the community. To accomplish this goal adequately, we must give careful scrutiny to all the relevant circumstances. We must decide which of the analogies alleged in the case reported here are appropriate. Does the successful prosecution of a war against terrorism, radically different in character from the country's past conflicts, warrant this kind of surveillance? Is this a situation so radically different that there are no analogies with past experience? Is it appropriate to compare the situation to one in which civil rights activists and peace protesters were targets of investigation by an out-of-control administrator like J. Edgar Hoover? On the other hand, in view of the recent revelations of the errors and heavy-handedness of investigative authorities, must we be concerned with the fair and equal treatment of our ethnically diverse citizenry by authorities? What evidence do we have about the adequacy of current FBI and CIA reforms to prevent ineptitude on the part of investigative agents and possible civil rights violations of innocent persons? Is the analogy suggested by the Supreme Court between government monitoring activities and news reporting a sound one? Does the possibility that the new monitoring will turn up important evidence of dangerous terrorist activity outweigh possible threats to the civil liberties of the innocent?

At the time of the secession from the Union of the Southern states, President Lincoln suspended the writ of habeas corpus, an instrument that prevents the executive from indefinitely detaining a prisoner without a hearing or without the possibility of bail. According to the Supreme Court, this was not the president's prerogative but that of Congress. To justify taking this action, Lincoln said that when the integrity of the state is concerned, acts otherwise unconstitutional become constitutional because of the extreme peril. Are today's circumstances analogous to those faced by Lincoln in 1861? What evidence must we collect to come to a prudent judgment in rank-ordering the values at issue in this case?

CONCLUSION

The prudent pragmatist approach to ethical analysis presents the ethical agent with elements of a systematic method for weighing and balancing conflicting values that define hard cases of policy choice. It also focusses one's attention on the special characteristics of the situation in hand, those which make it different from the routine case. Prudent pragmatism can also be of service in eliminating the strong ideological content that often attaches to what are represented as purely technical methods of policy analysis. The scientific systems analysis of the Great Society days carried a heavy welfare-liberal load, while cost-benefit techniques, so central to the policy analysis during the days of the Reagan administration, are underpinned by free-market values. Prudent pragmatism, by virtue of its focus on the circumstances of a particular choice situation and on the need to honor self-consciously all our diverse and conflicting basic values, should provide a way to avoid the pitfall of insinuating ideological doctrines wholesale into analytical instruments. The prudent pragmatist method cannot, however, guarantee a correct answer to an ethical question. Ethics is not an area in which absolute certainty can be obtained. Sound ethical decision requires conscientious deliberation and prudent judgment. But it does not have slide-rule accuracy in its result.

We want to emphasize that it is the process of reasoning with others, deliberating about a dilemmatic case at hand, that is the core of ethical decision making. No prudent person makes up his or her mind about important public questions in a vacuum. It is incumbent on decision makers, whether they are citizens pondering rival slates of candidates in an election, legislators in a parliamentary body, or administrative officials implementing a policy, to take counsel with others before deciding. One must hear and weigh arguments from all sides simply because there are no algorithms, no deductive procedures that one can employ in reaching an ethical decision. This is why legislatures are called deliberative bodies; laws are never the result of mathematical calculation; they are the result of comparisons of reasons. The prudent person is one who can distinguish good from bad reasons.

Ethical decisions are also tentative and experimental. If experience shows that a law does not work well or has evil results, there must be a new round of deliberation and a new decision. The same is true of elections, of course. Only experience can demonstrate the soundness or error, the goodness or badness of a decision on public policy.

We accept the Wittgensteinian assumption that language is the carrier of an entire culture, of a form of life (Wittgenstein 1968). A stable culture includes a social agreement about what is good and how goods are legitimately to be pursued as public values, albeit at a fairly high level of abstraction. We, therefore, suggest that the ethicist's role is to understand, clarify, systematize, and complete the common language conceptions of reasoning that lead to a decision about public good and evil, right and wrong. The politics of interest gives rise to an American penchant for utilitarian solutions, and the politics of conscience, together with our populist leanings, produces a Kantian thrust in our ethical makeup. Pragmatism in American culture serves to balance these penchants and the values embraced by them. Prudent pragmatism supplies a homegrown method for putting this all together in systematic ethical analysis.

The emphasis we have placed on weighing and balancing values—and on compromise—should not be taken to mean that prudent pragmatism is inescapably a middle-of-the-road philosophy. In times of crisis ethical choice may require radically new "ends in view" (a phrase of Dewey's) and new means. It may require abandonment of meliorism in favor of radical change. It may require startling redefinitions of the culture's basic moral concepts. It will, therefore, require moral imagination and moral leadership, not compromise. But if it is to be prudent, ethical choice will remain pragmatic (i.e., tentative and experimental in its procedure). Ethical leaders will always be ready to present their reasons to the community and be willing always to engage in rational debate with those who embrace other points of view. When rational deliberation gives way to passionate action without forethought, ethical choice becomes impossible. In such a situation the idea of ethical action becomes meaningless. There is a growing literature, especially in the fields of bioethics and public administration, that compares, evaluates, and attempts to amalgamate the methods of ethical analysis we have discussed in this chapter. (In particular see Ainslie 2002; Arras 2002; Bohmann and Rehg 1997; Brandt 1983; Chandler 1994; Cooper 1987; Dobel 1990; Dunn and Fozouni 1976; Fishkin 1984; Jonsen and Toulmin 1988; McGee 1999; Miller et al. 1996; Pugh 1991; Wolf 1994.)

REFERENCES

Ainslie, Donald C. "Bioethics and the Problem of Pluralism." *Social Philosophy and Policy* 19, no. 2 (2002): 1–28.

Arras, John D. "Pragmatism in Bioethics: Been There, Done That." *Social Philosophy and Policy* 19, no. 2 (2002): 29–58.

Aristotle. *Nicomachean Ethics.* In *The Basic Works of Aristotle,* ed. R. McKeon, 959, 1025–29. New York: Random House, 1941.

Bohmann, James, and William Rehg, eds. *Deliberative Democracy.* Cambridge: Massachusetts Institute of Technology Press, 1997.

Brandt, Richard B. "The Real and Alleged Problems of Utilitarianism." *Hastings Center Report* 13, no. 2 (April 1, 1983): 31–43.

Chandler, R.C. "Deontological Dimensions of Administrative Ethics." In *Handbook of Administrative Ethics,* ed. T.L. Cooper, 147–56. New York: Marcel Dekker, 1994.

Cooper, T.L. "Hierarchy, Virtue, and the Practice of Public Administration: A Perspective for Normative Ethics." *Public Administration Review* 47 (1987): 320–28.

Dobel, Patrick. "Political Prudence and the Ethics of Leadership." *Public Administration Review* 50 (1990): 74–81.

Dunn, W.N., and B. Fozouni. *Toward a Critical Administrative Theory.* Beverly Hills, CA: Sage Publications, 1976.

Fishkin, James S. *Beyond Subjective Morality: Ethical Reasoning and Political Philosophy.* New Haven: Yale University Press, 1984.

French, Peter A. *Ethics in Government.* Englewood Cliffs, NJ: Prentice Hall, 1983.

Haley, Kathleen, and Melinda Lee, eds. *The Oregon Death With Dignity Act.* Portland, OR: Center for Ethics in Health Care, 1998.

Jonsen, Albert J., and Stephen Toulmin. *The Abuse of Casuistry.* Berkeley: University of California Press, 1988.

Kant, Immanuel. *Grounding for the Metaphysics of Morals,* ed. J.W. Ellington. Indianapolis, IN: Hackett, 1981.

Kovesi, Julius. *Moral Notions.* New York: Humanities Press, 1967.

Liptak, Adam. "Traces of Terror: News Analysis." *New York Times,* May 31, 2002, Sec. A, Col. 4, National Desk, 1.

Lissy, Karen S. *Cellular Phone Use While Driving.* Boston, MA: Harvard Center for Risk Analysis, 2000.

McGee, Glenn, ed. *Pragmatic Bioethics.* Nashville, TN: Vanderbilt University Press, 1999.

Miller, Franklin, et al. "Clinical Pragmatism: John Dewey and Clinical Ethics." *Journal of Contemporary Health Law and Policy* 13, no. 1 (1996): 27–51.

Pugh, D.L. "*The Origins of Ethical Frameworks* in Public Administration." In *Ethical Frontiers in Public Management*, ed. J.S. Bowman, 9–33. San Francisco: Jossey-Bass, 1991.

Tong, Rosemarie. *Ethics in Policy Analysis*. Englewood Cliffs, NJ: Prentice Hall, 1986.

Wittgenstein, Ludwig. *Philosophical Investigations*, 3rd. ed., trans. G.E.M. Anscombe. New York: Macmillan, 1968.

Wolf, Susan. "Shifting Paradigms in Bioethics and Health Law: The Rise of a New Pragmatism." *American Journal of Law and Medicine* 20, no. 4 (1994): 395–415.

CHAPTER 4

Prudent Pragmatism and Consensus: Case Ethics in Monist and in Pluralist Society

ow did casuistry (case-by-case ethics) develop into prudent pragmatism? The pluralist character of our society and the distinction
between the private and public spheres of life set important parameters for the use of prudent pragmatism as an instrument of ethical decision
today. But pluralism and the private–public distinction are relatively new in
the history of human society. Casuist ethics developed in a very different
social environment, one that was monistic (monolithic, homogeneous)
rather than pluralist. And its function in that earlier milieu was different
from its function now. It was to provide an instrument for established
authority to guide and control individual conscience and action by interpret-
ing and applying settled law rather than to furnish, as today, a framework
for reaching free public agreement about what the law ought to be. In each
case it could be fruitfully employed because of an underlying value consensus that had to be interpreted and fitted to the circumstances of daily life.

THE FUSION OF RELIGION AND POLITICS
IN MONIST SOCIETY

Ancient polities were either ethnically and religiously homogeneous, or else
they enshrined the gods and values of a dominant group while ghettoizing
and subjecting all others. The latter was the usual case. In Lacedaemon the
Helots, a non-Greek people, were slaves of the dominant Dorian minority,
the Spartans. The Jewish people, though allowed by their Egyptian masters
to practice their own religion, provided forced labor for Pharaoh's architectural projects and were forbidden to mingle socially with their overlords.
After the exodus from Egypt, the Hebrews built their own monolithic state
and pledged it to serve only Yahweh. Despite many fallings away from this

covenant and the introduction of foreign gods, such as Baal and Astarte, into public life, the main line of the Hebrew political tradition remained both monolithic and monotheistic. Even in democratic Athens, persons of non-Athenian blood, called Metics, were forbidden a share in civic life, which included public religious rites. Imperial Rome was a kind of pluralistic society, in which cultures of all kinds mingled in the streets of the capital city and in which temples to Isis and Osiris stood side by side with those of Roman gods such as Venus, Jupiter, and Mars. Indeed, individuals and whole cities of non-Romans were admitted to Roman citizenship. But all were required to burn incense to the image of the deified emperor or, like thousands of nonconforming Christians, face death in the arena.

After the decline of the Greek *polis*, with its vital civic life, an individualistic lifestyle developed in the polyglot kingdoms that succeeded the Macedonian empire and later composed the empire of Rome. On the one hand there was the amoral, aggressive individualism that grew out of the teachings of the Sophists, and on the other the gentle but withdrawn self-sufficiency of the Stoics. But though some varieties of Stoicism did enjoin public participation as moral duty, no correspondent conception of individual right against the political order developed.

CASE MORALITY IN MONIST SOCIETY

The beginnings of case morality and case law are found in this ancient world of monistic polities, in which liberal democratic pluralism and the distinction between private and public were unknown. (For a history of casuist reasoning in western society, see Jonsen and Toulmin 1988, esp. chaps. 3–8. The following paragraphs rely heavily on this account.) We have already discussed in Chapter 3 the Aristotelian distinction between scientific reason and practical reason (*phronesis*), and also the observation that circumstances determine the way in which general principles should be applied. The college of pontiffs of the early Roman Republic proceeded in this way in arbitrating cases that could not clearly be settled by established rules of law. And toward the end of the republic, we find the Stoic philosopher Cicero recommending the same method in applying the law of nature. In his essay *On Duty*, Cicero wrote that one must consider what is most needful in each individual case:

> In this way we shall find that the fundamental moral claim of social relationship (*humanitas*) is not identical in every circumstance... These different circumstances should be carefully scrutinized in every instance of duty, so that we can become skilled evaluators of duty and by calculation perceive where the weight of duty lies, so that we may understand how much is due to each person. (quoted in Jonsen and Toulmin 1988, 79)

Still another origin of the case method of moral reasoning is found in the body of principles built up by Jewish rabbinical scholars out of the community's moral experience. These writings constitute interpretations of the Mosaic law of the Torah as well as applications of that law to particular cases.

The early Christian church carried the practice of casuist interpretation forward, and we find in the writings of the church fathers' advice on how to apply the general principles of Christian living to the specific and varied circumstances of everyday life. The generic problem was how to reconcile the apparently conflicting demands of religion and the needs of temporal life. The casuist distinction between strict commandments and counsels of perfection, on the one hand, and the principle of the lesser evil, on the other, also grew out of the work of the patristics. The writings of Pope Gregory the Great even admit the possibility of moral dilemmas with no adequate resolution. In the penitential literature of the early church, which was written to guide a Christian's examination of conscience, we also find a rich appreciation of the importance of an individual's special circumstances in judging his or her acts and a recognition of the great diversity of circumstances.

CASUISTRY IN MEDIEVAL EUROPE

During the period from the eleventh to the fourteenth centuries, the socio-political structure that has been dubbed the *Respublica Christiana* of Europe came into being and flourished.

By contrast with the earlier agrarian and pastoral centuries, this was an urbanizing society, but still a decentralized and feudalized one of small interlocking political units that rose hierarchically to the crown of the Holy Roman Empire. Alongside this temporal order stood a more centralized ecclesiastical authority, one capped by the Papacy. In theory the "two swords" controlled matching jurisdictions, each with its proper sphere of governance. In practice, political life was marked by constant competition between the civil and spiritual jurisdictions, as well as among the feudal nobility and royalty.

The System of Medieval Casuistry

Ideologically, the *Respublica Christiana* was a consensual society, one with a value system embracing the dictates of natural and divine law, which were authoritatively interpreted and detailed by papal decrees, by conciliar pro-nouncements, and by an elaborate system of civil and ecclesiastical courts as well as by individual consciences. An educated clergy staffed the admin-istrative and judicial offices of both civil and ecclesiastical institutions.

It was in the hands of this elite that an elaborate system of case law developed, and the expression *casuistry* emerged as the name for the process of refining general principles in the light of the multiform circumstances both of civil and ecclesiastical life.

Based in the universities that grew up in urban centers, such as Paris and Bologna, the scholars of the time built elaborate codices of law, which they developed taxonomically, beginning with agreed cases and moving analogically to more complicated ones rather than theoretically (deductively) from axioms and general principles. Often these codices took the form of restatements of the ancient law of Rome as well as collections of church canons. Jonsen and Toulmin summarize the characteristics of the method employed as follows:

> The methods of medieval law, politics, and ethics were . . . interconnected . . . Sound judgment in resolving problems of moral practice depended on recognizing crucial resemblances and differences between new and problematic cases and available paradigmatic cases. Ethics was not a "moral geometry" in which one could "prove" that any case fell unambiguously under some strict universal and invariable definition of, for example, courage or temperance, treachery or murder. Nor were the merits of a case formally entailed by any such definition. Rather, arriving at sound resolutions required one to see how far and in what respects the parallels between problematic cases and more familiar paradigmatic cases could justify *counting them as* cases of "courage" or "treachery." (Jonsen and Toulmin 1988, 108)

The clerics who presided over this work constituted an international assemblage, a single Europe-wide cultural unit, one sharing a single professional vocabulary and system of thought whose members expressed themselves in a single professional language, Latin. Surmounting the work of the canonists was that of theologians, the *Summae* of men like Albertus Magnus and Thomas Aquinas, who detailed and explicated the general principles of right with which the codices of applied law were suffused.

The Decline of Casuistry

New ideological currents along with vast changes in political, economic, and social structures introduced by the Renaissance and Reformation were to bring the elaborate system of casuist reasoning to ruin. Protestantism introduced into European life a new spirit of independence that was incompatible with the clerical oversight of conscience embodied in the work of the casuists. To signify his disdain for casuistry, Martin Luther ceremoniously burned a popular work, entitled *Summa Diabolica*. And even within Catholic France, the philosopher Blaise Pascal attacked casuistry as an overrationalized system of argument with which excuses could be made for any position one wished to take. As a countercurrent to the religious individualism of Protestantism, the Renaissance produced a secular individualism, that of Machiavelli's *Prince*, which in a very different way repudiated the elaborate moral structures of medieval casuistry. In Machiavelli's view the problem of successful political endeavor consisted in learning how not to be "good" (in the traditional sense), and then to use that knowledge, or not use it, as the occasion required—an abandonment of traditional moral ideas altogether.

The sixteenth and seventeenth centuries were also a time of vast political and economic change, as centralized states and capitalist economic structures began to take form in the midst of religious wars of great ferocity. Rulers faced challenges to their authority, challenges against which traditional moral maxims seemed to offer inadequate defense. This led to the casuist fashioning of complicated excuses for behavior that in more settled times were unacceptable, a practice from which the term *casuistry* acquired the connotation of laxity and false morality that it retains to this day.

With the development of capitalism, the casuists found it necessary to revise radically a centuries-old understanding that usury—the taking of interest on loans—was immoral. The new ecclesiastical toleration of the institution of interest led some to the view that casuistic reasoning could produce any kind of rationale desired by the powerful. But, in fact, circumstances of economic life had changed so much that the old conception of usury became meaningless.

From Casuistry to Theoretical Ethics

Along with religious change and the crumbling of traditional moral notions in the face of social and economic revolution, the sixteenth and seventeenth centuries also ushered in a radically new worldview in the form of natural science. In place of a conception of natural law as a system of divine purposes working themselves out to fulfillment in the life of the world (the Scholastic worldview), natural law came to signify instead a system of regularities of motion. Prediction and control of these regularities rather than uncovering the divine will gradually came to be the ends of the new science. It is true that the idea of God as prime mover and first cause continued for a time to loom large in the language of scientists such as Isaac Newton. But by the time of Leibniz, *God* had become an unnecessary hypothesis. In the philosophies that developed in conjunction with the emergence of natural science, such as those of Descartes, Hobbes, and Locke, there was an assumption that the search for truth leads through the understanding of the regularities of process in the natural world. And for all of these men, the beginning of this search had to be the autonomous mind of the individual. Descartes, for example, held that human existence is grounded in the self-conscious thought of the individual—"I think; therefore, I am." And with this intellectual revolution the ground disappeared from under the communitarian categories of scholastic thought.

Systematic ethics had to be rebuilt from the ground up on an entirely new foundation. And this was taken to mean that ethics emerged from an abstract and self-evident first principle rather than from social agreement. Pure reason, as in mathematics, rather than the practical reason of Aristotle would be the instrument of discovery. And the new concepts would have to be expressed as Cartesian "clear and distinct ideas" rather than as ambiguous and open-ended notions that could be clarified only by the careful examination of circumstance.

Most of modern ethical speculation has been in this mode—deductive argument from some first principle, such as Kant's categorical imperative or Bentham's "greatest good of the greatest number." An exception, as we have seen, is American pragmatism. And in the background, courts both in the United States and in England have continued to develop law by building from precedent to precedent, as in the casuist tradition. Our hope, in this volume, is to work these traditions together with elements of casuist ethics in the form of what we have called in Chapter 3, "Prudent Pragmatism."

CONSENSUS IN PLURALIST SOCIETY

It was not the collapse of religious uniformity as such that led to the unworkability of casuistry in European society after 1517, but rather the loss of the value consensus that depended on that uniformity. Pluralism and moral consensus are quite compatible. In fact the idea of pluralism is embraced as a value by a liberal democratic agreement, such as the one we described in Chapter 2. It derives from the ideal of individual autonomy. While the details of that consensus are specific to American political culture, the principles of liberty and equality, complexly defined and paradoxically combined and opposed, are the core elements of every liberal democratic polity and movement in the world today. They also are the substance of the worldwide liberal democratic consensus embodied in the United Nations Organization.

Levels of Consensus

In an article entitled "The Tyranny of Principles," the philosopher Stephen Toulmin reviewed the experience of the National Commission for the Protection of Human Subjects of Biomedical and Behavioral Research, of which he was a member (Toulmin 1981, 31–39). The commission was charged with making recommendations for guidelines for the treatment of human subjects in medical and psychological research. The commission was especially asked to determine the conditions under which certain vulnerable groups, such as children and prisoners, could participate in such research without moral objection. The members of the commission came from a number of different walks of American life—science, the law, the study of theology, and others. Toulmin noted that despite the disparity of their backgrounds, the members of the commission were able to reach quite detailed agreement in almost every case. He attributed this to the fact that they proceeded taxonomically in their work, moving from clear, agreed cases to more difficult ones, on a case-by-case basis, rather from general principles. For at the level of principle, their ideas were a veritable babel. When asked to justify what they had done, "Catholics appealed to Catholic principles, the humanists to humanist principles, and so on." But Toulmin may have been mistaken in concluding that the work of the commission was carried on without reference to principles. We would argue that behind the self-conscious embrace of the moral language specific to their particular religious groups lay tacit agreement on the principles of the American political consensus we adumbrated in Chapter 2, and we would also maintain that this explains their ability to agree so quickly on the particular recommendations of their report. After all, the problem they faced was to find a way to bring the liberty of autonomous individuals together with the community's need for scientific research about human subjects.

Development of the Pluralist Ideal

The essential aspect of liberal political consensus is its procedural character. The political system is not supposed to espouse, promote, or enforce any particular vision of the good life. *How to live?* is a question that must be answered by the individual on the basis of his or her autonomy. There thus arises a plurality of groups, formed by free individuals who seek out like-minded persons to develop and share a variety of conceptions of the good life. Each group is pledged to "live and let live," not to encroach on the freedom of others to live as they please. This is the philosophical formulation of the idea of pluralism. In this view, public policies are created for common purposes only, which boil down to enhancing the ability of each social group to live a satisfying, fulfilling life. (See Moreno 1995, 56–57.)

This very broad view of what pluralism means was not, however, the consensus that informed early American political culture. Pluralism originally meant a plurality of churches. The Lockean agreement set down the defense of persons and property as the proper work of public government, leaving conscience free to express its autonomy in private religious associations. But it was expected that everyone would belong to some church. In Locke's own view, atheists were not to be tolerated, since without an oath on a Bible, he feared that contracts would not be kept.

To this day there remain disagreements among Americans about the boundary line between public and private in the realm of religion. School prayer and the reading of the Judeo-Christian scriptures in school were common practices until late in the twentieth century, and these issues were frequently the subject of litigation before the U.S. Supreme Court. As late as

2003, there was a rousing dispute about whether a marble monument displaying a carved representation of the Ten Commandments belonged in a public courthouse. (A federal court decided that it did not.) The name of God remains on our currency, however, and the clergy of various faiths continue to invoke divine blessings on the proceedings of Congress and other public bodies. Furthermore, the political rhetoric of American conservatism continues to refer to the United States as a Christian country. The development of consensus on the secularization of the political community has been gradual, and it has been carried forward through peaceful litigation in the federal courts.

Limits on Pluralism

Lockean religious toleration did not extend to any practices that are inimical to the security of life and property, whose protection is the main business of government in his view. In his *Letter Concerning Toleration* Locke made it clear that human sacrifice could not be tolerated. The federal courts in America have gone beyond that stricture to forbid religious groups from rejecting scientifically grounded medical therapies that have shown promise in the pursuit of saving life. Parents, following scriptural injunctions not to consume blood, have been required to allow transfusions to save the lives of children who are not yet able to exercise autonomous choice. Similarly, parents may not refuse established cancer therapies for their offspring in favor of a prayer-only policy. Working from case to case, the courts have modified the consensus about pluralism in this way.

In an analogous fashion, the courts have also regulated the institution of marriage. Mormon polygamy was outlawed toward the end of the nineteenth century as a threat to the democratic principle of government in favor of patriarchal order. (The authoritarian position of the father in a multiwife Mormon family threatened to establish patriarchically-governed clans as political units.) At present a large public debate is taking place about the appropriateness of extending the institution of marriage to same-sex couples. We can anticipate an eventual settlement of the question through legal interpretation of the meaning of marriage.

The Question of Abortion: Irruption of Violence

Only in one area of policy involving the interpretation of pluralist freedom is there conflict today that sometimes leads to violence—the legality of abortion. This conflict occurs because of a clash between the partisans of two views of individual rights—those who favor the right of women to absolute control over their bodies and those who insist that this right is limited by the right of unborn fetuses to live. The disagreement turns on the absence of a clear and agreed-upon definition of what it means to be a human person, and of when personhood makes its appearance in the life cycle. Is a newly-fertilized egg a human person? Or does human life appear only when the fetus is capable of life outside the womb? We have as yet not found answers to these questions that are acceptable to all. Pro-life and pro-choice advocates continue to square off against one another. Public debate continues on the issue of abortion from year to year, and the law changes as a shifting public opinion moves our courts and legislatures to act. It is not clear that the procedures of prudent pragmatism can ever produce a consensus on the crucial definition.

In September 2003 the pro-life activist Paul Hill was executed for the murder of an abortion provider. He went to his death without remorse, declaring that any means whatever was legitimate to stop the "lethal force" of abortion. A sign carried by a supporter outside the prison where the execution took place read, "Killing Baby Killers is Justifiable Homicide." And a member of the clergy from Mobile, Alabama, was quoted as saying that "[w]hat Paul Hill did was absolutely justified" (Wire Services, *Rochester Democrat and Chronicle*, 2003, 1). If large numbers of people agreed with these opinions, the social contract would be dissolved, and we would be reduced to Hobbes' "war of all against all." For the most part, however, the public seems ready to carry on the debate, and a large literature on the question of abortion continues to grow. This is not all defiant affirmation and rejection, either. Much consists of reasoned argument by professional ethicists and other informed writers in scholarly journals, who continue to seek a common ground.

Hopes and Fears

A continued public discussion of contentious issues such as abortion, at a variety of levels, displays a willingness of Americans to think of our democracy as a way of life, one modeled on the ideas of the pragmatist philosopher John Dewey. "There is an individualism in democracy," Dewey writes, "but it is an ethical, not a numerical individualism; it is an individualism of freedom, of responsibility, of initiative to and for the ethical ideal" ("The Ethics of Democracy," in Menand, ed. 1997, 199). It is as well an individualism that culminates in community. Differing and opposed perspectives, in dialogue with each other, constitute the shared life of the community. In this context, the pluralism we have been discussing can be understood as the necessary starting point for the generation of public policies that construct a healthy community of purpose. As Thomas Alexander puts it, "[B]y exploring the idea of communication in the democratic process, one comes to see the *need* for pluralism, for a style of intelligence that relies upon imagination as well as reason, and for an erotic care above and beyond mere self-centered toleration of differences" (Alexander in Langsdorf and Smith, eds. 1995, 133).

If this kind of debate is to take place, however, a present worrisome trend must be reversed. This is a trend toward social separation and insulation that results from groups' fear of losing deeply prized values as a result of cooperating in the life of the greater society. A leading example is the practice of home schooling, the abandonment of the communitarian experience of the public school. In part this development has come about as a result of the increasing secularization of the public order we discussed earlier, with religious groups feeling unable to compensate for their loss without withdrawal from the democratic process. In part it has resulted from a decline in the quality of education offered by the public school system. This trend could be fatal to our democracy. As Alexander has put it, "[D]emocracy is based on fostering an educated imagination and the social dispositions to engage others through a mutual contextual understanding of . . . beliefs, needs, desires, feelings, traditions and identities" (ibid.).

REFERENCES

Alexander, Thomas M. "John Dewey and the Roots of Democratic Imagination." In *Recovering Pragmatism's Voice: The Classical Tradition, Rorty, and the Philosophy of Communication*, ed. Lenore Langsdorf and Andrew P. Smith, 131–54. Albany, NY: SUNY Press, 1995.

Jonsen, Albert R., and Stephen Toulmin. *The Abuse of Casuistry: A History of Moral Reasoning*, Berkeley: University of California Press, 1988.

Menand, Louis, ed. *Pragmatism: A Reader*. New York: Vintage Books, 1997.

Moreno, Jonathan D. *Deciding Together: Bioethics and Moral Consensus*. New York: Oxford University Press, 1995.

Toulmin, Stephen. "The Tyranny of Principles." *The Hastings Center Report* XI, no. 6 (1981): 31–39.

Wire Services. "Abortion Provider's Killer is Executed in Florida." *Rochester Democrat and Chronicle*, September 4, 2003, 1.

CHAPTER 5

Prudent Pragmatism and Democratic Polity: Citizen, Representative, and Policy Analyst

In what kind of a democracy is prudent pragmatism the characteristic instrument of public choice? In that good society, are the rules of ethical choice the same for all? Will the differences in their political roles affect the ways in which citizens, their representatives, and the professional experts who engage in policy analysis apply the procedures of prudent pragmatic decision?

CITIZENSHIP IN A DEMOCRACY

Not only does *democracy* have a thousand different definitions. So too do many of its chief varieties—*liberal democracy*, for example. As employed by political scientists carrying out empirical survey research, the liberal democratic model posits a world of instrumentally rational atoms, who are politically aware, oriented to issues, self-interested, able to make independent and reasoned judgments, and strategic in their behavior. Rational choice theorists make similar assumptions about the populations of their model worlds. (See Dryzek 1990, 168–69.)

The Classical Liberal Model

In ethical theory the classical liberal view described here corresponds in general to the model espoused by utilitarians. As we saw in Chapter 3, these proponents hold that society is a collection of self-interested individuals who believe that the social good is equivalent to the greatest quantity of individual preferences, summed. Pluralist constitutionalists think that the realization of this end comes about through a system of bargaining and compromise.

There are many critics of these individualist conceptions. Some find that they diminish our full human nature. John Dryzek writes that "an instrumentally rationalized world is one in which individuals are like economic men—calculating machines with an impoverished subjectivity and no sense of self and community" (1990, 5). Some argue that observation shows these "economic men" to be empirically incorrect. Many people fail to participate in politics, either because they feel marginalized and alienated, or out of a sense of satisfaction with the outputs of the system. In the latter case people prefer to optimize the use of their time by pursuing individual goals. Still others believe that widespread political apathy indicates that the polity is working well and that to encourage greater participation would be to invite conflict and instability. Some scholars have pointed out that though the public at large may be politically disengaged, increased ideological division and acrimony among political elites are making compromise difficult and thereby produce political stalemate. These scholars cite recent U. S. congressional sessions as evidence that supports this view. "Political and governmental processes are polarized, the participants self-righteous and intolerant, their rhetoric emotional and excessive," writes Morris Fiorina. "The moderate center is not well represented in contemporary national politics" (Skocpol and Fiorina 1999, 411–12). While American political culture remains fundamentally consensual, in that we all share the same political vocabulary of liberty and equality, the national dialogue required to redefine these terms as circumstances change sometimes breaks down, thus causing political fronts to harden.

Prudent Pragmatism and Deliberative Democracy

Prudent pragmatism as a method of ethical assessment finds its proper place in a different sort of democracy from this one, one which remains more a matter of aspiration than of daily empirical reality. Its proponents call it by two names: discursive democracy and deliberative democracy. Learning to approximate discursive (deliberative) democracy by learning to practice prudent pragmatism gives hope that the ills of the empirical models described earlier may be healed.

"As one moves toward the participatory pole of the spectrum, . . . politics becomes increasingly discursive, educational, oriented to truly public interests, and needful of active citizenship" (Dryzek 1990, 13). John Dryzek, a proponent of deliberative democracy, expressly embraces Aristotelian rationality, which we earlier identified as the ancestor of prudent pragmatism, as an alternative to the maximizing variety. "Aristotelian practical reason," he writes, "involves persuasion, reflection upon values, prudential judgment, and free disclosure of one's ideas" (ibid., 9). He describes this process as a "communicative rationality" that consists in discourse between two or more people, which can both generate normative judgments and principles of action, as well as involve more than the selection of means to achieve specified ends (ibid., 14). It is a process in which ends are changed and evolve, as an examination of circumstances reveals that one's earlier judgment was mistaken, that what one took to be a desirable end was either wrong or illusory. In this view "the only remaining authority is a good argument," one which can verify the accuracy of an empirical description or explanation as well as the "validity of normative judgments" (ibid., 15). "Free, public, and reflective subscription to coordinated action in their pursuit," Dryzek writes, "inhibits subsequent subversion by narrow self-interest" (ibid., 70–71).

In deliberative democracy people understand that political behavior is appropriate to the forum rather than to the market. Classical liberalism, by contrast, assimilates politics to the market. In the market the consumer is sovereign, because he or she chooses there between courses of action that affect only him or her. In politics, however, the citizen expresses preferences over states of being that affect other people. (See Stone 2002, 17–22.) Rational choice theorists think of governmental procedures simply as a means for coping with market failures, for efficiently supplying social goods the market cannot. But while a social choice mechanism may indeed resolve market failures that would produce "unbridled consumer sovereignty," considered as "a way of redistributing welfare, it is hopelessly inadequate" (Elster in Bohman and Rehg 1997, 10). Paraphrasing the views of Jürgen Habermas on deliberative democracy, John Elster tells us that instead of conceiving the political system as a means of aggregating or filtering individual preferences, we should understand it as "set up with a view to changing [preferences] by public debate and confrontation. The input . . . . would then not be the raw, quite possibly selfish or irrational, preferences that operate in the market, but informed and other-regarding preferences" (in ibid., 11).

In this sort of participatory democracy, deliberation is the central element. Its purpose is to induce reflection on their preferences by citizens, who must be willing to change these preferences in the light of evidence uncovered by the act of deliberating. Its instrument is persuasion, rather than coercion (Dryzek 2000, 1–3). Prudent pragmatism, as a method of analysis, insists on the thorough investigation of the circumstances of a choice situation, which may well be revealed and enriched by deliberation with others.

Obstacles to Deliberative Democratic Development

Numerous obstacles to deliberative democracy and to prudent pragmatic reasoning have arisen in recent years in American politics. One is the deep erosion of civil society, testified to by such insightful scholars as Robert Putnam of Harvard University. (See Putnam 1995.)

Since the time of de Tocqueville, observers of American society have pointed out the important place of the spirit of association that has historically informed American political culture. Americans have been joiners, spontaneously organizing themselves as trade associations, parent-teacher associations, church groups, charitable organizations of all sorts, bowling leagues, and civic groups such as the Rotary and Kiwanis—all aimed at accomplishing some social goal beyond the power of the individual and obviating governmental action in many areas of endeavor. These groups have been training grounds of civic virtue, activities in which individuals learn democratically to cooperate with one another for public purposes. As de Tocqueville saw it, this penchant for association has drawn individuals out of their purely private concerns and made social beings of them. In the context of these mutual endeavors, they have learned to deliberate and to reason with one another about what ought to be done for the common good. Doing these things has also made citizens of us and taught us how to perform our proper roles in democratic polity.

1. Decline of "Social Capital"

Robert Putnam has dubbed these participatory habits "social capital."

> Individuals who regularly interact with one another in face-to-face settings learn to work together to solve collective problems. They gain social trust, which spills over into trust in government. Wise public policies, robust economic development and efficient public administration all flow from such social trust grounded in regular cooperative social interactions. (Skocpol and Fiorina 1999, 13)

But Putnam has found that this spirit of cooperation declined markedly during the last part of the twentieth century. Using General Social Survey (GSS) data, he discovered that between 1974 and 1994, membership in fraternal groups, school service groups, veterans groups, among others, had declined by about 25 percent. And with this development has gone a decline in social trust. The causes of the phenomenon are manifold and difficult to pin down. Economic anxieties during a long period of corporate downsizing have led people to work ever harder at two or more jobs. Feminism has led women in ever larger numbers into the marketplace. Television has kept people at home when they might be elsewhere engaged in some sort of civic activity. The net result, according to Putnam, has been to unravel social bonds, to atomize American society into a population not of self-reliant, independent citizens, but of lonely and alienated beings who do not understand themselves or their society.

2. Oligarchy in Civil Society

Other scholars, however, have denied that American associationism has declined. Jeffrey M. Berry, for example, argues that some measurements indicate quite the opposite—"that community participation is stable or even rising" (in Skocpol and Fiorina 1999, 367). Investigating this counterclaim, Morris Fiorina found that people are indeed still joiners but that in the last decade the kind of organizations that have grown in membership are of an entirely different sort from the local associations that in the past have produced America's social capital. They are large national organizations such as the AARP, the Nature Conservancy, the National Rifle Association (NRA), the National Right to Life Committee, and the Concord Coalition. Membership in such associations involves paying dues, but little more in the way of individual action. These are advocacy groups, whose policies are made by staff rather than by the membership, and they are, therefore, oligarchical rather than democratic in character. As Fiorina puts the matter:

> Privileged and well-educated citizens have led the way in reshaping the associational universe, withdrawing from cross-class membership federations and redirecting leadership and support to staff-led organizations. The result is a new civic America largely run by advocates and managers without members and marked by yawning gaps between immediate involvements and larger undertakings. (Skocpol and Fiorina 1999, 462)

Members of these new civic organizations are not citizens, who are participating in democratic endeavor, but rather they are "consumers with policy preferences" (ibid., 492). The polity has been converted into a market. There are no longer many interactions between leaders and members, with leaders sounding out the policy opinions of their membership; now the leaders are acting on their own to set both agendas and policy (ibid., 494).

All this is corrosive of the attitudes and habits which make citizens capable of deliberative democratic practices and of prudent pragmatic reasoning. The new structures sometimes also fall into contradictions and produce democratic outrage by their grass roots. A case in point was the negative reaction of the AARP membership to leadership support of the Medicare reform bill of 2003, which introduced a prescriptions benefit into the program. The journalist Paul Krugman claimed that the AARP leadership, which had some years earlier begun selling prescription insurance to its membership, had in the process taken on the mentality of an insurance company and lost sight of its advocacy function on behalf of the aged (*New York Times* 2003).

Fiorina illustrates the difference between the democratic character of legislation, such as the GI Bill of 1944, and the effort of the Clinton administration in the 1990s to introduce a national health insurance system. In the 1940s it was not political elites who planned the veterans' entitlement legislation; rather it was the American Legion, a very large voluntary membership federation, that drafted the bill. In the 1990s advocacy groups did not mobilize mass support for a generally acceptable reform plan. Instead, "[h]undreds of business and professional groups influenced the Clinton Administration's complex policy schemes and then used a combination of congressional lobbying and media campaigns to block new legislation" (Skocpol and Fiorina, ibid., 503). The result was that the extension of health coverage to a large number of low-income families failed to pass.

3. Ideological Tensions and Policy Impasse

Fiorina's discussion of the Clinton health plan failure illustrates the effect of ideology on the new structure of civic engagement. Ideological stance is one of the factors that accounts for the growing rigidity in the policymaking process, the increased tensions between the major political parties, and the growing inability of congressional leaders to reach compromises. Instead, we have increased name-calling by our political leaders and heightened animosity, acrimony, and ideological division among political activists in general.

By contrast the decentralized system of civic engagement in the 1950s and early 1960s put to work our social capital of the time, which took the form of the civil rights movement. This movement, in turn, spread into still other rights movements in the 1970s, leading to the empowerment of women and gays, to the unionization of farmworkers, and to the mobilization of other nonwhite ethnic minorities. This was a period in which peaceful political protest went hand in hand with increased deliberative democracy. People reasoned together, information about the condition of unequal minorities was spread before the public, education took place, and minds were changed. The policy process worked to produce results acceptable to all. Today's oligarchic structure of political engagement has brought instead policy impasse, uncivil behavior in our legislative bodies, and anger. In December 2003, James Poniewozik, writing in *Time* magazine told of "The Rise of 'the Anger Industry.'" Illustrative of this event were books such as Al Franken's *Lies and the Lying Liars Who Tell Them*, Bernard Goldberg's *Arrogance: Rescuing America from the Media Elite*, David Corn's *The Lies of George W. Bush*, and Ann Coulter's *Liberal Treachery from the Cold War to the War on Terrorism*. Then there are the talk shows featuring the angry rhetoric of broadcasters such as Rush Limbaugh. By way of reaction, a boom in the conservative publishing industry has begotten a whole spate of books written by and talk-radio shows hosted by angry liberals. None of these "emphasize the substantive matters that define one as liberal or conservative," Poniewozik wrote. Those who tune in want to be told "at Wagnerian volume and in Proustian detail—what a bunch of S.O.B.s the other guys are" (38). All of these things make the practice of deliberative democracy and prudent pragmatic policymaking a far-off ideal.

The Restoration of Deliberative Democracy

The Republic has been in better shape before, however. And it can be so again. What kinds of experiences do we need to return us to more deliberative and rational habits?

A willingness to experiment has always been a characteristic of American democracy. We find the theme sounded as early as *The Federalist Papers*, whose authors wrote of the new Constitution as an experiment. Later, in his Farewell Address to the nation, Andrew Jackson announced that political life under this instrument "was no longer a doubtful experiment." Much later, during the crisis of the Great Depression, Franklin Roosevelt rejected all ideological panaceas in favor of an experimental approach to grappling with the nation's ills—the New Deal's program of political, social, and economic reform.

1. Experiments in Participatory Governance

During the last two decades, as the affirmative state that grew out of Roosevelt's experimentation of the 1930s became unwieldy and inefficiently bureaucratized, new and different experiments have contributed to renewal and reform. Two such efforts, undertaken at the level of city government, may be of special significance for the development of habits of deliberative democratic practice. Both have to do with the creation of neighborhood governance councils in the city of Chicago in the 1980s. One involved an effort to take school affairs out of the hands of a stagnating bureaucracy, the other was an attempt to devolve control over policing into the hands of the public.

In a study devoted to a number of such experiments, in the United States and abroad, Archon Fung and Erik Olin Wright classify the experiences in Chicago as examples of *Empowered Participatory Governance* (EPG) (2003). Their object was to enlist ordinary citizens, especially from the lowest levels of society, in the effort to solve the problems that bedeviled them. The authors write that the reforms "are participatory because they rely upon the commitment and capacities of ordinary people to make sensible decisions through reasoned deliberation and empowered because they attempt to tie action to discussion" (ibid., 5).

Since 1988, Chicago public schools have been governed by their own elected local school councils, which are composed of parents, teachers, community representatives and a nonvoting student. These councils are authorized to hire and fire principals, spend discretionary funds, and develop strategic plans. They are also held accountable for their actions. In each case the councils are confronted with tangible problems—there are no abstract exercises. In the policing experiment, the method employed was to have patrol officers and sergeants on beats meet regularly with residents to identify safety problems and to develop strategies to deal with them. The focus has been on creating situations in which people used to competing with one another for resources are led both to cooperate with one another instead and to work out problems by reasoned discussion. Participants listen to one another's positions and then work together to generate group choices. Their work does not involve adding up or compromising individual preferences, but rather working out group preferences. In the judgment of the researchers, the citizen councils were able to invent effective solutions superior to those worked up by school and police officials alone. In part this was because citizens and officials working together were able to generate relevant information broader than what the officials alone disposed of. As we saw earlier, generating detailed understanding of all the circumstances relevant to a given ethical problem is the essence of the prudent pragmatist method.

2. Virtue

The ability to implement the principles of prudent pragmatism or to engage effectively in the practice of deliberative democracy is not only a matter of following certain procedural rules. It is also a matter of developing *virtue*, which is simply another word for *excellence*. (The Greek word used by Aristotle in this connection is *arête*, which can be translated by either English word.) The specific virtue involved is that of prudence. Aristotle argued that it is not the young who display the most prudence, but rather the old because of their experience. It was for him experience in public deliberation that generated excellence in deliberative decision making. One becomes virtuous by doing virtuous acts. The experience of Chicago's citizen councils has demonstrated the truth of Aristotle's idea.

3. A National-Level Experiment

Another example of grass-roots democracy, at the national level, dates from 1983. This involved an effort by William Ruckelshaus, then administrator of the Environmental Protection Agency (EPA), to obtain public input concerning standards for arsenic emissions from the copper smelting and glass manufacturing industries in the United States. While arsenic is regarded as a dangerous air pollutant, adequate regulation ran counter to important economic values in one particular part of the country—the Tacoma, Washington, area. Here was located the American Smelting and Refining Company (Asarco), the only smelter that used ore with a high arsenic content. It was also the only domestic producer of industrial arsenic, and it produced one-third of the U.S. supply of arsenic. The EPA calculated that standards existing at the time caused one cancer death a year in the Tacoma area, in addition to those attributable to other factors. To raise the standards sufficiently to eliminate this result ran the risk of driving production costs up so high that Asarco would be forced to close its doors. There thus appeared a plain conflict between two important values—jobs and human life. Ruckelshaus decided that in issuing new regulations, he had to add the voice of the people affected by his regulations to the calculations of risk-benefit analysis.

This decision situation differed from the local school and policing problems we discussed earlier in several ways. For one, it was not a decision that could be completely devolved upon the people of the Tacoma area as part of an ongoing policymaking system. It was to be a one-time affair—and advisory only. It still remained Ruckelshaus' job to make the decision. Furthermore, the technical information the public needed to absorb in order to produce rational input was detailed, complex, and ambiguous. Whether the existence of a threshold of safety for carcinogens should be assumed was also being debated by scientists. In addition, whether the extent of emissions had been properly measured was also in question. This was the context in which the public was asked to contribute to a decision as to what was a reasonable public health risk to accept from arsenic emissions.

The EPA decided to provide technical information to the public via a series of workshops conducted by EPA employees. Before the workshops took place, both the local and national media gave the matter very extensive coverage of a highly dramatic kind, which triggered widespread emotional reactions. Some complained that EPA's role was to protect public health, not to ask a community what it was willing to sacrifice to avoid death by cancer. In addition, it was not clear what kind of guidance Ruckelshaus was seeking from public advice. He told the press he was not seeking a referendum, yet he remarked that he was in a quandary as to how to proceed if the advice given by the public was evenly divided. This was obviously not going to be an exercise in deliberative democracy, as we described it earlier.

Nevertheless, there was general agreement that the EPA workshops had value. EPA analysts were impressed by the high level of sophistication of questions raised by some citizens in the workshops. One remarked that in the give-and-take of the workshop discussions, the technical staff of the EPA had received a valuable education about the issue. Employees in the regional EPA office thought the consultation process had proved beneficial by improving both image and trust. If the questions could not be settled by democratic public decision, the policy analysts involved at least profited by the public role in the process. Information gathered for their work turned out to be at least equal to the value of public enlightenment by the process. If the decision was not the product of grass roots democracy, one may conclude that the democratic character of both citizen and analyst roles had been enhanced by the popular consultation. (See Scott in Gutmann and Thompson 1990, 163–76.)

4. National Deliberation Day

During the presidential election campaign of 2004, political scientists James Fishkin and Bruce Ackerman organized a National Deliberation Day in order to bring the public into a rational discussion on the leading issues of our time—foreign policy, healthcare policy, social security policy, and education policy. On October 21, focus groups met in the various regions of the country. These meetings were followed by plenary sessions in which several focus groups came together with experts on particular issues that were being considered. The experts were people with special knowledge acquired from their life experiences—public officials, both elected and appointed, union leaders, leaders of business groups, and local party leaders. Members of the focus groups came from all walks of society, and they were in some cases core members of the two major parties, in others, independents.

Various age groups were represented as well. There was an opportunity for members of the focus groups in a plenary session to question the experts on the details of policy issues under consideration (e.g., the relationship between the armed occupation of Iraq and the establishment of democracy there, the expectations of the Bush administration for the building of democracy there as an example to the rest of the Middle East and as a stimulus for the development of democracy elsewhere).

Participants spoke of their experience during the day as one of growth and of rational development as a result of the exchange of views in a nonpartisan context. They contrasted this experience with listening to partisan speeches by candidates, and they spoke of the importance of getting beyond abstract political slogans into a detailed rational consideration of issues in their contexts. In effect, these people had spent the day in an exercise in prudent pragmatism. Jane Mansbridge, a political science professor at Harvard, speaking on the Jim Lehrer *NewsHour*, contrasted the frustration expressed by citizens at the mudslinging and, sloganeering of the stump speeches of the presidential campaign, with the rational discourse of the Deliberation Day events.

The October Deliberation Day was an acting out of the prescriptions for such a national discussion described by Professors Ackerman and Fishkin in a volume devoted to the subject, which they published in 2004. In their book the authors write of their project as a preparation for future presidential campaigns. "If Deliberation Day succeeded, everything else would change: the candidates, the media, the activists, the interest groups, the spin doctors, the advertisers, the pollsters, the fundraisers, the lobbyists, and the political parties. All would have no choice but to adapt to a more attentive and informed public. When the election arrived, the people would have a better chance of knowing what they wanted and which candidates were more likely to pursue the popular mandate" (Ackerman and Fishkin, *Legal Affairs* January/February 2004, 34). They would have undergone an experience of prudent pragmatic therapy in rational discourse.

The creators of the Deliberation Day project believe that institutionalizing the day as a part of national elections would radically transform the nature of opinion polls. "Today," they write, "what polls of citizens generally measure are raw, poorly informed preferences based on very weak information" (ibid., 36). If large numbers of the electorate were to participate in National Deliberation Day, this situation would change fundamentally. As a result, the candidates, who closely follow the results of national polling, would have to change their approach to getting elected. "If Deliberation Day is established and a critical mass shows up to participate, . . . sophisticated politicians will no longer be so interested in monitoring the existing patterns of raw preferences. They will want to know about their constituents' refined preferences: what the voters will think after they have engaged in the discussion and reflection precipitated by Deliberation Day" (ibid., 37).

That this would indeed be the result is predicted by the experience of Professor Fishkin, who has spent the last ten years engaged in a social

science experiment called deliberative polling. In the experiment participants first take part in an initial survey, conducted in the usual manner of
opinion polling. They then read materials on public issues prepared by the
project directors, materials that have been tested for accuracy and balance.
These participants then go on to join in discussion groups, with panels of
competing experts present. At the end of a weekend of deliberation, they
take the initial survey over again. The results have been dramatic, showing
a change in the balance of opinion on as many as two-thirds of the policy
questions asked (ibid.). Most significantly, these changes are driven by better information. It has also been found that preferences become more pub-
lic-spirited as a result of the deliberative assemblies as well as more collectively
consistent. Professors Ackerman and Fishkin hope that Deliberation Day
may someday be enacted as the law of the land.

5. The World Wide Web and Deliberative Democracy

Have the amazing advances in the communicative capacity of individuals
made possible by television, computer technologies, and the Internet
provided instruments for the enhancement of deliberative democracy in our
time? The potential is there, but students of the matter find that as yet
"there is little push either from civic-minded consumers or from social,
economic or political leaders in that direction" (Bennett and Entman, eds.
2001, 19). At present the tendency seems instead to be in the opposite
direction—toward increasingly personalized communication and an
increasing fragmentation of interests and political direction. "Current communication fashions," write two students of the subject, "treat members of
the public as isolated consumers who pilot their own personal destinies."
They do not offer outlets "for effective and satisfying participation in the
policy sphere" (ibid.). These scholars find that the amount of space allocated
to detailed issues of public policy is actually shrinking, both because of its
high cost and also because people prefer to be treated as consumers of information about entertainment and lifestyles. These scholars conclude that "the
political tendency is for relatively isolated communities to develop and to
see government and policy intrusions as antagonistic" (ibid., 20).

There are some contrary indications, however. Political debate and political display have crept into the entertainment agenda. Public figures like
Arnold Schwarzenegger have announced their political candidacy on talk
shows in recent times. (What we are to make of the fact that entertainers like
Schwarzenegger and Ronald Reagan have become successful candidates for
public office, however, is not clear.) It is also noteworthy that the surprise
support of the AARP for the Republican-sponsored Medicare reform bill of
2003 was answered by massive membership protest expressed in part
through outraged postings on the AARP's website.

For those interested in political expression and recruitment, the Internet
now offers a greatly expanded range of possibilities—for the creation of

newsgroups, political chatrooms, and action groups. Dennis Thompson has praised the Democracy Network as a paradigm of the kind of site that accomplishes this (quoted by Peter Levine in Anderson and Cornfield, eds. 2003, 57). There have also appeared websites such as Debate America, which present public policy debates on both national and local issues. There are also Govote.com and Speakout.com (Anderson and Cornfield, eds. 2003, 60).

One student of participatory democracy points out that with regard to one large public issue in particular, the media have provided a way of integrating events in the world of everyday life into policy discourse—the issue of abortion. The media have given grass-roots organizations the opportunity to be heard and taken seriously in a national policy debate. Women have been shown as active agents in their own right, rather than as mere objects for protection by public policy. "Taken as a whole," writes William Gamson, "media discourse on abortion concretizes public discourse and helps to counteract excessive abstraction. It helps to bridge private and public spheres by translating between political policy discourse and the language of the life-world" (in Bennett and Entman, eds. 2001, 69). Whether it can facilitate the kind of discourse that will bring the public together on the abortion issue in the way that the media helped congeal national consensus on civil rights, however, remains an open question.

On the issue of nuclear power, media discourse produced some integration linking world opinion and policy discourse by helping to shape and give legitimacy to the anti–nuclear power movement. With regard to Arab-Israel relations, affirmative action, and troubled American industries, however, there has not been similar success (ibid., 70, 71). That organizations around the country have been learning to use the Internet for issue advocacy, rather than turning to candidates, however, cannot be denied. That this may result in more and better information available to the public in issue advocacy campaigns is a possibility (Anderson and Cornfield 2003, 72–73, 77–81). This would improve at least one dimension of democratic public discourse—detailed information available about relevant circumstances.

The public has shown its appetite for this. A 1999 Democracy Online Project study showed that two-thirds to three-quarters of the online electorate want information on community problems and candidates for public office (ibid., 24). "The most optimistic scenario," write Carpini and Keeler, "is that the Internet will help increase the mean level of knowledge while not exacerbating. . . existing gaps in knowledge across socio-economic groups" (Carpini and Keeler, in ibid., 136).

Conclusion: The Role of the Democratic Citizen

We have seen that if we wish to be prudent pragmatists in our public decision making, we must learn to practice deliberative democracy. We need to be as well informed as possible about the circumstances relevant to the issue at hand. And in the final analysis, we must consult our values as citizens, not as consumers, because our canvass of an issue is not to the end of satisfying a preference, but of deciding what kind of policy is for the common good. The prudent pragmatist does not ask what he or she can get out of tax reform, but in the light of the circumstances, what is required for the country's well-being as a whole. So far as feasible, we should make up our minds about policy issues in the context of discussions with our fellow citizens, discussions in which we stand ready to revise our opinions as sound argument and new information are conveyed to us. In presenting these conclusions to our representatives, we make it easier for them to review and amalgamate the ideas of their constituents in the drafting and negotiation of policy.

The citizen must also supply representatives and analysts with information that these people need to play their roles effectively. We should convey the substance of our interests in a policy decision as well as our judgments about the common good, since those who draft legislation and administrative rules can do so appropriately only if they know all the relevant facts. And our interests are part of that factual picture. We also need to use available media efficiently, from letters to e-mail, to protests, to focus groups, to messages posted on websites. The more we can do these things in conjunction with other citizens, in the context of pressure group organizations, public interest organizations, and party caucuses, the better. We should also make communication with our representatives as much as possible a two-way street.

REPRESENTATION AND REPRESENTATIVES

The size and diversity of our polity make it impossible for deliberative democracy and prudent pragmatic reasoning by citizens to suffice for our governance. Our views must be filtered and amalgamated at several levels of representation. Some of these levels are in our local communities, others in the nation as a whole. In some cases, representation will be by deliberative bodies, such as the houses of Congress; in other cases, by unified executives such as the president. Judges are also our representatives—in the sense that it is their role to interpret the laws that are our tentative judgments on the whole range of policy issues, and they perform this function in light of agreed fundamental principles of governance that we call the Constitution.

Legislators

What is the function of a representative? What does it mean to represent? Literally, the representative re-presents his or her constituents; the representative stands in their place. In the American Congress this has been construed in two ways. One is called the mandate theory of representation, according to which the congressional representative is a delegate of his or her constituents, a person who is mandated to do what they instruct him or her to do. In any strict sense, this would be a difficult thing to do, since constituents in the most united of districts will not speak with one voice. The representative must attempt to fuse or amalgamate, "filter" the ideas of his or her district in order to produce a unified voice. One may interpret this as a compromising function, finding a lowest common denominator.

In the tenth number of the *The Federalist Papers*, Madison spoke of the work of the representative as one of substituting for the passion of the constituent the congressman's own dispassionate reasoning. Representatives must replace the clash of individual interests with their own reasoning about what the common good requires. As Madison put it, the representative's role is "to *refine* and *enlarge* the public view by passing [the public's opinions] through the medium of a chosen body of citizens, whose wisdom may best discern the true interest of their country" (45). Representation thus makes possible a process of deliberation that does not take place at the grass roots. This is sometimes referred to as the "trustee" conception of representation. At the same time the interested demands of constituents supply raw material for the representative to reason about.

In a famous speech to the members of his parliamentary constituency in the English city of Bristol, the statesman-philosopher Edmund Burke presented another version of the trustee concept of representation. He remarked that what the member of Parliament owes his constituents is his judgment, which should operate for the good of the whole polity. His function is not to represent individual will but rather the reason of the whole.

While the Constitution, in the form of the system of separated powers and checks and balances clearly envisages the pushing and tugging of interests in the legislative halls, if this were all that was at work, even compromises would be difficult to achieve. Madison and the other authors of the *The Federalist Papers* wrote frequently of the importance of civic virtue in the makeup of legislators. By that they meant simply public spiritedness. Without this no mechanical system of balanced powers would be able to produce policies for the social good.

Executives

In American government textbooks the president of the United States is usually referred to as our Chief Legislator. The Constitution provides for his or her participation in the legislative process by giving the president a veto over the acts of Congress. In recent decades the president has also taken the lead in setting the legislative agenda of the national government. Presidents are annually expected to present Congress with a plan of action, a set of proposals to deal with the issues they think should have priority. In doing this, their role is to bring together the many interests and concerns of our pluralistic society and to lead the deliberative process of the national government in a successful grappling with the problems that beset us. Their office is perhaps unique in its need to see every piece of policy in relation to every other piece, not segmentally. This is especially important in bringing domestic policy into line with foreign policy. (See Gregg 1997, 6.) Sometimes wrenching decisions are called for, as when President Bush felt compelled to remove steel tariffs in 2003 in response to the demands of key foreign allies. This is deliberative democracy at the highest level.

The ethical demands of our country's pluralistic character place special constraints on executives and legislative representatives when they are leading the policymaking process. Unlike private citizens, they are foreclosed by their role from using their private value systems as guides in setting policy goals. As elected agents of the public, they undertake a commitment to act only within the common value system and not to attempt to impose their private ethical values by using the power of their office to do so. Not all of them, indeed, are aware of these constraints. But the more sensitive are.

Mario Cuomo, when governor of New York, gave an eloquent state-ment of this norm in an address on September 13, 1984, at Notre Dame University. The controversial subject in hand was abortion. As a Roman Catholic, he was committed to the view that the act of aborting an unborn child is grievously sinful. Constitutionally, he was empowered to work for a law against abortion. He could do this, not because of his religious beliefs, but because he thought that it was important for the good of the commu-nity to protect the life of the unborn. But he forbore to do so, he told his audience, because it would be divisive. It would "threaten our ability to function as a pluralistic society" (Cuomo 1993, 38). "Our public moral-ity," he continued, "depends on a consensus view of right and wrong. The values derived from religious belief will not—and should not—be accepted as part of the public morality unless they are shared by the plural-istic community at large, by consensus" (ibid., 38–39). On the other hand, it is certainly appropriate to fulfill one's religious values when they are part of the secular consensus. "The agnostics who joined the civil rights struggle were not deterred because that crusade's values had been nurtured and sustained by black Christian churches" (ibid., 39). The problem arises, rather, when religious values are brought forward to support positions that would impose on nonbelievers limitations they cannot accept.

Old ways die hard, however. The meaning of separation of church and state continues to evolve in our society. Some still do not realize that referring to our country as a "Christian nation" no longer fits our pluralistic reality. To suggest that God favors a particular political party or wants a church-state established is to withdraw from the common value consensus. Political lead-ers, especially those who aspire to high executive office—and, therefore, to be molders of national policy—must remain within the confines of the national value consensus.

POLICY ANALYSIS IN DELIBERATIVE DEMOCRACY

Policy Analysis as Technical Expertise

The work of the policy analyst seems on the face of it to be incompatible with deliberative democracy. For the result of policy analysis is expert opinion. The very idea of "expertise," with its technical connotations, does not seem to fit with the concept of democratic rule. Expert rule is based on special knowledge that is confined to a few, those with a special education. It is, therefore, aristocratic. Democracy, on the contrary, means rule by citizens who are equals.

Some kinds of policy analysis are, indeed, undemocratic, and they cannot be fitted into the system of deliberative democracy we sketched earlier. In its beginnings in the United States, policy analysis was a branch of economics and was devoted to determinations of allocative efficiency. Distributional equity was to be left to the political process. Grounded in welfare economics, policy analysis left "little room for social values." Its work was "to determine policies that will maximize the satisfaction of the preferences for which individuals are willing to pay rather than satisfying the goals or values of society as a whole." Its only social value was "overall utility, or social welfare defined in terms of the satisfaction of the preferences of . . . individuals" (Mark Sagoff in Carrow, Churchill, and Cordes, eds. 1998, 91). Beryl Radin, a past president of the Association for Policy Analysis and Management, notes that when she first entered the field in the late 1950s, policymakers were forced to "rely on overly technical and narrow experts who defined the policy issues in very incomplete ways, focusing only on efficiency criteria and driving out other values" (Radin 2000, vi). Over the years, however, she observed large changes in the policy analysis profession, which she judged had by 2000 "moved closer to the role that seems to [her] to be central: setting the activity in a pluralistic and fragmented policy world that operates in a society characterized by diversity" (ibid., vii). She sees the profession as one that has become "classically American as it has become more pluralistic and open," in contrast to its earlier condition which "had more in common with societies that had traditions of elitism and secrecy" (ibid., 2).

Policy Analysis as Value Clarification and Assessment

Policy analysts are now attuned to the fact that their clients have a very broad range of values to serve that are not amenable to the simple analytical models that analysts first employed. One consequence has been that analysts more and more have training in specialist fields, such as prison reform, treasury matters, medicine. Analysts have also had to become sensitive to the values of the public at large. Aaron Wildavsky in his classic work, *Speaking Truth To Power*, has urged analysts to devise means for greater public participation in the policy process, since so much depends on getting straight the relevant values in a policymaking situation. Interest groups such as the Sierra Club, Common Cause, professional and trade associations, and specially constructed focus groups may be used to develop relevant information. In one year, forty-five federal agencies employed more than 1,250 advisory committees with more than 22,000 members (Tong 1986, 51). "Analysts cannot insulate themselves from the dynamics of politics, interest groups, and deadlines. Information takes on particular meaning when it is attached to specific positions and articulated by participants in the decision-making process" (Radin 2000, 92).

The policy analyst also cannot assume that his or her client's values are given and fixed. It is the analyst's role to maintain a detailed dialogue with the client, in which they together explore the consequences of various kinds of actions. In the process the client's goals and values may be changed as well as clarified. If an analyst works for a lobby, it will be his or her job to show the consistency of the client's goals with the public interest—and to some extent modify and adjust these goals accordingly (Sagoff in Carrow, Churchill, Cordes, eds. 1998, 100). Weimer and Vining write that "clients are often ambiguous about their goals and they sometimes appear to have goals that you may consider inappropriate. You may be able to help your client ask a better question by identifying the ambiguity and by indicating why you believe that certain goals are inappropriate" (Weimer and Vining 1989, 182).

Policy Analysis as Prudent Pragmatic Reasoning in Policymaking

Good policy analysis requires that those who perform it engage in a continuous conversation about problems, alternative approaches, resources, and objectives that reaches backward to a plethora of information sources at the grass roots and forward through the planning structures and plans of policymakers. It, therefore, involves at every point the exercise of methods of prudent pragmatism in the context of a multiform, many-level system of deliberative democracy.

Ethicists as Policy Analysts

The proliferation of new technologies in the past three-quarters of a century, in giving rise to new and astounding capabilities for human control over nature, has also produced a string of problems in which public policy has become enmeshed in large ethical quandaries. Medicine, for example, now makes it possible to produce life in a laboratory and to modify the genetic makeup of plants, animals, and human beings. How do these new possibilities fit with our human moral sense? Is everything that has been made possible also to be deemed desirable? Society has to make up its mind about these things, and it has to adopt policies regulating the use of the new technologies for the common good. Advances in healthcare have made it possible to extend the life of ill patients almost indefinitely. What parameters should be set on the use of such capabilities? Should the suffering of the terminally ill be alleviated by medicine even to the extent of the practice of euthanasia? Should parents who can afford the money be free to modify the features, physiques, and brain power of their offspring by using these new tools? If the incidence of illnesses such as Parkinson's disease is determined by genetic makeup, should insurance companies have access to information of this sort about applicants for insurance coverage? Should society be willing to accept the risks of increased reliance on nuclear energy along with the benefits of abundant and inexpensive fuel?

If our society is to find sound answers to questions such as these, it must do so on the basis of ethical consensus. Recently there have appeared on the policy scene a new kind of expert and a new kind of institution that presumptively can be of help in establishing such a consensus—the professional ethicist and the ethics commission.

Professional ethicists today serve on the staffs of hospitals and teach in academia. They populate ethics think tanks, such as the Hastings Center, and hold conferences to discuss public policy questions. They advise physicians in hospitals on hard moral questions that come up daily in medical decisions about patient treatment. Should a neonate with spina bifida be kept alive with artificial means? Should life support systems be removed from patients who have become brain dead? Whose judgment should be followed in the event of differences of opinion among relatives and others intimately concerned? A recent decision on a matter of this sort by an ethics committee in the Florida Schiavo case was objected to by parents of the patient. This brought court intervention, followed by political action in the state legislature that sought to overturn the judicial judgment. The ethics committee judgment, however, finally prevailed. Ethicists publish articles in learned journals and also produce a quite extensive monograph literature. The most well known are asked to serve on governmental commissions. They profess a wide range of approaches to ethical analysis, and their ethical views are normally paired with a standard ideological position in the political spectrum, from conservative to radical.

That new technologies have given rise to genuine ethical problems, however, cannot be disputed. The term bioethics grew out of the national discussion on the study of syphilis at the Tuskegee Institute in Alabama, from the 1930s to the 1970s, when black men who were involved in the study were denied access to drugs such as penicillin so that the effects of the disease might be observed in their bodies. It was this study and the experience of the inhuman experiments carried on in the name of science by doctors connected with the Nazi regime in Germany that sparked in the United States an awareness of the ethical problems implicit in scientific discoveries. (See Mooney 2001.) The saliency of these problems is attested to today by the existence of a Presidential Council on Bioethics.

A leading figure in the bioethics profession is Leon Kass, Harding Professor on the Committee on Social Thought of the University of Chicago.

Trained as a biochemist and as a physician, Kass served for a while as a biochemist at the National Institutes of Health. Profoundly conservative in outlook, he developed over the years a distrust of the new technologies that have given human beings an extraordinary power to modify natural life processes. When cloning became a leading topic of the day, Kass left his biochemical work to become a philosopher and ethicist who periodically makes broad pronouncements on bioethical subjects. He has also been concerned with what he considers a threat of dehumanization implicit in the development of techniques for assisted reproduction. Over the years he has made common cause with the conservative theologian Paul Ramsey. Liberals on the other extreme of the ideological divide consider him an irrationalist and obscurantist.

The appointment of Leon Kass as chair of the president's commission raises a problem we canvassed earlier when discussing the role of one's private values, especially religious ones, in filling a role as public representative. As Chris Mooney has pointed out, "The objection is not that Kass has religious views, but that he thinks it's fine to base his arguments on them when making policy recommendations for a pluralistic society" (ibid.).

Tristram Engelhardt Jr., another Christian bioethicist who is aware of the problem, has remarked that "if all do not listen to God so as to be united in one religion . . . . the only source of common moral authority among moral strangers will be consent" (quoted in ibid.). The importance of these considerations for current public policy is clear from President Bush's decision to ban further stem cell research in the United States. He did this after seeking advice from Leon Kass. When asked to propose someone who would furnish a counterpoint to his advice, Kass suggested Daniel Callahan of the Hastings Center, where the two have worked together for many years. But it is well known that the views of Callahan, a liberal Catholic, are close to those of Kass on the stem cell question. At the meeting on stem cell research policy, the president heard no one articulate reasons to carry on the research.

Other presidential commissions have revealed a different, more consensual approach to public policy recommendations. Their function has been seen as "sanctioning delay in government action on a controversial matter or recommending unpopular policies, ensuring that competing interests are represented in policy deliberations through diverse membership, and building support for public policies" (Moreno 1995, 75). All these things can be seen as aiming at consensus building, not policy imposition from above. Important work was accomplished by the National Commission for the Protection of Human Subjects of Biomedical and Behavioral Research, which was appointed by President Jimmy Carter. This group articulated three ethical principles designed to guide research using human subjects—respect for persons, beneficence, and justice—all of which derived from a long moral tradition that included Judeo-Christian, Enlightenment (Kantian), and ancient Greek (Aristotelian) elements, plainly a consensual document. It was from the respect-for-persons concept in this pronouncement that the value of autonomy, central to the treatment of patients in American medical institutions today, derived. (See Moreno, 76.)

According to Jonsen and Toulmin, it was this commission that adopted a typically casuist—or prudent pragmatic—approach in their deliberations: "The Commissioners typically reached conclusions by working inductively from specific examples to general principles. By moving from a common core agreement outwards to its edges, they also showed just how extensive that core is. If the Commission had initially approached many of these issues as a matter of principle, areas of pronounced disagreement might have emerged" (quoted in Moreno, 78). The principles that Jonsen and Toulmin had in mind here, however, were those specific to particular worldviews, which might have become bones of contention. In commenting on this formulation, Moreno in his commentary wondered how an agreement could have been possible if the members of the commission had had no core principles. What he had in mind, however, were shared principles, not conflicting ones, saying that it was because "the moral principles held by the commissioners had a somewhat open texture that their group consensus could be enriched and expanded as they went" (ibid.).

This commission, therefore, had considerable influence on research ethics, though not on the Department of Health, Education, and Welfare that it was created to advise. In some cases the secretary either delayed responding to recommendations of the commission or completely ignored them, Moreno reports. Such is the power of established bureaucracy in the administration of broad policy.

Other kinds of expert commissions have had a different kind of impact on healthcare practitioners. The National Institutes of Health have sponsored more than sixty consensus conferences since 1980 to provide a forum in which the public and medical practitioners are exposed to the ethical implications of new and existing technologies. The bioethicist Robert Veatch, in a study of these conferences, has questioned their value, suggesting that ethicists and laypeople value facts very differently from one another, perhaps because the practitioners are immersed in them and the ethicists are not. In any case the conferences have not seemed to draw the attention of most practitioners, probably because the discussions at the conferences tend to be academic in quality. The preference of practitioners seems to be to rely more on their own clinical experience than on the ethicists' abstractions. As we have seen in an earlier chapter, ethicists of a utilitarian and of a Kantian persuasion tend to render their judgments more in abstracto than in the light of the circumstances. (See Moreno, 74.)

CONCLUSION

We have attempted in this chapter to put the concept of prudent pragmatism into the context of public decision making in a democracy. And we have examined the roles of the citizen, the representative, and the expert policy analyst in the making of democratic policy. We have observed that in each case, role players must act as members of a community, and also that they must construe their work as that of rational deliberators. The role, whether that of citizen, representative, or analyst, must fit the terms of reference of deliberative democracy. This is not to say that the citizen should never consult his or her own private interests. What one's interests call for are part of the information that the individual should supply to his or her representative—or to an analyst who is gathering data. This is necessary if representatives and analysts are to do their work properly. But the citizen is not simply an individual with preferences. He or she is also a citizen who is required to take part with others in the processes of deliberative democracy—and in that role to formulate conceptions of policy for the common good. This needs to be done if one is to understand one's interests correctly as the interests of a social and political being, not as the interests of a producer or consumer in a market only. The appropriate mode of reasoning in the capacity of citizen is that of prudent pragmatism.

REFERENCES

Ackerman, Bruce, and James S. Fishkin. *Deliberation Day*. New Haven, CT: Yale University Press, 2004.

———. "Presenting Deliberation Day: A Radical Proposal to Help Voters Make Better Decisions." *Legal Affairs* (January/February 2004): 34–45.

Carpini, Michael X. Delli, and Scott Keeler. "The Internet and an Informed Citizenry." Ch. 9 in *The Critic Web: Online Politics and Democratic Values*, eds. David M. Anderson and Michael Cornfield, 129–53. New York: Rowman and Littlefield, 2003.

Cuomo, Mario. *More Than Words: The Speeches of Mario Cuomo* New York: St. Martin's Press, 1993.

Dryzek, John S. *Discursive Democracy: Politics, Policy, and Political Science*. New York: Cambridge University Press, 1990.

———. *Deliberative Democracy and Beyond: Liberals, Critics, Contestations*. New York: Oxford University Press, 2000.

Elster, John. "The Market and the Forum." In *Deliberative Democracy: Essays on Reason and Politics*, eds. James Bohman and William Rehg, 3–33. Cambridge, MA: MIT Press, 1997.

Gamson, William A. "Promoting Political Engagement." In *Mediated Politics: Communication in the Future of Democracy*, ed. W. Lance Bennett and Robert Entman, 56–74. New York: Cambridge University Press, 2001.

Gregg, Gary L. II. *The Presidential Republic: Executive Representation and Deliberative Democracy*. Lanham, MD: Rowman and Littlefield, 1997.

Krugman, Paul. "AARP Gone Astray." *New York Times* (November 21, 2003), A31.

Levine, Peter, "Online Campaigning and the Public Interest." In *The Civic Web: Online Politics and Democratic Values*, ed. David M. Anderson and Michael Cornfield, 47–62. New York: Rowman and Littlefield, 2003.

Madison, James. *The Federalist Papers*, 10. New York: E.P. Dutton & Co., Inc., 1966.

Mansbridge, Jane. "Practice-Thought-Practice." Ch. 6 in *Deepening Democracy: Institutional Innovations in Empowered Participatory Governance,* eds. Archon Fung and Erik Olin Wright. The Real Utopias Project IV. London: Verso, 2003, 175–99.

Mooney, Chris. "Irrationalist in Chief." *The American Prospect* 12, no. 17 (September 24–October 8, 2001): www.prospect.org/print-friendly/print/V12/17/mooney-c. html.

Moreno, Jonathan D. *Deciding Together: Bioethics and Moral Consensus.* New York: Oxford University Press, 1995.

Poniewozik, James. "The Rise of the Anger Industry." *Time* (December 1, 2003), 38.

Putnam, Robert D. "Tuning In, Tuning Out: The Strange Disappearance of Social Capital in America." *PS: Political Science and Politics* 28, no. 4 (1995): 664–83.

Radin, Beryl. *Beyond Machiavelli: Policy Analysis Comes of Age.* Washington, DC: Georgetown University Press, 2000.

Sagoff, Mark. "Policy Analysis and Social Values." In *Democracy, Social Values, and Public Policy*, ed. Wilton A. Carrow, Robert P. Churchill, and Joseph F. Cordes, 91–106. Westport, CT: Praeger. 1998.

Scott, Esther, "The Risks of Asarco." In *Ethics and Politics: Cases and Comments*, 2d ed. Amy Gutmann and Dennis Thompson, 163–74. Chicago: Nelson-Hall, Inc., 1990.

Skocpol, Theda, and Morris Fiorina, eds. *Civic Engagement in American Democracy*. Washington, DC: Brookings Institution; and New York: Russell Sage, 1999.

Stone, Deborah. *Policy Paradox: The Art of Political Decision Making*, rev. ed. New York: W.W. Norton and Co., 2002.

Tong, Rosemary. *Ethics in Policy Analysis.* Englewood Cliffs, NJ: Prentice Hall, Inc., 1986.

Weimer, David L., and Aidan R Vining. *Policy Analysis: Concepts and Practices.* Englewood Cliffs, NJ: Prentice Hall, Inc., 1989.

Wildavsky, Aaron. *Speaking Truth to Power: The Art and Craft of Policy Analysis.* Boston: Little, Brown, 1979.

PART TWO

ISSUES AND CASES

Preface to Part Two

The purpose of this part of our book is to give the reader practice in applying to specific policy issues the material on American values and the analytical frameworks that we developed in Chapters 2 and 3. We present the cases in six different policy areas, both in historical and contemporary perspective.

Each case involves confronting value conflicts (and, therefore, moral dilemmas) experienced by American society. One of these cases opposes individual freedom to smoke to the requirements of public health. Two others balance control of illegal drugs and antiterrorist measures against racial nondiscrimination. Another measures welfare for the very poor against tax relief for burdened taxpayers. Still another canvasses the rights of the unborn against the need for scientific research to serve the living. Yet another case balances the environmental needs of the future against present economic well-being. The last case measures the needs of national security against the sanctity of international law.

In each case the descriptive material is followed by a brief outline of the ethical analysis, using deontological, utilitarian, and prudent pragmatist methods. Readers should flesh out each of these analyses for themselves. This should include adding recent developments in the case history. Remember that prudent pragmatism requires that the reader weigh and balance conflicting values by referring to specific political and social circumstances that affect their rank-ordering. Many of these circumstances will be found in the "thick descriptions" we present in the case material and in the historical background we furnish for them. Some may be researched by the reader. In applying the principles of prudent pragmatism, the reader is asked to consider whether a paradigm case is available in the issue area that can serve as an acknowledged standard of judgment (e.g., cigarette smoking identified as serious health hazard rather than as an agreeable pastime).

Readers should decide which method yields the most complete and subjectively satisfying judgment—and why. We also pose questions that address the manner in which one's social role—as citizen, representative, executive, or policy analyst—affects the way in which one goes about resolving an ethical dilemma. Readers should elaborate this material themselves.

The last chapter is devoted to an overview of the book's goals and arguments, and to the question of whether it is possible to move from national to universal values as the basis of ethical policy judgment. If there are universal values, how are they to be identified? We also discuss the dilemma of a developing cultural conflict between the major values of globalizing secular democracy and traditionalist religious and ethical norms, and we look at the problem this dilemma poses for consensual ethics in today's world.

CHAPTER 6

National Healthcare Policy

Ideally, the student of public policy would like to consider ethical problems in any one policy area within a comprehensive perspective. For example, one would like to decide how much of the national income should be allotted to healthcare expenditures, both public and private, in relation to expenditures for other national needs. Or from another standpoint, since the health of individuals varies with social position, do we need to create greater equality in society at large in order to equalize health status and to affect the nation's attachment to equal treatment for all? To illustrate, is the prevention of lead-based paint poisoning of children best accomplished by public health measures or by diminishing poverty? One would also like to know how the condition of the environment affects individual health.

Questions like these, linking one policy area to another, are appropriately raised by policy-planning institutions of the federal government, such as the executive and congressional budget offices, and by White House and congressional planning agencies. Private research organizations, such as the Rand Corporation, the Brookings Institution, and the American Enterprise Institute, also deal with policy problems at this level of generality. But not all meaningful analysis can be done at this high level. We also need to deal with ethical issues within a more segmented framework in order to reach down to specific and detailed problems.

At this lower level of generality, we identify two fields of endeavor within the scope of national healthcare policy. These are the sustenance of a healthy community through a public health system and the maintenance and enhancement of individual health through medical treatment. The discussion that follows begins with a consideration of the national public health system and then moves on to the medical care of individuals.

THE U.S. PUBLIC HEALTH SYSTEM

Historical Perspective

During the nineteenth century New York City in many ways served as a model for public health policy. Attempts to improve the urban environment through adequate sanitation facilities and housing conditions were given additional support by the acceptance of the germ theory of disease propounded by Pasteur and Koch in the latter part of the century. Their discoveries provided the basis for extensive public health measures into the twentieth century. It was generally accepted among public health professionals that protecting the weakest and most vulnerable in society protected everyone because this effort eradicated or limited microbial diseases. However, Americans' attachment to individual freedom of choice has continued to stand in the way of effective action for society as a whole. In 1998 Daniel Callahan of the Hastings Center could declare, "As the scientific case for public health becomes stronger, politics and popular support have not kept pace" (quoted in Garrett 2000, 266).

The political dilemma—one found in many other regulatory areas as well—was that of providing diffuse benefits for many at a direct cost to a few. Randall B. Ripley and Grace A. Franklin have shown in their classic study of bureaucracy and policy implementation that when this dilemma occurs, the result will almost invariably be that the organized and intense few will have policy influence out of proportion to their numbers. As Ripley and Franklin state, "At the stage of implementation they [those regulated] may continue to view themselves in an adversarial relationship . . . , or they may attempt to capture the regulators as sympathetic friends" (Ripley and Franklin 1996, 77). American public health policy has been no exception to this phenomenon. By the 1940s in the United States, doctors and hospitals were effectively determining health policy. Moreover, the approach taken was not to bring health issues into the arena of policy discussion, but as far as possible to keep such issues off of the public agenda entirely.

Until the Great Depression and the New Deal, public health was primarily a state and local concern. An exception was the area of epidemics. Here the U.S. Public Health Service (USPHS) was increasingly active. In 1912 Congress gave it the authority to intervene at the local level on its own initiative. The federal government has also offered some aid for maternal and child healthcare since early in the twentieth century. More federal aid was forthcoming during the 1930s as the Great Depression played havoc with state and local public health programs. Laurie Garrett states that "[t]he New Deal's impact on the nation's public health infrastructure was profound and would prove lasting. A dozen agencies were created between 1933 and 1938, each of which affected the health of Americans" (Garrett 2000, 312).

World War II stimulated federal concern about the health problems caused by the mass concentration of people. Two especially important health threats—venereal disease and malaria—emerged, and the Communicable Disease Center was established in 1946. This agency evolved into the Centers for Disease Control and Prevention (CDC) in 1992.

With the advent of the Great Society, government expanded its role of providing for the nation's health. In particular, issues of the equitable distribution of healthcare came to the fore. The most important movement in this direction was the enactment in 1965 of Medicare and Medicaid. Both of these programs originally focused on individual healthcare, but they now serve as mechanisms for controlling medical costs generally. Later, in 1970, creation of the Environmental Protection Agency (EPA), the Occupational Safety and Health Administration (OSHA), and the National Institute of Occupational Safety and Health (NIOSH) provided authority for broader health measures aimed at community interests.

To date, no coherent, comprehensive health policy at the national level has emerged. Nor, given the institutional structure of American government, are we likely to see this happen. With the possible exception of national emergencies, incremental, fragmented change remains basic to the American policy process. Today, the recurring question is whether such a policy process, reflecting as it does fundamentally competing norms, can effectively cope with the rapid and massive threats to public health that may occur.

We turn now to a specific issue area that has been rife with both ethical and political dilemmas over the past few decades.

Controlling Tobacco as a Hazardous Substance: Development of a Policy

The battles over controlling cigarette smoking in the United States have been similar to those in the public health field generally. Antismoking advocates have sought to apply an epidemiological framework to the threats posed by smoking. Illnesses caused by smoking have been characterized as an epidemic, and the high correlations found between smoking and certain diseases are treated in causal terms. At the same time, private interests have forestalled a coherent preventive policy against smoking. Although progress in reducing smoking has been made, the approaches in this direction have been both incremental and fragmented.

1. Changing American Views of Smoking

Tobacco policy in the twentieth century reflected the evolution of basic American norms as the country responded to changes in knowledge and to deliberate attempts to refashion those norms. Most persistent among them has been the American belief in one's right to choose even if that choice results in personal risk. Increasingly, the concerns for social welfare, generally in terms both of health costs borne by taxpayers and of those involuntarily exposed to health risks, have emerged as strong counterarguments to those of individual right. A strongly populist flavor has also permeated this policy area. State and local governments have consistently acted aggressively against smoking behavior, while attempts to create effective federal regulation have seen only modest success. Activist groups appear to have been more focused at the state and local levels, and in many jurisdictions they have been able to make use of populist policy instruments such as the initiative and referendum. However, the 1998 Master Settlement Agreement (MSA) reached between the state attorneys general and the major tobacco companies suggests that certain kinds of serious policy questions may be beyond the reach of the normal democratic process.

At the beginning of the twentieth century, smoking cigarettes was seen as a disgusting habit and was not socially acceptable among elites. However, by the 1950s cigarette smoking was not only widespread, it was also often seen as highly fashionable. The change seems to have started during World War I, a time during which the supply of cigarettes to the fighting forces was seen as important to morale. In the interwar period, efforts were made by tobacco companies to induce media stars to smoke, and women were assured that smoking cigarettes was acceptable. Pop icons became purveyors of the chicness of the cigarette. The cigarette functioned especially well in the movies and later on TV as a ubiquitous prop. World War II further reinforced the desirability of smoking, and, as Richard Klein has shown, numerous novels and movies of the time featured characters and actors smoking cigarettes (Klein 1995). Throughout this period the convenience of the cigarette on the assembly line or in the office made it especially desirable as a source of relief from both tension and boredom. In its advertising the cigarette industry also utilized widespread and effective commercials to promote the manliness, sophistication, and femininity of smoking. As a result of these factors, cigarette consumption reached a peak in 1963.

2. Report of the Surgeon General's Committee and Its Aftermath

By the 1960s cigarette smoking had become ingrained as a habit in American culture. Yet in the 1950s American medical research had already begun to raise danger flags. Studies were beginning to find significant correlations between cigarette smoking and health problems. In 1958 the Consumers Union advised its members to quit smoking or at least to reduce their use of cigarettes (U.S. Department of Health and Human Services 2000, 39). The turning point in the policy arena—perhaps the defining moment—was the release of the report of the Surgeon General's Advisory Committee on Smoking and Health on January 11, 1964. This advisory committee of twelve highly regarded medical people with expertise largely in respiratory and circulatory diseases was for the most part divorced from any of the interested constituencies in the debate over tobacco. After more than a year of study, this carefully selected committee concluded that "cigarette smoking contributes substantially to mortality from certain specific diseases and to the overall death rate." It urged "appropriate remedial action" (quoted in Derthick 2002, 10). Government had entered the fray. Congress responded to the committee's report by passing legislation requiring warning labels on cigarette packages that informed consumers that smoking could be hazardous to their health, an action that preempted the states from undertaking more drastic steps.

Throughout the battle to reduce smoking, two basic American values have stood as obstacles. First and foremost has been Americans' belief in the importance of individual choice. Second, most Americans assume that individuals must make their own decisions as to the level of risk that they wish to experience in their lifestyles and should accept responsibility for the effects of such decisions. Antismoking advocates have thus had to struggle against the cultural bedrock of American individualism. In recent years, however, the public has shown itself increasingly ready to hold tobacco companies responsible for disabilities suffered by those who choose to smoke, although many continue to place sole responsibility on the individual smoker.

3. Congress Acts Incrementally

In the first instance many antismoking activists sought relief in Congress. Congress, however, remains an elected body reasonably representative of the variety of attitudes distributed across the nation, and, thus, it is ill-fitted for fashioning a national consensus on anything. Congressional policy decisions are for the most part brokered decisions. They result from compromises fashioned over extended periods of time. If national opinion on an issue remains partly inchoate, Congress is structurally incapable of making it jell. Consequently, despite such exceptions as Congressman Henry Waxman (D-CA) and Senator John McCain (R-AZ), no great enthusiasm for national control over or prohibition of smoking emerged. The results of congressional legislation in this area have been—and remain—decidedly mixed.

4. Action at the State and Local Levels

Whereas at the national level, efforts to reduce smoking proceeded slowly and placed heavy reliance on persuasion, more forceful actions were occurring at the state and local levels. These efforts generally took two forms: increased taxation on cigarettes and bans on smoking in public places.

State excise taxes on cigarettes have illustrated one fundamental dilemma in smoking policy. At the same time that such taxes are justified as penalties for unhealthy behavior, states have become more dependent on them for revenue. As scientific evidence about the health hazards of smoking accumulated and as the social acceptability of smoking declined, states moved to increase excise taxes on cigarettes. Some of these efforts were encouraged by funding from the Robert Wood Johnson Foundation, which in 1994 dedicated $10 million to movements in nineteen states to increase cigarette excise taxes (Sullum 1998, 125). By 1998 these taxes were 50¢ a pack or more in sixteen states. In 2000 cigarette excise taxes ranged from 2.5¢ a pack in Virginia to $1.11 in New York. Paradoxically, as its social acceptability declined, smoking became increasingly useful to cash-strapped state treasuries.

Although a few states were quick to enact statewide smoking restrictions, antismoking advocates found early success chiefly at the local level of government, because they were able to target receptive communities and focus their organizational efforts most effectively there. By the end of the 1980s, 44 states and approximately 400 U.S. cities and counties nationwide had banned smoking in public places (U.S Department of Health and Human Services 2000, 47). During the next decade, local and state bans against smoking generally increased in number and severity.

5. Changing Social Norms

Antismoking activists realized that they had to move on additional fronts if they were to eliminate smoking or at least substantially reduce it. Increasingly, they turned their attention away from smokers themselves to others who were victims of cigarettes. "Equal rights" rather than "right to choose" gradually moved to the forefront of the debate. Smoking opponents began to focus on the effects of smoking on the young and the threats posed by environmental tobacco smoke (ETS) on nonsmokers. Much of the legislation that followed was based on the premise that innocent victims of smoking had to be protected; nonsmokers had rights against smokers. In the words of Alan M. Brandt, "[t]he new focus on innocent victims became the entering wedge for the moral calculation of the meaning and nature of the cigarette in the last two decades of the twentieth-century" (Brandt 1998, 172).

Meanwhile, efforts to reduce smoking among young people were becoming more sophisticated and effective. The states, stimulated by federal monetary incentives, became the primary actors in the battle against smoking by minors. Gradually, researchers and government agencies realized that underlying social norms were involved in smoking behavior, and they began to fashion programs involving family and peer relationships, which appear to have reduced smoking among students. In some cases the smoking rates of targeted populations differed by as much as 30 to 50 percent less than the rates among the control groups. Such programs are especially effective when combined with antismoking messages in the media (U.S. Department of Health and Human Services 2000, 61–94). The results have been encouraging. In May 2002, the Centers for Disease Control and Prevention reported a drop in smoking among high school students from 36 percent in 1997 to 29 percent, with a target of 16 percent or lower by 2010 (Manning 2002, A3).

6. Litigation

While government officials at various levels were trying to restrict smoking through regulation, numerous individual suits against the tobacco companies were being initiated and litigated. Initially, almost none were successful, primarily for two reasons. First, the tobacco industry was very effective in utilizing every possible procedural delay in order to drain the financial resources of the plaintiffs. Second, when cases did finally reach the verdict stage, juries were receptive to arguments that a smoker was aware of the risks that he or she undertook. Such judgments were even more likely after warning labels appeared on cigarette packages and in print advertising.

The first major breakthrough for those attacking Big Tobacco through litigation came in Mississippi. In that state Attorney-General Michael Moore brought suit against the tobacco industry to recover the costs of Medicaid payments attributable to health problems from smoking. The argument was essentially one of economic fairness: The tobacco companies should help pay for the medical costs that use of their product engendered. At this point the issue of reducing smoking began to take a backseat to the question of how much money the states could obtain from the tobacco companies to offset the medical costs that were associated with smoking. The tobacco companies moved to settle out of court with Mississippi, and a series of suits soon ensued in Florida, Minnesota, and Texas.

Impressed by Mississippi's success and encouraged by its attorney general, other state attorneys general began to cooperate in a massive class-action suit against the tobacco industry. After much negotiation, in 1997, they reached a settlement in which the tobacco industry agreed to unprecedented restrictions and payments. Before it could be implemented, however, this agreement required congressional approval of important provisions, and so the tobacco issue was once again returned to the forum that many of those striving to eliminate smoking had tried to avoid. Their concerns proved well founded.

Once in the congressional arena, the 1997 tobacco agreement rapidly unraveled, and no equivalent legislation was to emerge. Exploiting the parliamentary delays employed to prevent final passage of antismoking measures, the cigarette industry mounted an effective media campaign portraying the legislation as a huge money grab by trial lawyers and as unfairly discriminating against blue-collar workers. As a result of the media blitz, a wavering president, and Congress's sense that there was no overwhelming enthusiasm for comprehensive antismoking legislation, the Senate killed any kind of compensatory agreement with the tobacco companies—and it did so without forcing any senator to actually have to vote on the proposed legislation. By killing a measure that disregarded its penchant for incremental policymaking, Congress once again demonstrated its unwillingness to act definitively on the question of smoking.

7. The Master Settlement Agreement of 1998

Disappointed by Congress's failure to act, the state attorneys general and the tobacco industry returned to the bargaining table. The result was an agreement reached in 1998 that gave the states less than the original agreement and provided the companies less protection from liability. At the same time the agreement imposed heavy penalties on smaller companies that did not wish to participate in the agreement. In addition to offering specified monies to the states for the next twenty-five years and later unspecified payments in perpetuity, the agreement also insulated the industry from further state suits and from competition from new firms.[1] It protected both their market income and their market share. In return the industry agreed to pay the plaintiffs' legal fees, to accept restrictions on various forms of advertising, to disband the Tobacco Institute (the industry's lobbying organization), and to refrain from certain kinds of lobbying at the state and local levels. These last three provisions in particular raise serious First Amendment questions; however, the industry further agreed not to challenge the constitutionality of the settlement.

Perhaps the aspect of the 1998 agreement that has the most far-reaching ramifications is that it was implemented without legislative input. The state attorneys general hired accomplished tort lawyers on a contingency basis to extract money from the tobacco industry and to regulate its behavior under threat of litigation. In each state the agreement came into effect with the issuance of a consent decree by the appropriate state court. Provisions limiting lobbying and advertising seem vulnerable to charges of unconstitutionality. Yet the agreement was designed to prevent the industry from challenging them. Furthermore, in contrast to legislation, there appears to be no simple way in which the agreement can be modified or amended. The tobacco settlement constitutes a major shift in one area of American public policy, and the obligations that it imposes exist in perpetuity, a term and concept rarely found in the American policy process.

There is no question that the demonization of the tobacco industry and the scientific evidence of the health hazards of smoking contributed greatly to the final settlement between the states and the industry. Brandt concludes that by 1991; "Social convention increasingly defined public smoking as taboo, a violation of social norms and communal 'civility'" (Brandt 1998, 173). It seems equally clear that the unhealthy consequences of smoking are now only one issue in the formulation of tobacco policy. A substantially more important factor for the states has become the revenue to be expected from the tobacco industry. And perversely, the continuation of this revenue depends on the continued sale of cigarettes. Surveying the states' use of funds derived from the MSA, the *Economist* found that in 2002 only $1 in $20 of these funds was used to finance efforts to stop smoking. Reacting to these data, the article offers the observation that this "modest figure adds fuel to the notion that the 1998 settlement was a case of legalized extortion" (*Economist*, "Saved by Smokers," 2001, 33).

---

[1]Unlike the 1997 proposed agreement, the 1998 agreement did not protect industry from private suits or from being sued by the federal government. While action at the federal level faltered, the industry continued to be pressured by suits by private individuals, which in California, Florida, Kansas, and Oregon resulted in multimillion dollar awards.

CASE STUDY: NEW YORK STATE'S RESPONSE TO SECONDHAND SMOKE

In 2003 New York, a state that for much of the last two centuries had been a leader in the public health movement, was lagging behind other states in dealing with the health threats posed by smoking in public places. As with most states, the issue of limiting smoking had become an important agenda item there. However, New York possesses a political structure unlike any other state in the union, and the policy environment created by this structure seriously hampered statewide efforts to limit smoking.

New York has always been a strongly contested two-party state. This fact accounts for the tremendously tight control that flows from the political leadership in Albany, the state capital. In some ways, the political leadership in Albany resembles that of the Sun King of France. With regard to state politics, all power flows from Albany. Other than referenda on bond issues or constitutional amendments, no mechanism for direct popular policy influence exists, and neither party has any interest in promoting grass-roots input through initiative or referendum.

The partisan divisions within the state capital are both distinct and rigid. The New York State Assembly has been apportioned so that it is improbable that the Republicans will ever take control without massive reconfiguration of district lines. The Speaker of that body and his close advisers determine the outcome of all measures there. Their imprimatur assures passage in that chamber; just as their opposition constitutes the death knell for a bill. Over the past two decades, the state Senate has remained tenuously in the hands of the Republicans, and procedures there are somewhat more open. However, in this body as well, power is concentrated in the hands of the majority leader. Both houses of the state legislature make extensive use of legislative campaign committees (LCCs). These committees raise enormous amounts of money and funnel these funds into the campaigns of their members, further increasing dependence of the membership on the leadership. Both parties recognize that sufficient campaign funds are important to their continuing control.

The third player in this enclosed policy process is, of course, the governor. The office of governor remains reasonably competitive, with Mario Cuomo, a Democrat, in control from the mid-1980s until 1995, followed by George Pataki, a Republican. This troika of Assembly Speaker, Senate Majority Leader, and governor determine state policy. Rebellions in the ranks of either legislative body are almost unheard of and are swiftly and ruthlessly punished.

In the fall election of 2004, popular disgust at the failure of the legislature to pass a budget on time yet once more brought rumbles in the public that seemed to presage some kind of grass-roots revolt against the system. The election itself produced no upset, but the politicians have at least promised there will be reform.

If everyone is in agreement, this kind of closed policy process can accomplish much. Unfortunately for New Yorkers, agreement is not often forthcoming, and for years attempts to deal with control of smoking were no exception. As the concerns about secondhand smoke grew in the 1980s, the elected state policymakers in New York refused to act. Responding to this inaction, the State Public Health Council in 1986 proposed stringent nonsmoking regulations. The Public Health Council is a fourteen-member board appointed by the governor and has the authority to deal with "any matters affecting the security of life or health or the preservation and improvement of public health." The new regulations had the support of the state Department of Health, and at the six hearings it held, testimony was approximately 4 to 1 in their favor, despite heavy opposition from tobacco interests and business associations. The council formally adopted the regulations in February 1987 (Schmalz May 6, 1987, B1, B7; Uhlig 1987, B3).

The action of the Public Health Council soon ran into heavy criticism. Administrative agencies are exceptionally powerful in New York State, and many legislators viewed the council's decision as another attempt at power aggrandizement by unelected bureaucrats. In retaliation, in April 1987, the state legislature cut from the budget the $300,000 item that was to fund enforcement of the new regulations on the ground that the council had exceeded its legislative mandate. In November 1987, the New York State Court of Appeals, the state's highest court, struck down the new regulations (Titone, *New York Times* 1987, B6; Schmalz 1987, A1).

Although the actions by the Public Health Council came to a sorry end, that body's movement on the issue of prohibiting smoking stimulated public debate and eventually forced action by elected policymakers. This activity first occurred at the local level, and, within six months of the Court of Appeals decision, the New York City Council enacted a tough antismoking law that severely limited smoking in public places and places of employment. At the state level Governor Cuomo continued to lead the attack against smoking, and in July 1989, he signed an antismoking measure that was more restrictive than that of every state except Minnesota. The measure required that smoking in almost all public facilities be restricted to designated areas, and it required restaurants seating more than fifty to provide 70 percent of their space for nonsmokers. Exempted were bars and restaurants seating less than fifty people. For over a decade, this legislation was the high-water mark for antismoking advocates in New York State.

Demonstrating an exceptionally sophisticated understanding of New York State politics, the tobacco industry counterattacked very effectively. The tobacco lobby's response to antismoking measures took the form of spending large amounts of money to influence elected policymakers. In 1993 Philip Morris, which was not even listed among the top ten spenders in 1992, became the largest lobbying spender in New York State (Fisher 1994, B2). In September 1999 that company revised its lobbying reports for 1996 through 1998, apparently in the hope that an ongoing investigation by the state lobbying commission would thereby be brought to an end. The revised data showed that from 1993 through 1996, at least 115 of the

211 members in the state legislature had accepted gifts from Philip Morris. Despite this effort at greater accountability, in November the company was fined $75,000 by the state commission and agreed to keep its head lobbyist, who was also fined $15,000, from working the legislature for three years (*New York Times* November 16, 1999, A26).

These statistics tell only part of the story. The ability of the tobacco companies to channel funding through other groups increased their effectiveness by giving the appearance of broad opposition to antismoking legislation. Thus, groups such as the Empire State Restaurant and Tavern Association and the Business Council received tobacco funding. Within the state legislature the tobacco lobby built exceptionally strong ties with the powerful Black-Hispanic Caucus in the Assembly. Philip Morris and R. J. Reynolds provided funds for a variety of neighborhood and other projects dear to these legislators, and these companies were rewarded with support on policy issues. In 1998, in the Assembly Health Committee, four black and Hispanic Democrats crossed party lines to kill a bill banning smoking in restaurants (Levy 2000, B1). Given this lobbying blitz, it is little wonder that no effective antismoking measures were enacted after 1993 at the state level. By 1999 New York lagged significantly behind at least nineteen other states in per capita spending to discourage smoking. *The New York Times* quoted Blair Horner, legislative director of the New York Public Interest Group, as concluding, "There's no question that the political money of the tobacco companies has been a major factor in stalling action in New York" (Perez-Pena 1999).

In the 2001 session of the New York State Legislature, a turning point in the efforts of the antismoking activists appeared to have been reached. For the first time in twelve years, a strict nonsmoking bill prohibiting smoking in all public restaurants was introduced and passed the Assembly. Moreover, it appeared to have strong support in the Republican-controlled Senate. In the words of Russell Sciandra, director of the Center for a Tobacco-Free New York, "The gestalt has changed. . . These guys are beginning to realize it's what their constituents want. This is like a soccer mom's kind of issue" (Sengupta 2001, B1). It seemed that the conditions for consideration of such a measure had indeed become more favorable.

This changed environment could be attributed to a number of factors. First, everyone, including the Republican Senate leader, had become convinced that secondhand smoke was a serious health hazard. No one any longer seriously debated that point. Second, by 2001 New York City and four other counties had nonsmoking laws more restrictive than the state law. These areas encompassed about 70 percent of New York State's population. Moreover, in conservative upstate areas, like Chautauqua County, restrictive nonsmoking laws were being favorably considered, a fact that encouraged normally reluctant state senators from those areas to be supportive of further state action. Third, legislators were increasingly defensive about the fact that New York State, once a leader in policy change, was drifting farther and farther behind other states on this issue. The 2001 effort stalled and died, however, when Governor Pataki suggested that the bill would place too great a burden on small restaurants.

The prospects for the proposed Clean Indoor Air Act improved even more in the following session of the state legislature. Once again, Assembly passage was swift, and it appeared that the Senate would finally act favorably. Additional factors favoring passage included a study of tax data from five counties with restrictive nonsmoking laws that showed that spending in restaurants in those counties actually grew faster than sales in other retail businesses. At the same time a poll of its members by the New York State Restaurant Association showed that 53 percent of the membership supported a stronger nonsmoking law (Precious 2002, C1). However, the proposal's proponent in the Assembly unilaterally announced that a deal with the Senate had been reached, thereby irritating his Senate colleagues and giving the opposition—largely in the form of the Empire State Restaurant and Tavern Association, which claimed membership of 5,000 small establishments—time to organize a counteroffensive (Dewan 2002, B1).

Although the governor made no public pronouncements this time, it was again rumored that he did not want a Senate vote on the issue. He had negotiated a wide-ranging budget deal with the healthcare unions at the beginning of the session, and he had financed it with a large increase in cigarette taxes that for a time at least made New York State's tax the highest in the nation. Some commentators believed that he did not want to further antagonize the tobacco industry (ibid.). Another possibility was that in an election year, he was unwilling to allow the Democratic-controlled Assembly to take credit for moving against smoking. Whatever the case, the proposed Clean Indoor Air Act again died without coming to the floor of the New York State Senate.

The prospects for a rigorous statewide ban on smoking in any restaurant or bar continued to improve, however, when in August 2002, New York City Mayor Michael R. Bloomberg proposed such a ban for his city. Mayor Bloomberg based his position heavily on the right to be free from smoke in the workplace, and he identified bars and restaurants as workplaces in which workers were entitled to protection. The mayor saw a total ban as simply an extension of bans that had already been applied to more traditional work areas, such as offices and factories. With New York City moving toward a total ban and neighboring counties looking to follow suit, it was but a matter of time until the state legislature finally acted.

Finally, in March 2003 the New York State legislature passed one of the most restrictive smoking laws in the nation. Smoking in public, with the exception of cigar bars and Native American casinos, was prohibited. Governor Pataki signed the bill less than two hours after its passage. The costs of healthcare and the effects of secondhand smoke carried the day with some of the last holdouts in the Senate. These concerns were bolstered by aggressive leadership on the part of Majority Leader Joseph Bruno, who commented, "Sometimes when you are in government you have to do things for the people whether they like it or not. That's what government is all about" (Precious 2003, A1, A9).

In October 2004 a state Supreme Court justice threw out $650 in fines against three pubs in Suffolk County. A county Health Department inspector had found people smoking in the three locales and also discovered that the managements had set out makeshift ashtrays for customers. The inspector also testified that no efforts were made by the owners to challenge smokers, despite the presence of prominently displayed No Smoking signs.

The Supreme Court justice held that the law in question did not require that pub owners deny service to smokers, as the hearings officer who levied the fines claimed. Such a requirement, the justice held, would constitute an "onerous, substantive enforcement" burden on businesses that was not envisaged by the law banning smoking in bars.

The Empire State Restaurant and Tavern Association is preparing to challenge the constitutionality of the New York State ban in federal court, and it will use the ruling by the state's Supreme Court as evidence for its position. It will argue that the law unfairly puts the burden of its enforcement on proprietors of bars, restaurants, bowling alleys, and similar establishments. This results in making the owners rather than the smokers the regulated entities, according to the association. On the other side, organizations such as the New York Public Interest Research Group are taking up the cudgels for the law, claiming that the Supreme Court ruling effectively condones lawbreaking (*Rochester Democrat and Chronicle* November 1, 2004, 5B).

Elsewhere in the state, enforcement has proceeded more smoothly. In Allegany County, for example, the health department has been busy issuing warnings to offending bars and restaurants. If problems continue after two of these warnings, fines ranging from $100 to $1,000 are levied. Allegany's enforcement action is complaint-based. Citizens must submit their complaints in writing, and the county has so far fined about forty facilities on the basis of these complaints (Liebler 2005).

In New York City the state prohibition on smoking in public places was preceded by a city ordinance, as we have seen. Enforcement has not been a problem, and contrary to expectations, bars and restaurants have not experienced a fall-off of business. James McBratney, president of the Staten Island Restaurant and Tavern Association, reports that customers actually like the ban, and he says that visions of a mass exodus of patrons to New Jersey bars, where smoking was still legal at the time, did not materialize. Employment in bars and restaurants since inception of the ban has actually risen over the two years of its existence, as has the number of restaurant permits requested and held. City inspectors report a 98 percent rate of compliance with the ban. News of New York's success with the ban has been spreading, and a bill providing for a like measure has been introduced in Philadelphia's City Council (Rutenberg and Koppel 2005, A25).

Ethical Analysis of the Case

The history of tobacco control legislation in the United States well displays the workings of deliberative democracy. In recounting this story, we have seen what a prudent pragmatist would describe as a paradigm shift in the moral meaning of the act of smoking. Instead of being seen simply as a pleasurable pastime or as a chic thing to do in social settings (both "good" things), smoking has become viewed by the public as a potentially lethal practice, both for smokers and for those subjected to secondhand smoke (both morally "bad" things). A complex system of social and political conversation, involving authoritative pronouncements and explanations by medical experts, administrators, and educators, has been at work, and this conversation has interwoven with a process of partial and incremental political regulation. Through discourse, political action, and the experience by many of illness and death as the long-term effects of smoking, the American public has fundamentally altered its evaluation of the practice, from "good" to "bad." The public has significantly changed its preferences, and the change has been registered both in the tobacco control legislation we have described in this chapter and in smoking behavior itself.

It would be difficult to apply the utilitarian model for formulating the social good to these events. At no point could a Benthamite legislator have calculated the good of society as a whole by summing preferences. What would serve as a common term? Also, how can values such as social status, relaxation, and good health be quantified? In this case, preferences were in a process of change, and at any one time they were grouped into conflicting units of opinion. How could these have been summed?

To approach an understanding of the situation from a deontological standpoint would require thinking in terms of rights. Thus, we have the right of the individual to freedom of choice, a most valued, indeed central concept in American political culture. But this is countered by the equal right of nonsmokers to be free of unpleasant, and indeed, dangerous secondhand smoke. So we are forced into a process of weighing and balancing one right against another in a prudent pragmatist mode. Given the circumstances of developing evidence of the bad health effects of secondhand smoke, it was appropriate that legislators enacted the bans described in the case study. But questions remain as to how far government should go in limiting the individual's right to smoke. Is there a residual individual freedom in this area?

At present, smokers gather outside the doors of buildings, and some have even welcomed the new arrangements. One person has been quoted as saying, "There's a secondary scene now outside of bars—a smoker's scene . . . . You can meet a girl out here. Strike up a conversation" (ibid., 19). Another remarked that he liked going outdoors. "I like to get fresh air." Another reports that his dry-cleaning bill has gone down since bars have become smoke-free, forcing him to smoke outside. In speaking to the reporter he added, "And I'm smoking less," indicating that for him, smoking is not so much an exercise of freedom as a compulsion, which it might be well to resist. But this seems like an example of what Rousseau meant when he said that one may be "forced to be free" by obeying the "General Will," which in this case would be identified as the enacted smoking ban. This has always been cited as a problematical element in Rousseau's theory of democracy, and it is more to be associated with the totalitarian than with the liberal version of democratic theory. We are also reminded of Isaiah Berlin's distinction of positive and negative liberty in his magisterial book entitled *Two Concepts of Liberty*, as well as his warning about the positive version (Berlin 1958). Since the educational campaign about the dangers of smoking has had an enormous success, do we need coercive law as well? Does the anecdotal material reported earlier indicate that coercive law itself can have an educational effect? Or is that idea an oxymoron in a liberal society?

Is there an easily recognized boundary between places where one's right to smoke can and cannot interfere with another's right to be free from secondhand smoke? Some municipalities have been canvassing the idea of forbidding smoking on beaches and in public parks. In March 2006 one actually did so—Calabasas, California, which enacted a ban on smoking in all outdoor places where one could be subjected to secondhand smoke. This involved soccer fields, bus stops, parks, and sidewalks (Broder, *New York Times* 2006). Perhaps this is an area in which policy analysts could contribute empirical studies to the solution of the problem. Then there is the question of health costs. Would it be ethical to forbid smoking outright on the ground that smoking is deleterious and increases an individual's risk of contracting cancer? Perhaps we have here a question that might be answered by risk-benefit analysis. But a philosophical question would remain no matter what the analysis showed. Should social costs trump an individual's right to smoke? Also, not all smokers develop cancer, nor do those who are subjected to secondhand smoke. (In another policy area, several states have repealed laws requiring motorcyclists to wear helmets, even though research shows that highway motorcycle accidents account for large numbers of paraplegics in our hospitals and nursing homes, and that many of these people are cared for at public expense.)

Do the demonstrated high costs of public expenditures for caring for those who have developed cancer from smoking perhaps warrant banning the sale of cigarettes and other tobacco products altogether? Should nicotine be designated an addictive drug, one that's outlawed along with substances such as heroin? (Efforts have already been made to do so.)

The case study presents us with still other problems. New York was slow to enact a statewide ban on what had come to be recognized as a clear evil, whereas in other areas it had been a leader in the public health movement. Should New York legislators be blamed for lagging behind? The cause of their failure to enact a ban earlier was extensive lobbying activity by tobacco interests in the legislative halls during the 1990s. Should legislators have accepted money from tobacco lobbyists under the circumstances of the time, since it was shown that lobbyists had overstepped their legal bounds? But we know that lobbyists are always active in our legislatures, both at the state and national levels. How should a legislator balance his or her need for funds and other political support against his or her obligation to serve the public good? Does the universal dependence in legislatures on lobbyist money point to a fundamental ethical defect in the political system that should be remedied? Or is it simply a political fact of life that must be tolerated?

In 2001 a strong antismoking bill managed to work its way through both houses of the state legislature, but it died because of opposition from Governor Pataki. His concern that it might have placed too great a burden on small restaurants seems to have been unwarranted in view of the success of the recent legislation. Might a carefully designed policy analysis have shown his fear to have been unfounded? The following year, a simple poll of the membership of the New York State Restaurant Association showed a majority in favor of stronger legislation.

PAYING FOR INDIVIDUAL HEALTHCARE: THE INSURANCE DILEMMA

Historical Development

We turn now from the communitarian side of healthcare policy to the question of individual medical treatment. For most of America's history, the libertarian ethic has predominated here; until the end of World War II, Americans assumed that each individual was responsible for his or her healthcare, with medical care, when needed, supplied on a fee-for-service basis.

In the early years of the twentieth century, healthcare insurance became available for some through a variety of private sources. Unions, fraternal associations, and some corporations provided health plans for their members or employees. At the state level there were a few public programs. By 1932, for example, all but four states provided workmen's compensation for those injured on the job. But at the national level, despite its welfare programs, the New Deal did not encompass healthcare for Americans. Nonetheless, from 1939 onward, bills for a national health insurance program were introduced annually in Congress.

It was not until the Truman administration, however, that a sustained political effort was put into proposals for national health insurance. Truman campaigned on this issue in 1948, and in 1950 his administration gave additional impetus to national health insurance by sending a comprehensive proposal to Congress. After the defeat of the Truman proposal, the proponents of government-sponsored health insurance finally recognized the need to move in an incremental fashion. Accordingly, they decided to focus on a particular segment of the population for health insurance, and, unlike many European programs, which began by covering industrial workers and their families, these proponents chose the elderly as their target population. In this revised effort the Truman advisers recognized the ideological value of a program that carried some of the same entitlement characteristics possessed by social security.

Somewhat surprisingly, the idea of national health insurance again gained prominence in the closing years of the Eisenhower administration. In 1960 Congress passed the Kerr-Mills program, which provided federal funds for states that wished to initiate health insurance for the elderly poor. President Eisenhower supported the program because it was voluntary, and by 1964 over thirty-nine states were participants. Additionally, the Hill-Burton program for hospital construction, enacted in 1946, carried the stipulation that any hospital receiving construction funds from that program must agree to provide free healthcare for those unable to pay. Positive action on national health insurance under the conservative Eisenhower administration indicated that there was strong public sentiment favoring the provision of healthcare to those in need.

The defining moment for a form of national health insurance came in 1965. President Lyndon Johnson insisted upon including national health insurance among his Great Society programs. Moreover, he had substantial Democratic majorities in both houses of Congress to assist him. The battle over health insurance eventually centered in the powerful House Ways and Means Committee, led by Wilbur C. Mills (D-AR). Mills was justly known for his political skills and able leadership of Ways and Means, but in 1965 he confronted a policy issue over which the Johnson administration, the Republicans, and the American Medical Association (AMA) were at loggerheads. The administration wanted healthcare for the poor; the Republicans were concerned about cost, and the AMA wanted independence for the medical profession.

Mills confounded all parties by combining the three positions in the ensuing legislation. Medicare part A provided universal hospital insurance for the elderly through a payroll tax similar to that for social security. Part B of Medicare, which was voluntary, opened the door to supplementary insurance for physicians' costs and outpatient services; and Medicaid, in a separate title of the legislation, provided healthcare to indigents of whatever age. Without any public hearings at this stage, Mills satisfied the articulate interests of the time and moved into law the basic structure of the nation's health insurance, providing for the first time in American history publicly financed healthcare for the elderly and the poor throughout the nation.

Mills' action certainly was not incremental. It constituted a total reworking of healthcare policy at the national level. The policy window for such dramatic change was provided by the combination of large Democratic majorities in each house of Congress and a Democratic president elected by a huge landslide, who was pushing hard for action on healthcare.

Perhaps as important, by giving everyone something, Mills circumvented the ideological differences that had to that point stymied national healthcare proposals. It was as though Mills had taken differing American cultural norms and thrown them together in one big basket. These ideological differences, of course, would not disappear, but from this point forward they would be working within the framework of an established program. The politics of interest now had statutory boundaries. The American economic machine had produced a revenue cornucopia sufficient to submerge temporarily the basic divisions in the nation's culture, but in the following decades these divisions would emerge repeatedly to plague attempts at major healthcare reform.

It is, of course, understandable that Medicare quickly developed a solid constituency among the elderly. But political support for Medicaid also formed within a short time. Under Medicaid, hospitals and doctors receive reimbursement for patients who otherwise would not have been able to pay or might simply have not sought treatment. Additionally, children's advocates increasingly saw Medicaid as an important program for children. State governments also began to see a financial opportunity in the program. The financing arrangement for Medicaid, which was 50 percent federal and 50 percent state funded, encouraged the states to move as many programs as they could under the Medicaid umbrella, thus lessening by 50 percent the costs of these programs to the state coffers. As a result of these pressures, funding for Medicaid almost tripled from 1988 through 1994. (See Gruber, "Medicaid," in Moffitt, ed. 2003, 31.) Total federal expenditures for Medicaid increased from $1.7 billion in 1966 to over $219 billion in 2001 (see Table 1.4 in Gruber, 32), and federal and state expenditures were expected to double within ten years from the $265 billion expended in 2003.

Philosophical Frameworks

Programs of government-sponsored health insurance thus developed in this fashion down through the period of the Great Society. By then there were also signs, at least in the field of healthcare, that the individualist and communitarian strands of American political culture might be coming together. Philosophers began to canvass the possibility of adding a new right to healthcare to the panoply of socially guaranteed entitlements. This development occurred in tandem with the emergence of bioethics as a significant field of philosophical endeavor, itself a result of the many profound ethical dilemmas spawned by the mushrooming of discoveries and inventions in biotechnology.

The leading work of synthesis was done by John Rawls, a professor of philosophy at Harvard University, who attempted to weave together the libertarian and egalitarian values of American culture in a systematic contractarian philosophy. This philosophy's central concept is "justice as fairness." The individual, preparing to choose a political constitution for him- or herself, is asked to imagine principles of fairness while standing behind a veil of ignorance concerning social status and natural endowments. A leading principle emerging from this idea experiment was that each person should be granted a degree of liberty that is compatible with equal liberty for all. Another principle—articulating Rawls's concept of equality of opportunity—was that jobs and offices should be open to all on the same footing. The reconstituted society should not be radically egalitarian, but differences in status should be justified by a showing that they contribute to the well-being of the least well off—the difference principle. Thus, free public education is required in order to offset inequalities flowing from birth. Under this principle, health is a primary social good, since it is assumed that widespread good health is necessary for there to be fair equality of opportunity. In this way Rawls combined the traditional concern for individual freedom with the traditional concept of the equal value of human lives. Embedded in these principles as well is the idea of a right to healthcare as a prerequisite of fair equality of opportunity.

Working within the Rawlsian model, one might conclude that a two-tiered health system is most equitable. Every citizen has a right to basic healthcare coverage, an equal decent minimum. Those with the means would be free to purchase additional care, or insurance coverage, in the market. It would remain exceedingly difficult, however, to determine at what point basic coverage should end and the discretionary coverage begin. Who, after all, are the least well off in such a Rawlsian system—the poorest or the sickest? If the latter, then the wealthy would seem to have an inherent advantage in terms of the limits to their expenditures. Moreover, given the individualistic norms of American culture, it remains unclear how limits on an individual's healthcare expenditures could be enforced.

It does appear, however, that the idea of a right to healthcare as an entitlement has achieved a certain currency among the members of the public, as evidenced by the widespread acceptance of the Medicare and Medicaid programs. Some would also give weight to the fact that the United States has signed the U.N. Declaration of Human Rights, which calls for universal recognition of a right to healthcare (Daugherty 1988, 30). In the form of universal health coverage, this right has been endorsed by every industrialized democracy in the world except the United States and South Africa.

Rawlsian contractarianism remains a popular philosophical standpoint today, but it has by no means achieved the status of a generalized ideology. In fact, a libertarian retort to Rawls was made almost immediately upon the appearance of *A Theory of Justice* by a Harvard colleague named Robert Nozick. (See his *Anarchy, State, and Utopia*, 1974, which received great notoriety among American intellectuals.) In Nozick's work we have an elaborate restatement of the market principle, which posits free exchange as central to all but a very few social relationships. In Nozick's minimal state there is no place for (re)distributive justice, either in healthcare or anything else. For libertarians the only true rights are negative, and a healthcare entitlement would have to be based in norms of charity, not those of justice.

Libertarians define freedom as freedom from coercion, even though it is possible to argue that certain conditions (e.g., poverty, the ravages of nature, or threats to health) are coercive in themselves.

Continuing Efforts to Expand Healthcare Coverage

In the late 1980s the first major attempt to expand national health insurance led to what can only be described as a politically bizarre sequence of events. The issue that occasioned this upheaval in the policy process was the expansion of Medicare to provide for catastrophic illnesses (i.e., illnesses that exhausted previous Medicare benefits). Led by Otis Bowen, secretary of Health and Human Services under President Ronald Reagan, Congress in 1988 enacted the Medicare Catastrophic Coverage Act by large margins in each house. Incredibly, a mere sixteen months later, Congress repealed this legislation. In retrospect it appears that Congress had moved too far, too fast beyond the public's willingness to accept greater government expansion. In the words of Senator Dave Durenberger (R-MN), "We did too much all at once, and we decided we were going to charge them [senior citizens] for it" (*Congressional Quarterly Almanac* 1989, 150).

A major problem with the new legislation was that it charged for benefits that many elderly already had. Opposition was especially intense from organizations representing retired federal employees and military personnel, who gained no additional benefits from the catastrophic insurance but who were assessed the additional costs.

Finally, many elderly felt no immediate need for catastrophic insurance. They were already receiving Medicare, and they were often not aware of its limitations. Additionally, some had coverage through Medigap insurance that covered those areas not included in Medicare. For most elderly there was little sense that a personal health crisis was impending for them. Some representatives and senators, in particular Senator John McCain (R-AZ), fought repeal until the bitter end, but most members of Congress wanted to extricate themselves from what they saw as a politically untenable position as quickly as possible. That the legislation had to be repealed demonstrates that new policies are most successfully enacted through incremental rather than comprehensive change.

With the advent of the Clinton administration in 1993, the incremental approach to national health policy was again abandoned, again with negative results. This time, the cause was universal health insurance. Clinton made universal healthcare part of his campaign, and upon taking office, he assigned the task of formulating a legislative proposal to his wife, Hillary. The approach spearheaded by the president's wife was controversial both in terms of method and substance.

Mrs. Clinton strongly advocated the importance of proceeding on a grand scale. In her study of the early years of the Clinton administration, Elizabeth Drew describes Mrs. Clinton's views of how to deal with healthcare reform: "She scathingly dismissed behind their backs those who wanted to go slower—mainly, the economic advisers—as 'the incrementalists'" (Drew 1994, 305). Additionally, much of the planning and formulation of the Clinton plan was done in secret meetings among healthcare professionals and scholars. Major interests in the healthcare field were forced to obtain court orders to allow them to access records of the deliberations. Public policy scholars have often counseled against deciding controversial policy questions in a closed policy process. Mrs. Clinton's approach flew directly in the face of such wisdom, and the fate of her proposal served to confirm that view's validity.

The 1,342 page Health Security Act proposal that finally emerged offered a tremendously complex system that in essence would have provided universal health coverage financed largely by assessments on employers. In opposition to the plan, the Health Insurance Association of America, a group representing small and midsized insurance companies that were threatened by the Health Security Act, ran the famous Harry and Louise ads, which as Theda Skocpol states became "veritable icons among political insiders" (Skocpol 1996, 138). These ads featured a middle-aged, white couple discussing the Clinton proposal and decrying the layers of bureaucracy and manifold regulations involved.

Because of the secretive manner in which it was formulated and its girth, the Clinton plan was received in Congress with skepticism and, after ten months of compromise efforts and alternative proposals, disappeared from the legislative agenda for want of sufficient support. Nonetheless, reform of the healthcare system remained politically popular during the Clinton administration. Some proposals, such as the portability of health insurance for workers who change jobs, were later proposed and passed in Congress's typically incremental fashion. (See Skocpol 1996, 192.)

Throughout the policy history of Medicare and Medicaid, incrementalism has ruled supreme. Tinkering with the programs has proceeded pretty much continually, with efforts at fundamental reform failing consistently. In both programs, costs have continued to rise, and in times of fiscal distress at the national level, these costs have become important issues. Two other areas of concern that have appeared on a regular basis have been coverage for long-term healthcare and for prescription drugs, neither of which had been included under Medicare.

PRESCRIPTION DRUGS AND MEDICARE: A CASE STUDY

In his 2003 State of the Union address, President George W. Bush called for major Medicare reform that would include prescription drugs under Medicare. A number of factors prompted this initiative. Perhaps most important was that the effectiveness of drugs in the treatment of illness was growing exponentially, with many senior citizens paying substantial amounts for prescriptions that materially improved their health and quality of life. Politically, the president acted in the context of an off-election year, hoping that he could get congressional action before the legislators had to begin campaigning in 2004. Additionally, the president wanted a substantial domestic policy achievement of his own to take to the voters in 2004.

President Bush's position was strengthened by the Senate's selection of Bill Frist (R-TN) to replace Trent Lott (R-MS) as Majority Leader. Although Frist was a rookie in this position, he had been a solid supporter of the president and was personally and ideologically more flexible than Lott. Just as important, Frist was a medical doctor and had a serious interest in improving healthcare delivery for Americans.

In the first two years of the Bush administration, numerous unsuccessful attempts to revamp Medicare to provide funds for prescription drugs were made in Congress. Finally, in his January 28, 2003, State of the Union speech, President Bush put his full support behind reform of Medicare that would include prescription drug benefits at a cost of $400 billion over ten years. The battle was joined, and the budget resolution approved by Congress in the spring of 2003 included the $400 billion figure. In June the House and the Senate passed different versions of a Medicare prescription drug program. The two approaches diverged widely and in various forms embodied the ideological differences that had haunted Medicare since its inception.

Throughout the summer House and Senate conferees negotiated their differences. The conference committee consisted of ten Republicans and seven Democrats. Among the seven Democrats, Senators John B. Breaux (D-LA) and Max Baucus (D-MT) worked closely with the Republicans to push for a compromise bill. It was especially important for the Senate Republicans to stress bipartisanship, given the close party division in that body and the lurking threat of parliamentary maneuvers requiring extraordinary majorities. On November 15 a compromise conference-agreement was reached, with the prospect of intense opposition awaiting on the floor of each chamber. However, a key turning point in the negotiations came on November 17 when the twenty-one member board of the AARP voted to support a compromise Medicare prescription program. The Democrats were enraged, and Majority Leader Frist, who had reached out to the AARP over the previous several months, was rewarded for his efforts. As a number of congressmen noted, the AARP seal of approval made it much more difficult to oppose a Medicare reform bill.

The AARP (formerly the American Association for Retired People) has been characterized as the 800-pound gorilla within the Beltway. The *New York Times* suggests that it is "perhaps the wealthiest and most influential advocacy organization in the nation" (Stolberg and Freudenheim 2003, A1). Founded in 1958 to help provide health insurance for retired teachers, the AARP has expanded its membership and services to the point that it now boasts 35 million members and an income from services that it provides members that is close to $200 million. In 2001 the circulation of 20.8 million copies of its magazine, *Modern Maturity*, dwarfed that of all other popular magazines (Kucznski 2001, C1). The AARP has the preeminent position as an advocate for the elderly, but in the past several decades it has cast its net far beyond the retired elderly. In 1988 it lowered its membership age to 50; and in 2003, for the first time, a majority of its members were still working (Stolberg and Freudenheim 2003, A19). To reflect this turn to the younger generation, the organization in 1998 dropped the words in its name and now goes simply by the letters AARP (Holmes 2001, D8).

While expanding membership has given a new dynamism to the organization, this growth has inevitably been accompanied by a dilution of the organization's focus on the needs of the retired. In this respect retired Americans have been coopted by an organization that once spoke only for them but now seems at least equally interested in anticipating the needs of those older Americans still in the labor force. Also of concern to some of the more outspoken Democrats was the possibility that the AARP's various business interests might conflict with the best interests of senior citizens. After final passage of the prescription drug legislation, the *New York Times* quoted Senator John D. Rockefeller IV (D-WV) as charging that "[t]he AARP is a business, first and foremost. They have a product to sell" (Stolberg and Freudenheim 2003, A19).

The conference committee charged with fashioning a compromise between the two versions of the Medicare prescription drug coverage bill passed by the House and the Senate served as a kind of microcosm of the ideological differences existing in Congress and the nation. From the House side, where the conservative position was most forcefully articulated, the Republicans, in concert with President Bush, were determined to inject a significant private sector element into the Medicare program. Somehow, either through competitive opportunities for private providers or through some kind of government premium support for private accounts, these legislators wanted private action. The plan embodied features of President Bush's Ownership Society ideology. Also, this group of legislators voiced concern about the costs of a Medicare drug option. Congress in its budget resolution of 2003 (for FY04) had settled on a cost of $400 billion over ten years. In the face of spiraling budget deficits, due primarily to the costs of the Iraqi war and security needs, plus declining revenue as a result of tax cuts, many members of congress feared the fiscal effects of a major new domestic entitlement program. The Bush administration and the Republican leadership stood by the $400 billion estimate to assuage these concerns. Later, the Medicare actuary Richard S. Foster would reveal that he had been ordered by the administrator of the Medicare program to withhold from Congress estimates that projected at least $32 billion higher costs for the drug prescription program (Pear March 2004, A8). By February 2005 the figure had risen to $750 billion.

Many Democrats, on the other hand, proceeded from fundamentally different assumptions. They wanted government to remain the dominant

Medicare provider. They feared that greater private involvement would eventually lead to inequities in the provision of health services and healthcare. Such involvement might even produce a two-class system of insurance, with the poorest and the sickest constituting the clientele of the government program and the well-to-do and healthy subscribers to the private one. Medicare had worked well to this point; they saw no need for radical change. They wanted assurances that drug benefits would be provided universally and equally to the elderly. Likewise, some Democrats made no apologies for the cost, with several estimating that truly worthwhile Medicare drug reform should cost in the neighborhood of $800 billion over ten years, exactly double the figure contained in the congressional budget resolution.

Agreement developed that the time had come for including a prescription drug benefit under Medicare and that senior citizens should be able to choose between Medicare and private drug plans. Also, in provisions not directly related to drug benefits, both bills increased Medicare payments to some of the traditional providers, such as doctors and hospitals, under Medicare. The resulting legislation, then, was to be composed of incremental variations on the basic positions staked out by the protagonists, although the overall result constituted the most far-reaching reform of Medicare since its beginning. It also involved establishing two diametrically opposed insurance paradigms at its center.

Most of the major changes were delayed until 2006, safely after the 2004 election. In the meantime the bill provided for prescription discount cards to be issued in 2004 to provide some savings on drug purchases until the full drug plan went into effect in 2006. The full plan would not offer complete coverage, but instead it would provide coverage of 75 percent, with a $250 deductible, up to $2,250. At that point the beneficiary would have to soon pay a total of $3,600 out of his/her pocket. After the beneficiary had paid out this amount, the government would again enter the picture and provide 95 percent coverage of additional prescription drug costs. With both the discount card and the $3,600 deductible, the poor received additional help. Low-income clientele received $600 assistance in 2004 and 2005, and in 2006 those with incomes up to 150 percent of the poverty level would not have a gap in coverage, but they would have a sliding scale of premiums and copayments. The government would provide fallback coverage if qualified private plans were not available in a region. To mollify those wanting to move toward greater privatization of Medicare, the bill offered a pilot program beginning in 2010, under which traditional Medicare would have to compete with private insurance plans in six metropolitan areas to be selected later. Significantly, a number of congressmen and congresswomen agreed to vote for the bill only after they were assured that none of these areas would be located in their districts. There were, of course, numerous other provisions in the bill, including a provision for health savings accounts, other forms of means testing for Part B premium payments, and changed reimbursements for providers.

As anticipated, there was sustained criticism of the compromise, and, again, the vote in the House was a cliffhanger. In the Senate a number of procedural hurdles requiring extraordinary majorities had to be surmounted. President Bush signed the bill into law on December 8, 2003 (P.L. 108–73).

1. Problems with the New Law

The poorest (couples who earn under $16,862 per year) will benefit most under the new law, since in addition to discounts, they will receive a $600 annual drug subsidy. For those who are better off, however, the cards may be of dubious worth. Tom Daschle, the Democratic Senate leader who lost his seat in the election of 2004, remarked that the cards were expected to provide little significant value to seniors. At a forum on discount cards at a church in Bloomington, Illinois, in the summer of 2004, eight retirees talked about their inquiries about card benefits. None of them had signed up for the program, having found that their present private coverages were better than those offered with the discount card program. Most of these people were retired schoolteachers, and others had worked in private business. In fact, only 10 percent of seniors ever signed up for Medicare drug discount cards.

Seniors have found the cards complicated and confusing. In Missouri, the number of calls to a state-supported hotline to answer questions about Medicare almost doubled—from forty-five to eighty calls per day—after enactment of the prescription program. In California there was likewise a flood of calls to the State Health Insurance Counselling and Advisory Office. A spokesperson for the Senior Health Insurance Program of the Illinois Department of Insurance is reported to have said, "It's disappointing that Congress couldn't find an easier way to deliver a drug discount program for older Americans. It didn't have to be this complicated" (Swiech, *The Pantagraph* 2004). A resident of Seattle, Washington, remarked that "[u]nderstanding this plan is almost as bad as filling out an income-tax return" (Song, *Seattle Times* 2004).

Significant problems posed by the discount plan include the fact that a single card may not cover all drugs a Medicare recipient uses, that card sponsors may drop a particular drug needed by a card holder, and that prices can change weekly. The cardholder, however, is locked into a given program for a year.

Many elderly people have been purchasing drugs in Canada at much lower prices than are found at home. The new law makes it more difficult for them to continue to do so, because of alleged problems of safety. Another fear about the law among the elderly is that larger corporations that have had generous prescription plans for retirees will now retrench their benefits—and perhaps only match what Medicare provides. And those who have purchased Medigap insurance for their retirement will find that the law has made such policies unavailable.

The American Medical Association (AMA), the premier representative of organized medicine in the United States, lobbied enthusiastically for the Medicare

Reform Act during 2003. But with passage of the law secured, the association has gone on to argue that Congress ought to follow up with a bill authorizing the secretary of Health and Human Services to negotiate contracts with the pharmaceutical companies supplying drugs to enrollees. This would be necessary, it says, to prevent the companies from receiving windfall profits at the expense of seniors. To make the new law meaningful, drug prices would have to be controlled; its purpose, after all, was to give seniors access to affordable drugs. The law itself, however, forbade negotiated prices, because of the fear that the government would overwhelm the free market in drugs and produce price fixing. Thus, on the one hand, there was a fear of price gouging; and on the other, there was concern about an artificially low price. The government had hoped that under the new law, competing private care plans would produce large manufacturers' discounts. But what the actual economic outcome will be is not at all clear.

Another concern was the 1.5 million Americans who live in nursing homes. Experts on long-term care were reported in December 2004 to be concerned that the new law would be unworkable. (See Pear 2004.) Because of physical disabilities and brain disorders, many nursing home residents are not able to shop around for bargain plans, as Medicare beneficiaries are expected to be able to do under the new law. And nursing home patients typically take a large number of pills per day, eight on average. The new law calls into question the role of long-term care pharmacies that currently supply nursing homes and assisted living centers. It requires that each beneficiary choose between two or more government-subsidized plans, each with its own list of approved drugs (formularies) and its own retail pharmacy network. Since premiums will vary from plan to plan, Medicare beneficiaries are expected to compare them carefully for the best fit. But are nursing home patients able to do this and find a formulary that satisfies their current needs? A third of them suffer from Alzheimer's disease. A plan offered by Aetna, for example, might not include in its network the long-term care pharmacy a beneficiary has been using. Administration officials have recognized the problem, but they have not said how it would be addressed. Nursing home representatives say that they would not have the competence to advise patients on their choices. "If nursing homes have to deal with multiple formularies from multiple prescription drug plans, that will result in chaos, and an increased potential for medication errors, said Thomas P. Clark, policy director for the American Society of Consultant Pharmacists (Pear, 29). These problems were seen as most acute for those not on Medicaid. Those patients on Medicaid get their drug benefits from programs that are closely monitored by the individual states, which must assume 50 percent of the costs.

Thus, we have a law that after a fashion constitutes a major reform of the Medicare program. But it leaves public policy on health insurance a crazy quilt of essentially ad hoc decisions made over several decades, at the heart of which stand two incompatible insurance paradigms.

In March 2005 it was reported that the new drug benefit program had overcome a major obstacle when a number of large insurance companies decided to offer prescription drug coverage to Medicare beneficiaries beginning in 2006. Some programs will be offered nationwide, and others only in selected states or regions. Companies have stated that federal subsidies will minimize their financial risks and that they are reluctant to yield the market to their competitors. Blue Cross and Blue Shield, together with Aetna, are among the large firms that have decided to participate. The Bush administration is relying on competition among participating companies to make the legislation work. Some problems remain: the bewildering range of choice for consumers and the large deductible of up to $5,000 per year. The problem of confusion is largely due to the complexity of the program itself and the opportunities for private companies to enter the field. When the new program began in 2006, still further confusions ensued.

Ethical Analysis of the Case

Is the prescription drug law of 2003 a good law? First, what would utilitarians say? They would want to apply the test of overall increase in social well-being. Ideally, this analysis would require a comparison with the costs and benefits of all alternative social expenditures. Since this is not possible, utilitarians would confine their comparison to alternative expenditures for medically vulnerable populations. How would one establish priorities among those in need of medical services? Would it simply be a matter of choosing to support treatments with the greatest likelihood of success? Or would we have to establish priorities of vulnerability among groups? But utilitarians are not able to raise such a question, since their standard requires that all individual preferences be counted equally. One thing a utilitarian might do is complain that cost estimates were very badly carried out when the legislation was planned, since those estimates have risen from an original $400 billion to almost twice that figure over ten years.

A deontologist might ask, as one whose chief concern is equity, whether health technology has reached the point at which access to healthcare could be considered a universal right? A deontologist would also seem to be the one to establish a rank-order of vulnerability. An alternative to prescription drugs for the elderly, for example, would be basic healthcare for the 45 million poor who cannot afford health insurance. Another would be insurance for poor children, who today remain uninsured. What standard of equity the deontologist might employ, however, is not clear.

Prudent pragmatists might enter the argument by comparing the status of American health with that of other leading industrial countries. They might look at data showing that countries with universal healthcare policies also have lower infant mortality rates and longer life expectancy than the United States. This approach would also point to a more aggressive program of preventive healthcare, with a focus on the health of the young, not the aged. This would also allow the prudent pragmatist to finesse the equity question the deontologist could not answer.

Prudent pragmatists would weigh and balance the prescription drug expense against a variety of other programs, both in the health field and elsewhere. Though precise measurements are not possible, they would ask whether so expensive a program ought to have been weighed against the enormous expenditures required by the Iraq war and nation-building before passage. Does the circumstance that national security now necessitates extraordinary expenditures mean that this welfare priority should be put on a back burner? Might an open-ended growth of the national budget so unsettle financial markets as to deliver a catastrophic blow to the well-being of the society as a whole?

A prudent pragmatist might also wish to take seriously a comment on national health policy made by Daniel Callahan, a leading bioethicist, who argues that we have been allowing technological improvement to drive up the price of healthcare to unsustainable heights. Is it rational and efficient to allow healthcare costs to escalate in such an uncontrolled way? A case in point is the program of free kidney dialysis for anyone affected by kidney disease, which was enacted by Congress in an emotional moment, when the legislators viewed a kidney patient being dialysed on the floor of the legislative house. Perhaps a better use of scarce resources would be to ration healthcare and focus instead on "the amelioration of the social, economic, and cultural conditions that contribute . . . to population and individual health" (Callahan 1999, 81). Other societies engage in such rationing.

President Bush sees the drug law as a part of his Ownership Society program, which is intended to serve the traditional value of individual independence and freedom, and to reduce the individual's dependence on government agencies in serving his or her welfare. How important is this objective? What would a utilitarian or a deontologist say about this goal of the prescription drug program? Does it have to do either with efficiency or with equity? The prudent pragmatist would no doubt inquire into the circumstances surrounding the acts of choice involved. One would be the meaningfulness of free choice for aging minds, especially those affected by increasing dementia, and these inquiries would involve numerous technical questions. Policy analyses on questions of this sort would be called for in planning the implementation of the law in the years ahead. A prudent pragmatist would no doubt fault the policy analysts who did the planning for the interim and permanent programs whose shortcomings we have described.

Prudent pragmatists would not only wish to rank-order national goal values in assessing the prescription drug law. They would also want to establish their logical compatibility. For example, in introducing the possibility of subsidized private healthcare plans as an alternative to traditional Medicare, one opens the possibility of private coverage undermining the fiscal viability of the public system. How would one prevent the well-to-do from using their freedom of choice to constitute a pool of subscribers that would leave the poor and sick the sole contributors to the public pool? A policy analyst working for the Office of Management and Budget might do a study of the cost effectiveness of private vis-à-vis public insurance, or the degree to which private insurance might be subject to market failure, or the compatibility of two insurance paradigms within the same legislative project.

REFERENCES

Anonymous, "Saved by Smokers," *The Economist Newspaper Ltd.*, November 22, 2001, http://www.economist.com/world/na/displayStory.cmf?Story_ID= 8777061. Accessed 5/22/2006.

AP, "Panel that Set Smoking Curbs is Denied Funds," *New York Times*, April 14, 1987, B2.

Berlin, Isaiah. *Two Concepts of Liberty*. Oxford: Clarendon Press, 1958.

Brandt, Allan M. "Blow Some My Way: Passive Smoking, Risk and American Culture." In *Ashes to Ashes: The History of Smoking and Health*, ed. Stephen Lock, Lois Reynolds, and E.M. Tansy, 164–91. Atlanta, GA: Editions Rodopi B.V., 1998.

Broder, John M. "Smoking Ban Takes Effect, Indoors and Out." *New York Times* (March 18, 2006), A14.

Callahan, Daniel. *False Hopes: Overcoming Obstacles to a Sustainable, Affordable Medicine*. New Brunswick, NJ: Rutgers University Press, 1999.

Congressional Quarterly Almanac. "Catastrophic-Coverage Law Is Repealed." Washington, DC: Congressional Quarterly, Inc., 1989, 149–56.

Daugherty, Charles J. *American Health Care: Realities, Rights, and Reforms*. New York: Oxford University Press, 1988.

Derthick, Martha A. *Up In Smoke*. Washington, DC: CQ Press, 2002.

Dewan, Shaila K. "How a Popular State Bill to Restrict Smoking Faltered." *New York Times* (July 9, 2002), B1.

Drew, Elizabeth. *On the Edge of the Clinton Presidency*. New York: Simon & Schuster, 1994.

Editorial. "Smoke Filled Albany." *New York Times* 11-16-99, A26.

Fisher, Ian. "Philip Morris Tops List of Lobbying Spenders in New York." *New York Times* (March 16, 1994), B2.

Garrett, Laurie. *Betrayal of Trust: The Collapse of Global Health*. New York: Hyperion, 2000.

Gruber, Jonathan. "Medicaid," in *Means-tested Transfer Programs in the United States*, ed. Robert A. Moffitt, 15–77. Chicago: University of Chicago Press, 2003.

Holmes, Steven A. "The World According to AARP." *New York Times* (March 21, 2001), D1, D8.

Horner, Blair, "Court Ruling is Threat to State's Smoking Ban," *Rochester Democrat and Chronicle*, November 1, 2004, 5B.

Klein, Richard. *Cigarettes Are Sublime*. Durham, NC: Duke University Press, 1995.

Kucznski, Alex. "New AARP Magazine Is Courting Younger Readers." *New York Times* (January 22, 2001), C1, C11.

Levy, Clifford J. "Tobacco and Its Money Have Minority Allies in New York." *New York Times* (January 4, 2000), B1.

Liebler, Shawn M. "Allegany County Levies Smoking Fines." *Hornell-Wellsville Spectator* (January 9, 2005), 1A, 9A.

Manning, Anita. "Teenage Smoking Rates Drop." *USA Today* (May 17, 2002), A3.

Nozick, Robert. *Anarchy, State, and Utopia.* New York: Basic Books, 1974.

Pear, Robert. "Medicare Actuary Gives Wanted Data to Congress." *New York Times* (March 20, 2004), A8.

———. "Concerns Raised on Medicare Law: Nursing Homes." *New York Times* (December 5, 2004), A1, 29.

Perez-Pena, Richard, "State Efforts to Cut Smoking Leave New York Far Behind." *New York Times* (May 30, 1999), Sec.1, 1, 26.

Precious, Tom. "Smoking Bans Didn't Reduce Business." *Buffalo News* (June 14, 2002), C1.

———. "Pataki Signs Tough New Law That Bans Smoking in Public." *Buffalo News* (June 27, 2003), A1, A9.

Rawls, John. *A Theory of Justice.* Cambridge, MA: Bellknap Press of Harvard University Press, 1971.

Ripley, Randall B., and Grace A. Franklin. *Policy Implementation and Bureaucracy,* 2d ed. Chicago: Dorsey Press, 1986.

Rutenberg, Jim, and Lily Koppel. "As Air Clears, Even Smokers Are Converted." *New York Times* (February 6, 2005), A25.

Schmalz, Jeffrey. "Appeals Court Stays Rules in Smoking." *New York Times* (May 6, 1987), B1.

———. "Curbs on Smoking Are Struck Down in New York State." *New York Times* (November 26, 1987), A1.

Sengupta, Somini. "Though Smoking Bill Fails, Hopes for Ban Persist." *New York Times* (June 25, 2001), B1.

Skocpol, Theda. *Boomerang: Clinton's Health Security Effort and the Turn Against Government in U. S. Politics.* New York: W.W. Norton and Co., 1996.

Song, Kyung M. "Medicare Discount Cards: What Seniors Need to Know," *The Seattle Times*, April 29, 2004, http://seattletimes.nwsource.com/html/health/2001915367_medicare29m.html/

Stolberg, Sheryl Gay, and Milt Freudenheim. "Sweeping Medicare Change Wins Approval in Congress; President Claims a Victory." *New York Times* (November 26, 2003), A1, A19.

Sullum, Jacob. *For Your Own Good: The Anti-Smoking Crusade and the Tyranny of Public Health.* New York: The Free Press, 1998.

Swiech, Paul, "Carding Seniors," *The Pantagraph*, June 7, 2004, http://web.lexis-Nexis.com/universe/printdoc.

Titone, Vito J. "The Limits of Action by a Public Health Agency." *New York Times,* 11-26-87, B6.

U.S. Department of Health and Human Services. *Reducing Tobacco Use: A Report of the Surgeon General.* Atlanta: Centers for Disease Control and Prevention, National Center for Chronic Disease Prevention and Health Promotion, Office on Smoking and Health, 2000.

Uhlig, Mark A. "Smoking Rules Prompt Power Fight in Albany." *New York Times* (January 29, 1987), B3.

CHAPTER 7

Criminal Justice

The prudent balancing of social values in the area of law enforcement has posed a continuing ethical dilemma since the beginning of the Republic. The power of the law has been required to defend the lives and property of citizens against predators, to protect the nation's health from harmful drugs, and to guarantee national security against enemies both domestic and foreign. At the same time liberal democratic values dictate fairness in the pursuit of these goals—that arbitrary process be avoided and that the accused be guaranteed equal protection of the law. These standards have evolved over the past two centuries. In recent years, for example, increased sensitivity to the value of human life and doubts about the equity of the American system of criminal prosecution have produced a national debate about the legitimacy of capital punishment. Even more recently, changes in the character of modern warfare have created new ethical dilemmas for Americans. Concerns about the need for greater security from terrorist threats have had to be balanced against Americans' fundamental attachment to civil liberties.

THE ADMINISTRATION OF CRIMINAL JUSTICE: A HISTORICAL PERSPECTIVE

The story of criminal justice in America has been one of movement from local control and discretion to centralization and uniformity. Individual rights and equality before the law have always been essential parts of the language of American criminal justice. They have not, however, consistently been part of the practice of those in law enforcement. At the state and local levels, for much of this nation's history, the emphasis has been on punishing and controlling crime first, whatever the costs in individual rights, and on ensuring that criminal justice authorities have remained duly responsive to those groups in political power. Gradually, however, norms of equal treatment and of due process have gained greater force.

The Nineteenth Century: Crime and Local Politics

During the nineteenth century, it was understood that partisan political advantage entailed control of a locality's police. This meant that the dominant ethnic and racial groups in an area received favored treatment, both in recruitment for jobs in law enforcement and in the application of police and prosecutorial discretion. With regard to policing, August Vollmer, an advocate of police professionalism, described the period as "an era of incivility, ignorance, brutality, and graft" (Walker 1980, 61). These problems were exacerbated by the limited communications and transportation technologies of the time. Cops on the beat were essentially unsupervised and thus exercised a large amount of discretion. They were, in the words of Samuel Walker, "primarily tools of local politicians" (ibid.).

Inaction at the national level left the administration of criminal justice to the states and localities by default. Congressional legislation was minimal, and federal police authorities confined themselves to executing the basic constitutional mandates of Congress (e.g., protection of the currency and control of smuggling). The Supreme Court also limited national power in law enforcement in the case of *U.S v. Hudson and Goodwin*, 7 Cranch 32 (1812). In this proceeding Hudson and Goodwin were prosecuted by federal authorities for the common law crime of libeling the president. The Supreme Court, in a decision written by Justice William Johnson, declared that the national government has no criminal common law jurisdiction. For an act to be a crime at the national level, it must be specified in statute. That decision remains good law. Because the states had sole jurisdiction over criminal common law and because the national government did not extensively legislate, states and localities had pretty much free rein in dealing with crime and criminals throughout the nineteenth century.

During the 1800s, the concept of crime itself varied over time and from region to region. By the early part of the century, religious crimes had given way to economic crimes, or transgressions against property. Prosecutions for fornication, blasphemy, and Sunday law violations declined dramatically relative to property crimes. William E. Nelson concludes from his study of legal change in Massachusetts during this period that the criminal "was no longer envisioned as a sinner against God, but rather as one who preyed upon the property of his fellow citizens" (Friedman 2002, 258). Geographically, treatment of what constituted criminal behavior also varied depending primarily on which minority group was at hand. The southern states' abuse of African Americans was salient in this respect, but other areas saw the scales of justice weighted against Asians, Native Americans, or Hispanics.

Professionalization and Nationalization of Law Enforcement

By the close of the nineteenth century professional police associations began to appear. The Progressive Era of the early twentieth century engendered reform and efforts toward professionalism in criminal justice, just as it did in other areas of public service. Reformers stressed the need for trained specialists, the importance of insulating law enforcement from partisan political pressures, and the value of administrative efficiency. These steps toward greater professionalism undoubtedly contributed to greater uniformity in law enforcement standards across the country. This movement was eventually to spill over into uniform procedural protections for individuals in the criminal process. Emerging professional standards thus brought with them authoritative norms of equal protection.

The nationalization of law enforcement policy was accelerated by greater activity in Congress. The Progressive Era saw the enactment of numerous federal statutes that created federal crimes. With this effort came the establishment of the Bureau of Investigation in 1908, which evolved into the Federal Bureau of Investigation in the 1930s. Increasing national involvement in the nation's criminal justice efforts, however, was not without its negative side effects. The Red Scare of the 1920s resulted in persecution of radical aliens that overshadowed the protection of individual rights. The national enforcement of Prohibition seems to have encouraged the growth of organized criminal activity to circumvent federal law. On a positive note the FBI, with its national crime laboratory and training programs for municipal police officers, provided expertise and professional training to other law enforcement agencies.

Crime Control and Rights

Changes in the concept of crime continued during the twentieth century. At times these changes seemed driven by the goals of FBI director J. Edgar Hoover, who continually raised public concern about organized crime and the communist threat. The 1960s witnessed the waning of the FBI's influence and the appearance of activist groups that insisted on more equal treatment under the law. Beginning with the 1954 *Brown* v. *Board of Education* (349 U.S. 294) decision, the Supreme Court vigorously and consistently invoked the equal protection clause of the Fourteenth Amendment to protect against racial discrimination. Much of this judicial reorientation can be credited to the politics of interest and the politics of conscience exercised in sophisticated fashion by black groups, such as the National Association for the Advancement of Colored People (NAACP). Women, the disabled, the elderly, the poor, and gays and lesbians, among other culturally diverse groups, were also eventually to obtain protection under the expanding umbrella of judicial interpretation.

In the 1960s procedural criminal protections were given national status when most of the protections in the Bill of Rights were applied to the states through the due process clause of the Fourteenth Amendment. By gradually expanding the content of the term liberty in that clause to include almost all of the Bill of Rights guarantees, the Supreme Court gave individuals increased protection against state action. The judicial rules enunciated in these decisions became part of the standard operating procedures (SOPs) of police departments across the nation due to the spreading professionalism of law enforcement generally. (Professionalism carries with it norms of reasonableness and of dispassionate and impersonal justice.) The Supreme

Court's expansion of rights in the criminal process created a due process model of law enforcement that has served as a counter weight to balance what was previously the prevailing crime control model. For the issues posed by increasing American pluralism, the Court's focus on criminal procedure provided a solvent that the crime control model could not match.

However, the crime control component of the criminal justice system remained important, especially in the war on drugs. Here the federal government moved into a position of dominance with the establishment of the White House Office of National Drug Control Policy in 1988, which coordinated the work of over fifty federal agencies. Much of the effort to control drugs was headed by the Drug Enforcement Agency (DEA), which was housed in the Department of Justice. The involvement of drugs in a high percentage of physical assaults and homicides has made the attack on drugs exceptionally important in the public mind.

Advocates of the crime control model of justice appeared to have achieved an important breakthrough with application of a new conceptual approach in New York City under Police Commissioner William Bratton and Mayor Rudolph Giuliani. Bratton was favorably impressed by an article by James Q. Wilson and George Kelling entitled "Broken Windows," which appeared in the March 1982 issue of *The Atlantic Monthly*. Wilson and Kelling argued that the most effective crime control model was one that focused on quality-of-life crimes such as broken windows, graffiti, and other minor violations of the law. By punishing these kinds of activities, the police improved the quality of a neighborhood and began to make life difficult generally for those with little respect for the law. Additionally, following up on minor arrests of these people often led to the discovery of more serious criminal activity by them or their associates. Bratton also drew on the latest technology in communications and advances in data analysis to institute more stringent control over the discretion of police officers. Accountability and responsiveness to the public became the order of the day. In New York City the improvement in community life and the drop in crime rates were dramatic.

This systems approach to crime control, which integrated the latest technology with the prosecution of crime from minor infractions to the most serious felonies, gained adherents in many cities, and with its acceptance some of the more extreme claims of rights activists were pushed to the background. Fred Siegel (1997) asserts that one of the major problems in New York City had been that rights activists had essentially destroyed the ability of the police to enforce the law. Bratton, however, insisted that arrests be made—that minor crimes be punished. So, for example, when he took on the squeegee men, his aides discovered a traffic regulation specifically prohibiting approaching a car to wash the windshield. This silenced the New York Civil Liberties Union, which had been intent on preserving the right of a group of derelicts to continually harass motorists at traffic lights (Bratton 1998, 213–14).

Although New York City's experience showed that innovation in the control of crime was possible at the local level, the trend in this area has been toward greater intervention by the national government. Indicative of this development has been the increased number of federal crime-fighting statutes in the past several decades. Many of these laws are omnibus in scope, reflecting the wider range of activities monitored by the federal government. Chief among these are the Law Enforcement Assistance Act of 1965, the 1968 Omnibus Crime Control and Safe Streets Act, the 1970 Racketeer Influenced and Corrupt Organizations Act (RICO), the 1984 Comprehensive Crime Control Act, the 1990 Crime Control Act, and the 1994 Violent Crime Control and Law Enforcement Act. There are also important recent statutes dealing with the terrorist threat, which we discuss later. This list does not include statutes aimed at specific issues, such as drugs and guns. (A sense of the proliferation of criminal statutes at the national level can be gained from Baker and Bennett 2004.)

As America moved into the twenty-first century, ideas about crime and criminal behavior underwent further changes. The first of these changes was the rise to public prominence of white-collar crime, a term attributed by Lawrence M. Friedman to a sociologist, Edwin Sutherland, who first used it in 1949. With the proliferation of government regulations of financial activity and the tremendous growth in that sector, the opportunities for criminal behavior increased markedly. Thus, in the early years of the twenty-first century, Americans were shocked to learn of the extensive machinations by corporate leaders to mislead investors as to the true value of their corporations. Even more stunning—indeed cataclysmic—were the terrorist attacks of September 11, 2001. These attacks, which demonstrated dramatically the global reach of crime and terrorism in today's world, led the Bush administration, in its attempts to prevent terrorist attacks, to displace the rights orientation embedded in much of American criminal law.

RACIAL PROFILING AND THE WAR ON DRUGS: SEARCH-AND-SEIZURE JURISPRUDENCE AND RACIAL PROFILING

Probably nowhere in American criminal law do the general standards of constitutional rights and the particular circumstances of on-the-street policing collide more strikingly than in the realm of search-and-seizure jurisprudence. The legal and ethical questions in this area have become even more complicated with the emergence of the issue of racial profiling.

Prior to the tenure of Chief Justice Earl Warren (1953–1969), the states had wide latitude in how they conducted searches and seizures. Federal authorities since the early years of the twentieth century had been bound by the Fourth Amendment's protection against unreasonable search and seizure, primarily through the Court's imposition of the exclusionary rule, which required that evidence unconstitutionally obtained and any derivatives therefrom must be excluded from trial. It was not until 1961, in the case of *Mapp v. Ohio* (367 U.S. 643), that the Supreme Court applied the exclusionary rule against the states. From that point on, the due process clause of the Fourteenth Amendment, bound state and local law enforcement personnel to the same Fourth Amendment search-and-seizure standards as the federal authorities. Thus, the dragnet approach toward solving crimes, in which the police simply brought in, searched, and interrogated anyone in the area of a crime—while making for good television—was no longer permissible under the Constitution.

The issues involving on-the-street police stops were considered by the Supreme Court in the case of *Terry v. Ohio*, 392 U.S. 1 (1968), which began to spell out the right of officers to stop and frisk suspects. Basically, the Court justified a police officer's right to search for dangerous weapons when making a reasonable investigative stop on the street. In this case a Cleveland police detective, Martin McFadden, who had thirty-nine years of police experience, had stopped three men whom he judged to be acting suspiciously, and he found illegal weapons on two of them. There were two important points in this case. First, the Court accepted the fact that Detective McFadden "had developed routine habits of observation over the years" that gave credibility to his statement that "when I looked over, they [the defendants] didn't look right to me at the time." Second, the Court allowed police officers to make stops on the street based on reasonable suspicion that a crime was about to be committed or was being committed. Thus was justified the stop-and-frisk power of the officer on the street.

Although the Terry decision established an officer's right to frisk for weapons for self-protection, the logic of its search-and-seizure premise evolved to cover as well pat-downs that discovered drugs. The Court reasoned by analogy. Under the "plain sight" doctrine, if police acting lawfully observe contraband, they may seize it without a warrant. In *Minnesota v. Dickerson*, 508 U.S. 366 (1993), the Court concluded that an officer who is legally justified in patting someone down for weapons is constitutionally permitted to seize and use at trial any contraband discovered during that pat-down.

Surprisingly, despite decisions on almost any aspect of search-and-seizure that one can envision, the Supreme Court has not directly confronted the issue of racial profiling. The Court has advanced individual protections in the criminal process, and in parallel fashion it has moved to protect groups under the equal protection clause. But the twain have not met in Court doctrine. In fact, in a unanimous opinion in *Whren v. U.S.*, 517 U.S. 806 (1996), the Court specifically refused to merge the two.

Whren provided an opportunity for critics of racial profiling to interject the question of racially discriminatory intent into violations of individual criminal protections. In this case, Washington, D.C. police officers pulled over the defendants for minor traffic infractions in a high drug area in what was a classic example of a pretextual stop (i.e., the officers used the traffic violations as a pretext for creating a situation in which they could search for drugs). In the defendants' vehicle the police discovered two large bags of crack cocaine. The defendants, who were both black, argued that the evidence should be excluded from trial because the police really were acting on the basis that their race created suspicion that they possessed drugs. Justice Antonin Scalia, speaking for the Court, roundly rejected the defendants' contentions. In his words, ". . . the constitutional basis for objecting to intentionally discriminatory application of laws is the Equal Protection clause, not the Fourth Amendment. Subjective intentions play no role in ordinary, probable-cause Fourth Amendment analysis" (Whren 98). Here the police had reasonable cause to believe that the traffic code was being violated, and the Court was absolutely unwilling to delve into the subjective intent behind the officers' actions.

The Whren decision has given local law enforcement agencies latitude in their use of profiles to apprehend criminals. Most of these profiles have focused on drug control, but in areas near the Mexican border, illegal immigration has also been a concern. And since September 11, 2001, homeland security efforts have made individuals of Arab descent targets of profiles. Those fighting the use of profiles in these areas have been placed on the defensive because it is exceptionally difficult to prove equal protection clause violations from particular cases. One approach has been to try to gather sufficient empirical data to be able to show statistically that discriminatory police action is taking place.

The Supreme Court has always allowed the states broad discretion in their handling of crime on the highways. It has recognized that for the most part the states have primary control over their highways, and it has also emphasized the importance of supporting professional judgments by the police in the field. It has, however, insisted on the need for "particularized suspicion" to justify searches of automobiles for criminal activity other than drunken driving (*City of Indianapolis v. Edmond*, 531 U.S. 32 [2000]). Thus, when Indianapolis established roadblocks to check groups of cars by open-view inspection and the use of drug-detection dogs, the Supreme Court demurred. Justice Sandra Day O'Connor insisted that for most criminal activity, the state must demonstrate particularized suspicion to justify a stop and search. In her words, "[w]e cannot sanction stops justified only by the generalized and ever-present possibility that interrogation and inspection may reveal that any given motorist has committed some crime" (*City of Indianapolis*, 44). The Court, however, was careful even here to allow police some leeway. Justice O'Connor noted that exceptions remained for patrols close to the border and for purposes of safety on the highways. She also suggested that carefully tailored roadblocks might also be appropriate for imminent terrorist threats or dangerous fleeing criminals. Nonetheless, particularized suspicion remains the search-and-seizure prerequisite for the common, garden variety criminal on the nation's highways.

Today the Constitution, then, requires in most instances particularized suspicion for a warrantless search to be constitutional. This suspicion must be based on probable cause if it results in an extensive search or seizure. However, temporary and brief stops may be valid based on reasonable suspicion, and, if the suspect subsequently consents voluntarily to a search, it is very difficult to raise a Fourth Amendment challenge. It is this latter area that has caused the most controversy on the nation's highways.

The debate over racial profiling is one in which professional law enforcement goals have clashed with racial sensitivity in our pluralist society. Both Presidents Bill Clinton and George W. Bush have reacted to this sensitivity with statements condemning racial profiling. The problem with these condemnations and much of the press coverage is that racial profiling is largely misunderstood. No reasonable American would justify stopping and searching people simply because of their race. Profiling has been an attempt, begun largely by the DEA, to formulate characteristics that indicate an individual may be a drug courier. These profiles have often included race or ethnicity as one component. It has been this factor and its abuse by the police that have led critics to level charges of racism.

1. Forfeiture and Perverse Incentives to Profiling

The profiling approach at the state and local levels received an important stimulus from Congress's efforts to encourage more cooperation between the DEA and state and local agencies. In the 1984 Comprehensive Crime Control Act, Congress specifically provided authority for the DEA to share forfeited property in drug cases with state and local agencies that give "significant" assistance in such cases. For this purpose the statute established an Assets Forfeiture Fund in the Department of Justice, and, to assist further in drug enforcement, the DEA shared its profile methodology with these agencies. Everyone involved recognized that domestic law enforcement efforts in the United States are heavily dependent on personnel and knowledge at the local levels.

The result at the state level was a perverse set of incentives that encouraged aggressive stops and searches, ones that were often based on the DEA-supplied profiles. State and local law enforcement agencies that seized large caches of money that could be drug related turned this money over to the DEA, which then returned a large share back for their use. Some departments did very well under this arrangement. The Justice Department, for example, in fiscal year 2001 reported accepting $357.9 million in forfeited cash (U.S. Department of Justice, June 2002). It would not be unusual for the Feds to return 40–60 percent of this money to state and local police agencies.

As one would expect, several serious problems emerged from this approach to drug interdiction. First, it provided substantial incentives for state and local police agencies to treat individual protections against unreasonable searches and seizures in a cavalier fashion. Second, the search-and-seizure efforts to end drug trafficking became more aggressive just as minority sensitivities heightened and activists' organizational ability to protest such law enforcement behavior increased. The legal questions about using race or ethnicity as a factor in a stop and search arise most graphically on the nation's highways—and especially on those like I-95, which is a major thoroughfare down the East Coast. Finally, an additional complication introduced by the forfeiture monies is that they increase the autonomy of local police forces by providing a source of funding independent from legislative oversight.

Because of its reluctance to mesh equal protection concerns with search-and-seizure protections, the Supreme Court has been of little assistance to defendants who believe that they are the victims of racial discrimination by police stops. Moreover, with regard to search-and-seizure protections, the Court has been willing to permit police officers considerable discretion in the field. A traffic violation is obviously grounds for a police stop, and suspicion aroused from the stop may easily justify a search. In practice many stops yield nothing beyond a traffic warning. Legal recourse in these cases is virtually nonexistent. Nor is there much recourse when a driver consents to a search, which appears to happen in most cases.

2. Problems of Discrimination

There is evidence from around the nation that blacks have been subjected disproportionately to stop-and-search procedures. An American Civil Liberties Union (ACLU) study of police stops on I-95 found that blacks and whites violated traffic laws at the same rate. But, although blacks constituted only 17 percent of the driving population, they made up 72 percent of those stopped and searched—strongly suggesting a racial profiling stance by the police. This discriminatory treatment appeared to occur without regard to social class or gender. In some cases African American legislators have been victimized, and, in response, they have introduced traffic stops statistics bills—for example, in North Carolina and California. (See Taslitz 2003, 221–98.)

Increasing the administrative procedures required of the police has been a fairly common way of trying to cope with racial profiling complaints. Some states now require extensive paperwork on each stop to determine the race of those stopped and the reason for the stop. What appears to be behind this gathering of data is an effort to establish equal protection standing against the police. But as several commentators have pointed out, this approach may reduce the willingness of the police to make stops at all, and it appears to have lowered significantly the apprehension rate for drug couriers. Peter H. Schuck notes that in many jurisdictions, "the officer must decide what the motorists' race, ethnicity, or national origin is and then record the data for the profiling monitor—without asking them [motorists], much less allowing them, to self identify" (Schuck 2003, 146). He is sympathetic to the criticism that such data will necessarily be inaccurate.

RACIAL PROFILING IN NEW JERSEY: A CASE STUDY

The federal incentives for state and local law enforcement officials to pursue drug couriers aggressively were especially attractive to state troopers along the New Jersey Turnpike, a major north-south route along the East Coast. With the passage of legislation at the national level encouraging the sharing of forfeited monies and proceeds from forfeited goods, law enforcement activity on the turnpike became significantly more noticeable, particularly to minorities.

As part of their cooperative effort against drug trafficking, the New Jersey State Highway Patrol was provided with training from the DEA and with profile formats that included race and ethnicity as one factor to be considered when stopping and investigating for drugs (Kocieniewski 2002). Many black drivers complained that their race was the sole reason for their being stopped, and statistics consistently showed that a larger proportion of African Americans than Caucasians were stopped for investigation. New Jersey officials, however, denied that racial profiling of this sort was occurring. Governor Christine Todd Whitman stated this position vehemently. "Profiling is not only not the policy," she stated, "but it is illegal. . . . I don't believe the state police engages in illegal activity" (Wiggins 1998, A1).

The issue of racial profiling really exploded into the headlines in April 1998, when two state patrol officers stopped a van with an out-of-state license plate whose four occupants were African American and Latino. Asserting that the driver of the van tried to back over them, the officers fired eleven times into the vehicle, seriously wounding the three passengers. The resulting controversy changed entirely New Jersey's stance on the issue of racial profiling. No drug-related charges were ever filed against those in the van.

Legal action dragged on for several years. The serious state charges against the patrol officers were eventually dropped, but civil charges against the state remained. In the meantime, black organizations became aroused over the profiling issue. Although African Americans comprise only 13 percent of the New Jersey population, the black vote in that state's elections has often been crucial. There is no question that the black community in New Jersey is organized and politically articulate. Elected officials ignore its concerns at their peril. The Rev. Al Sharpton appeared on the scene to lead protests and met privately with Governor Whitman. At the same time the state, in order to ward off further bad publicity, moved from a stonewalling position to one of concern. In April 1999, Governor Whitman fired State Police Superintendent Carl Williams for stating, "Today with this drug problem, the drug problem is cocaine or marijuana. It is most likely a minority group that's involved with that. . . . They aren't going to ask some Irishman to be a part of their gang because they don't trust them" (McGraw 1999, A1). On April 20, 1999, State Attorney General Peter Verniero declared, after a study of the issue, that unconstitutional racial profiling did exist in the state patrol. While criminal

charges were still pending against the police officers involved in the van shoot-
ing, the state negotiated a $13 million settlement with the plaintiffs. This set-
tlement, which included $912,000 for the driver, who was uninjured, was
widely viewed as excessive in terms of previous settlements.

To some, it appeared that the pressure on the Whitman administration
from critics of racial profiling had led to an attempt to remove this issue
from public discussion as quickly as possible. Both Governor Whitman and
Attorney General Verniero may have been looking to their political futures.
Despite aggressive questioning about his role in racial profiling policy,
Verniero was later approved for a seat on the New Jersey Supreme Court—
and, of course, Governor Whitman obtained the position of administrator
of the Environmental Protection Agency in the Bush administration. At the
same time that he announced the civil suit settlement, Attorney General
John Farmer Jr. also stated that his office was dismissing 128 drug and gun
cases in which defendants had alleged that racial profiling led to their
apprehension (Mansnerus 2002, B6).

The state's action was soon followed by a consent decree agreement
with the Division of Civil Rights of the Justice Department in the closing
days of the Clinton administration. The December 1999 agreement provided
for a judicially appointed monitor to report on state steps to prevent racial
profiling. This consent decree, of course, placed state troopers in between
two agencies in the Justice Department. One—the DEA—provided incentives for aggressive search-and-seizure. The other—the Division of Civil
Rights—was prepared to prosecute based on the troopers' implementation
of DEA guidelines.

In an important sense, the controversy over racial profiling on the
New Jersey Turnpike achieved closure with the conclusion of the criminal
proceedings against the officers whose shots into the van in April 1998
ignited the issue. In January 2002, both officers pled guilty to charges of
obstructing the investigation of the incident and to lying about the race of
those whom they had stopped in other instances. Both officers stated that
they had been directed by their superiors to focus on blacks and Latinos
because they were thought more likely to be drug couriers. Both agreed to
resign from their jobs as state troopers and not to serve in law enforcement
in the future. In return they were fined $280 each, and the U.S. Justice
Department agreed not to pursue further charges. The judge appeared to
be moved to leniency by the claims that both officers were following depart-
mental policy by targeting black and dark-skinned drivers for stops.

Later, in the case of *State v. Steven J. Carty*, 170 N.J. 632, (March 4,
2002), the New Jersey Supreme Court narrowed dramatically the basis for
consent searches. Moving beyond previous precedent, which had provided
that consent merely be voluntary and knowing, the Court in *Carty* insisted
that there be a "reasonable and articulable" suspicion of criminal activity
before a consent search could even be requested. The Court contended that
this requirement would help to prevent a routine traffic stop from becoming

"a fishing expedition for criminal activity unrelated to the lawful stop." Moreover, the Court based its decision on the state constitution, thereby making it more difficult for the legislature to limit or overturn its position. The state court had taken aim directly at pretextual stops.

Finally, in March 2003, the New Jersey State legislature got into the picture by making racial profiling a criminal offense. This legislation was the result of three years of negotiating between organizations representing law enforcement personnel and those representing minorities and civil rights agendas. In the meantime the state implemented the use of cameras on the turnpike to record stops and searches, and it required all 2,700 troopers to take training on how to classify a motorist racially from his or her skin color and facial characteristics (Schuck, op. cit., 146). While this narrowed the discretion of the state troopers in the field, it may also have provided greater protection for both them and motorists.

Ethical Analysis of the Case

The settlement of perceived instances of injustice in this case was achieved not by any change in ethical attitude on the part of the police involved, but only through political pressure. It was also not a process of deliberative democracy, leading to an improved understanding between the police and blacks that produced the result, but rather it was a contest of interests, one mediated through our system of representation and our courts, that brought resolution. It was just such a politically produced approximation of justice that James Madison had in mind when he defended the system of representative government combined with separated and balanced powers embodied in our constitutional system.

Our focus in this book, however, is on ethics—and on ways of ethically evaluating public policies. The intention of the arrangement for highway stops and checks for drug couriers was, of course, an ethical one—to interfere with trafficking in drugs, which is a clear evil in each of the three systems of ethical analysis we have been studying. We may question, however, the system of forfeiture that was introduced into the search process in order to furnish a motive to the police for rigorous investigation. A deontologist and a prudent pragmatist would not think this a moral way to proceed, though a utilitarian would be indifferent. Utilitarians recognize self-interest as a motive that exists both universally and as a given of human nature. The ethical problem for them is simply to sum the preferences of self-interested individuals in such a way as to produce the greatest amount of satisfaction possible in society.

Utilitarians looking at the drug problem might first point to the general agreement that drug consumption and trading are not in the public interest—that they diminish the overall good of society. The utilitarian's ethical intention would, therefore, be to achieve the greatest efficiency possible in controlling this traffic. Thus, John Derbyshire, writing in *National Review* in 2001, says, "A policeman who concentrates a disproportionate amount of his limited time and resources on young black men is going to uncover far more crimes—and therefore be far more successful in his career—than one who biases his attention toward, say, middle-aged Asian women" (Derbyshire 2001, 39). Jackson Toby, a sociology professor at Rutgers, claimed in a 1999 op-ed piece in the *Wall Street Journal*, "If drug traffickers are disproportionately black or Hispanic, the police don't need to be racist to stop many minority motorists; they simply have to be efficient in targeting potential drug traffickers" (A22). Clayton Searle, president of the International Interdictor Association, has written in a report, "Those who purport to be shocked that ethnic groups are overrepresented in the population arrested for drug courier activities must have been in a coma for the last twenty years. The fact is that ethnic groups control the majority of the drug trade in the United States. They also tend to hire their underlings and couriers from others of their same group" (in Callahan and Anderson 2001, 3).

But what does the empirical evidence show about the efficiency of racial profiling? No definitive national study has been done, but narrower analyses call the idea into question. A study of "hit rates"—the percentage of cases in which contraband was turned up—at stops by Maryland state troopers on Route I-95 showed the same for black and white drivers: 28 percent. A New Jersey attorney general's report in 1999 showed a hit rate of 13.5 percent for black drivers stopped by state troopers and 10.5 percent for whites. The U.S. Customs Service reported hit rates for stops and searches in airports as 6.7 percent for blacks, and 2.8 percent for Latinos (Institute on Race and Poverty 2001). Legislators concerned with problems of drug trafficking as related to the racial profile of couriers should put their policy analysts to work on the question. All the evidence needed to make the utilitarian judgments cited earlier is not yet in. The utilitarian might also be persuaded to consider the ramifications for American society of an increased tendency toward racial stereotyping and heightened prejudice. These concerns have increased with the advance of the war on terrorism.

Deontologists would deny that efficiency should be the criterion of judgment in evaluating racial profiling in drug courier stop cases. Their primary concern would be that equal justice be done and that everyone's rights be secured. Would definitive empirical evidence about the comparative number of blacks, Hispanics, and whites arrested in traffic searches for having contraband in their possession be of interest to deontologists who wanted to settle the rights question? What if hard evidence were developed that blacks and Hispanics do greatly outnumber whites in such arrests? Would deontologists then find the practice acceptable? This would still leave open the possibility—perhaps the likelihood—that innocent blacks and Hispanics would be stopped and harassed. Would their concern for equity allow deontologists to accept this fact?

How would a prudent pragmatist deal with the question? Again, the ethicist would like to have on hand reliable empirical evidence about the proportion of whites, blacks, and Hispanics found with contraband on them by the police at drug stops. If the numbers were found to be equal or roughly equal, this would show that the utilitarian value of efficiency would not be served by racial profiling, and there would be no rational ground for engaging in the practice. But if the evidence did show a strong correlation between racial profiling and drug arrests, the prudent pragmatist would have to weigh and balance the value of controlling drugs and risking the unjust treatment of innocent persons of color. Pragmatists would no doubt want to get detailed evidence about the degree and nature of harassment experienced by blacks and Latinos at drug stops in order to weigh this evil against the positive good achieved. But would pragmatists be comfortable with this strategy? To weigh and balance the achievement of conflicting positive values in an ethical assessment is one thing, but weighing positive good against positive evil is another. Is there an alternative for prudent pragmatists who are facing this dilemma? Might they explore alternative methods of drug control that would not involve either drug stops or racial profiling? Legalization of drugs has already been suggested by policymakers as an alternative to police enforcement, with an increase in the availability of treatment for those who wish to get rid of the habit. Prudent pragmatist legislators might well establish a battery of policy analyses aimed at assessing the feasibility of this approach to the problem of drug use.

The Fight Against Terrorism: An Addendum

That it causes injustice to innocent individuals makes racial profiling a problematical technique in an ethical struggle against drug runners. Would this objection also arise in the war against terrorists? Are the circumstances of this conflict sufficiently different from those encountered in day-to-day policing to render the ethical issues themselves essentially different? Would prudent pragmatists, deontologists, and utilitarians have the same or different views on this question?

The terrorist attacks of September 11, 2001, on the World Trade Center in New York City and the Pentagon brought a new dimension to the battle against crime in the United States. These events culminated a rising incidence of anti-American terrorist acts over a period of three years that began on August 7, 1998, when nearly simultaneous car bombs hit U.S. embassies in Tanzania and Kenya, resulting in 231 dead, including 12 Americans. Then on October 12, 2000, an explosive-laden boat rammed the USS *Cole* off Yemen, killing 17 American sailors. The September 11 events demonstrated conclusively that terrorism was a major domestic threat as well. Law enforcement agencies throughout the nation recognized that terrorism must become a major priority on the policy agenda.

Although prior to September 11, he had flatly stated that racial profiling was wrong and should be ended, in his June 17, 2003, announcement prohibiting racial or ethnic profiling by federal authorities, President Bush specifically excepted investigations of terrorism or matters related to national security. It seems clear that after September 11 the Justice Department focused on those individuals of a particular ethnic and religious persuasion; furthermore, public opinion supported this approach. A Gallup poll of late September 2001 found that 71 percent of African Americans, as compared to 57 percent of white respondents, agreed that those of Arab background should be subjected to more intensive security checks than others before being allowed to board airplanes. In the words of one of the respondents, an African American public school teacher, "[i]t's better to be safe than sorry. I know it's wrong, but we'll apologize later" (Scales 2001, A16). When the Census Bureau revealed in July 2004 that it had given to the Department of Homeland Security detailed breakdowns of the Arab American population, critics immediately pointed out that that agency had provided similar information on Japanese Americans during World War II (Clemetson 2004). Given the omnipresent threat of domestic terrorism, the global reach of technology, and a pattern of violence committed by fundamentalist Muslim Arabs, does a general focus on young male Muslims from the Middle East represent an acceptable policy?

The issue has been clouded in the public mind by unfortunate incidents in which Arabs have been singled out for unfair treatment simply because of their background. One could argue, however, that these incidents do not illustrate the injustice of racial profiling, but rather that they are examples of inept implementation of procedure. One student of public management, David Lapin, has called for "descriptive profiling." Under this approach, individuals would be detained not as individuals but as members of a group suspected of containing terrorists. In his view this would not imply that all members of a group were terrorists, but it would assume that all terrorists sought were members of this group. Resources would thus not be wasted screening people who were not members of the suspect group. This seems compatible with the position of Charles Krauthammer, who argues that "random searches are a ridiculous charade, a charade that not only gives a false sense of security but, in fact, diminishes security because it wastes too much time and effort on people who are obviously no threat" (2002, 104).

The point of most concern for terrorist attacks was, of course, air travel. Here the issue of ethnic profiling came dramatically to the fore with the position taken by Department of Transportation Secretary Norman Mineta. Mineta, a Japanese American whose parents were interned during World War II, remained adamantly opposed to the inclusion of any racial or ethnic characteristics in airport screening. He was strongly criticized on this point. When questioned as to the status of a seventy-year-old Caucasian grandmother, he replied that such an individual was just as suspect as someone with an Arabic background. Mineta's view appeared to be at odds with that of Attorney General John Ashcroft, whose agencies clearly targeted Arabic communities in their search for terrorists.

Descriptive profiling would not legitimate racial profiling in conventional crime prevention, in which there is no identifiable group in which most lawbreakers are to be found. But is this a valid distinction? Does it adequately differentiate between the problems of racial profiling when used against minorities in drug enforcement and those of racial profiling for airport security? Are the differences in circumstances (e.g., religiously inspired violence against the United States) sufficient to allow such distinctions? Or does descriptive profiling, as proposed, brush too close to the constitutional strictures against guilt by association?

COMBATING SUBVERSION: CRIME CONTROL OR WAR

Prior to September 11, a variety of statutes provided authorities with surveillance powers over suspected subversives within the United States. Most extensive among these statutes was the Foreign Service Intelligence Act of 1978, P.L. 95-511, also known as FISA. Under this act a secret surveillance court consisting of seven federal judges was established to authorize the clandestine surveillance of suspects. Evidence gathered under the court's secret authorizations has been used in trials, but the primary purpose of Congress appears to have been to keep some limits on federal activity in this area. Thus, for example, the court consistently refused to allow prosecutors to direct intelligence activities and thus stood as a deterrent that prevented prosecutors from using secret searches as fishing expeditions. The legislative responses of the Bush administration and Congress to the 2001 attacks on the World Trade Center and the Pentagon built heavily on FISA. Facing a form of terrorism never before experienced, policymakers turned to tools with which they were familiar.

The earlier 1993 attack on the World Trade Center and the 1995 Oklahoma City bombing increased congressional concern about terrorist attacks within the United States. One response was the 1996 Antiterrorism and Effective Death Penalty Act (P.L. 104-132). This act authorized the secretary of state to designate terrorist organizations, and it instituted heavy penalties for those convicted of giving aid to these organizations. This response was in many ways reminiscent of the approach taken during the McCarthy era, a time of fervent anticommunism, during which the Attorney General compiled a list of communist-action, communist-front, and communist-infiltrated organizations. Not surprisingly, portions of the 1996 act have encountered judicial criticism.

The USA PATRIOT Act

At the national level the response to the September 11 terrorist attacks was remarkably swift. On September 19, Attorney General John Ashcroft proposed to Congress legislation designed to combat domestic terrorism. Congress considered and passed the USA PATRIOT Act (an acronym for Uniting and Strengthening America by Providing Appropriate Tools Required to Intercept and Obstruct Terrorism Act) within the short span of less than six weeks, and President Bush signed it into law on October 26, 2001 (P.L. 107-56). The atmosphere was one of crisis and national danger. During House debate on the bill, the FBI website warned of the probability of imminent additional attacks, and President Bush declared at an October 11 news conference that the nation was "on full alert" for more terrorist activity. Attorney General Ashcroft urged the congressional leadership "to send the President a bill to sign right away. I can say with enthusiasm that [it] should not delay; we need these anti-terrorism tools now" (Palmer 2001, 2400). Adding additional pressure on the congressional process were the anthrax attacks that forced the closing of several congressional offices during consideration of the USA PATRIOT Act.

Largely as a result of this sense of urgency, Congress acted quickly and decisively. While understandable given the circumstances, congressional haste left almost no opportunity for debate. The effort in the House, which featured a day of hearings before the Judiciary Committee, was preempted by Speaker Dennis Hastert (R-IL), who after secret negotiations with administration representatives and a few congressional leaders, introduced an alternative to the White House bill. House members voted on this version the same day that it was printed (a document of several hundred pages) without any opportunity to read it carefully. In the Senate there was no Judiciary Committee consideration, and debate lasted a short three hours before final passage.

Many of the complaints during the legislative discussion centered on the speed with which Congress was acting. Several speakers contended that lack of debate and of a record of congressional intentions would have serious repercussions as the courts and the public dealt with how the USA PATRIOT legislation was to be implemented. With regard to the courts, some such as Senator Arlen Specter (R-PA) were concerned that Supreme Court precedents appeared to require a fuller legislative record (Palmer 2001, 2533–35). Specter seemed to be saying that without a clear indication of congressional findings supporting the statute, the courts might be reluctant to endorse some of the restrictions on individual liberties that it contained. As for the public, the lack of give-and-take in debate or of legislative findings had the potential to undercut the act's legitimacy. Following enactment of the legislation, a number of commentators suggested that the real meaning of the statute would be established by how it was implemented. Without a clear congressional statement of intentions, implementation became less a matter of congressional policy and more a strategy of bureaucratic initiative.

During Senate consideration, Senator Russell D. Feingold (D-WI) raised questions about the long-term threats to civil liberties posed by the act. After reviewing past instances of injustice in the name of American patriotism and security, he said,

> Now some may say, indeed we may hope, that we have come a long way
> since those days of infringements on civil liberties. But there is ample reason

for concern. And I have been troubled in the past 6 weeks by the potential loss of commitment in the Congress and the country to traditional civil liberties. (*Congressional Record*, October 25, 2001, S 11020)

Despite the issues raised by Senators Specter and Feingold, the sentiment in the Senate was overwhelmingly supportive. The House of Representatives passed the bill by a 357–66 margin under suspension of the rules, and the Senate, which had added extensive powers to track money laundering, approved it 96–1, with Senator Feingold in dissent. Because congressional leaders and the administration had negotiated continuously behind closed doors to achieve agreement, there was no need for a conference committee.

The hasty passage of the measure may have contributed to the numerous challenges to it that soon emerged. A basic problem with the war on terrorism is that to the extent it is successful, it undercuts a sense of urgency about the danger of attack among Americans. Because the need for secrecy makes an informed citizenry impossible in this policy area, there is a tendency, in lieu of manifest terrorist activity, for those concerned about threats to civil liberties to move this issue more prominently onto the public agenda than those actually engaged in the battle against terrorism. In November 2003, former Vice President Al Gore called for repeal of the USA PATRIOT Act. Before a crowd of approximately 3,000, he bitterly charged that the Bush administration had ". . . exploited public fears for partisan political gain and postured themselves as bold defenders of our country" (Doty 2003, A18). Acting on similar concerns, as of December 2003, ad hoc civil liberties groups had obtained resolutions from 200 cities, towns, and counties symbolically repealing the USA PATRIOT Act at a time, one might argue, when the lack of domestic terrorist activity may well have been demonstrating the law's success. Legally, the ACLU and other civil liberties organizations mounted challenges to the act and other antiterrorist actions taken at the national level. In short, the USA PATRIOT Act quickly precipitated a nationwide ethical debate that in some ways served as a surrogate for the lack of discussion during its passage.

There is no question that the 342 pages of the USA PATRIOT Act contain the potential for a fundamental reworking of American liberties in the area of privacy. Where terrorist activity is suspected, the act authorizes extensive surveillance beyond that constitutionally allowed for criminal investigations. In addition to mail and telephone communication, Congress extended this authority to all electronic communication, including Internet use. The act also allowed so-called sneak-and-peak searches. With the proper warrant from the secret FISA court, authorities were now able to search an individual's property without notification and could wait an undefined "reasonable time" before informing the suspect of the search or searches—and with court approval, these authorities could delay informing suspects even further. Moreover, federal authorities were granted the power to obtain nationwide search warrants that allowed them to search in any jurisdiction in the country. Congress also authorized—indeed directed—all federal agencies to share all intelligence information on individuals suspected of activities that could be related to terrorist activities. Extensive provisions on money laundering opened banking and financial records to investigators and imposed on financial institutions regulations designed to prevent the clandestine movement of funds.

Broad as it was, the act did contain limitations in the form of sunset provisions for some powers. These were to expire on December 31, 2005, and they applied to many of the sections on surveillance powers, nationwide search warrants, and money laundering. (After several delays, President Bush signed the reauthorization of the Act on March 9, 2006, P.L. 169-178.) Michael T. McCarthy argues that the act illustrates Congress's belief that executive power must be balanced by congressional and judicial oversight. In his words, "Congress modified the Administration's original proposals in important ways to ensure a continuing oversight role for Congress and the courts. Although these modifications do not ensure that the USA PATRIOT Act will never infringe upon civil liberties, they do make it more likely that the political and judicial processes will protect them" (McCarthy 2002, 436). The national government's system of checks and balances retained some life, while allowing prompt and powerful action in a time of crisis.

Commentators on the Act were, of course, unaware that President Bush had authorized warrantless surveillance by the National Security Agency of domestic electronic communications with suspected foreign terrorist organizations. He contended that the battle against terrorism constituted a war and, as such, enabled him to circumvent the limits of both the FISA and the USA PATRIOT Act. Moreover, he noted that eight congressional leaders had been informed of this activity from its beginning.

Also ominous for those concerned about civil liberties—and echoing the comments of Senator Feingold—the USA PATRIOT Act specifically allowed its surveillance powers to be used for criminal investigations other than terrorism. Under this act, warrants and surveillance procedures need show only that foreign intelligence information is a "significant" purpose—but not necessarily the only purpose—of a proposed investigation. On November 18, 2002, a special review court, one established under FISA, ruled that the USA PATRIOT Act swept away the barrier between intelligence gathering activities and criminal prosecution that had been based on previous judicial interpretations of FISA. Attorney General John Ashcroft declared that "[t]his revolutionizes our ability to investigate terrorists"(Lewis 2004, A1).

An associated concern with the USA PATRIOT Act is the effect of some of its provisions on recruitment to our universities of foreign graduate students. The number declined by 6 percent during 2004, the third decline after ten years of growth. Our universities are dependent on foreign students for teaching and research assistants. This is particularly true in engineering and the natural sciences, where foreign students comprise half the graduate enrollment. A large factor in the decline has been the perceived difficulty of obtaining student visas within the confines of American immigration policies. More generally, foreign students have been turned off by American foreign policy changes stemming from the 9-11 crisis. Our felt need to enhance national security seems to be having an indirect adverse effect on the economy's future.

THE LACKAWANNA SIX: A CASE STUDY

In his "Report from the Field: The USA PATRIOT Act at Work" (U.S. Department of Justice 2004), Attorney General Ashcroft stated that the freer exchange of information among intelligence and law enforcement agencies was crucial to the successful prosecution of six Yemeni-American citizens known as the Lackawanna Six (ibid., 3). When the Justice Department became aware that six individuals from Lackawanna, New York, had participated in training camps in Afghanistan prior to September 11, it subjected their activities to intensive monitoring. Despite this scrutiny, no evidence was ever produced that they were terrorists or intended any terrorist acts.

The surveillance activities of the law enforcement community appeared to bear fruit in Lackawanna with the arrest on September 14, 2002, of five Yemeni Americans for aiding al-Qaeda terrorists. A sixth Yemeni American, Muktar al-Bakri, was arraigned on September 16. Al-Bakri had been arrested in Bahrain, where he and his family had flown for an arranged marriage to a girl of sixteen. These individuals, all American citizens, ranging in age from twenty-three to thirty years of age, were long-time members of the Yemeni community in the former industrial steel town. With the exception of al-Bakri, all had been born in the United States, all were married, and most had children. Their friends and neighbors were aware that they had visited the Middle East in the past year, although most believed that the trip was for religious instruction in Pakistan. Since returning from that trip, they appeared to be more strongly devoted to Islam, with several of them visiting the mosque many times each day. Their arrests were greeted with surprise and dismay by members of the Yemeni American community.

No one claimed that the defendants were plotting any kind of terrorist activity or had been in contact with al-Qaeda operatives since returning to the United States. The closest indication of some kind of activity was an e-mail sent by al-Bakri in July 2002, in which he wrote of a coming "Big Meal" that would be "very huge" and that only those of great faith would be able to withstand it (Herbeck 2003, A6). At the initial arraignment of the five defendants, U.S. Magistrate Judge H. Kenneth Schroeder asked, "What is it that these defendants were planning?" Assistant U.S. Attorney William Hochul responded that the government was unable to say at that time. Even so, Magistrate Schroeder denied bail to all but one of the defendants. Later evidence showed that in the spring of 2001 they had attended an al-Qaeda training camp in Afghanistan, imbibing radical Islamic teaching and learning to use various kinds of weaponry. Four of the defendants, however, left before completing the camp. One of these men, Shahim Alwan, faked an injury in order to be allowed to leave early. Although the government made full use of surveillance powers authorized under the USA PATRIOT Act, the Justice Department prosecuted under a 1996 antiterrorist statute, the Antiterrorism and Effective Death Penalty Act. Section 2339B of this statute in volume 18 of the U.S. Code provides:

> Whoever, within the United States or subject to the jurisdiction of the United States, knowingly provides material support or resources to a foreign terrorist organization, or attempts or conspires to do so, shall be fined under this title or imprisoned not more than 15 years, or both, and, if the death of any person results, shall be imprisoned for any term of years or for life.

Five of the six defendants pled guilty to the government's charge that by attending the training camps in Afghanistan, they had given material aid to terrorist organizations and activities. The sixth pled "to conducting transactions unlawfully" with al-Qaeda (U.S. Department of Justice 2004, 3). After initial reluctance on the part of two of the group, all had cooperated with federal authorities.

The six were sentenced over a period of two weeks in December 2003. With the exception of al-Bakri, the first sentenced, all made statements of profound remorse. Yahya Goba, who along with al-Bakri received a sentence of ten years in prison, apologized for his conduct and stated, "I love my country. I'm proud to be an American." The four others, who received sentences ranging from seven years to nine and one-half years, made similar statements of contrition and support for the United States. Yasein Taher, who received an eight-year sentence, said, "I'm sorry for what I've done. I accept full responsibility and I know it was completely wrong for me to go. I want to apologize to my family, my community and, most of all, my country" (Staba 2003, A29). The government's case was based on the proposition that by attending the al-Qaeda camp and raising money for the trip, the six young men had provided material and personnel support to al-Qaeda. At the camp they received training in firearms and heard lectures on Islamic fundamentalism. At least two of them were reported to have met Osama bin-Laden. Another, Shafal Mosed, refused the opportunity to meet with bin-Laden when it was offered to him in an attempt to persuade him to stay.

Critics of the government's action in this case have pointed to the lack of evidence that the defendants were actively engaged in terrorist activities or that they were contemplating such activity. David D. Cole, professor of law at Georgetown University, has charged that this is the first time in American history that individuals have been imprisoned for attending a training camp. In his view the government's case was patently unconstitutional, and he pointed out that two lower federal courts had held parts of the 1996 act unconstitutional. Other critics of the government argued that the case was a prime example of guilt by association and punishment for holding particular ideas. In this respect it should be noted that the sentencing judge, U.S. District Court Judge William M. Skretny, stressed his concern that Goba had been teaching Islam to children in the community and asserted that he should have stayed clear of al-Qaeda's teachings.

Ethical Analysis of the Case

Some of the ethical questions raised by this case are fundamental. In the words of Robert Precht, director of the public service program at the University of Michigan, "[i]t used to be considered un-American to prosecute people on the basis of who they know or where they travel or what they think or say. But when you have prosecutors saying, 'We have to prevent terrorism,' what jury is going to say, 'We will not convict'?" (Locy and Johnson 2003, 1A). This view has found some support in the federal courts. On December 3, 2003, the U.S. Court of Appeals for the Ninth Circuit ruled unconstitutional the provisions of the Antiterrorism and Effective Death Penalty Act to which the Lackwanna Six had pled guilty. In the case of *Humanitarian Law Project et al. v. U.S. Department of Justice, et al.* (2003) which dealt with humanitarian aid to Kurdish and Tamil groups officially identified as being affiliated with terrorism, the Court of Appeals ruled in a 2–1 decision that the act's use of the terms *personnel* and *training* was unconstitutionally vague under the First and Fifth Amendments "because they bring within their ambit constitutionally protected speech and advocacy." This decision was rendered just as the Lackawanna Six were being sentenced for previous guilty pleas to charges that they provided personnel for terrorist activities through their attendance at al-Qaeda training camps.

Whatever their doubts about the constitutionality of the statute under which they were being prosecuted, the Lackawanna Six and their attorneys faced the practical dangers of going to trial before a jury in highly charged times. All were young men and several had children. Despite President Bush's pleas for tolerance toward those of Muslim faith, young men of Middle Eastern background were being interrogated across the country, and, although fairly isolated, instances of social persecution of those of Arabic appearance were occurring. (See for example, Cole 2003, 47–48.) A plea negotiation might have appeared to be the safest route. On the other hand, some of the six might have been more deeply involved and committed than the others. Juries in separate trials might have been able to distinguish between those who sincerely regretted their brush with Islamic terrorism and those who were committed to it.

However, it may be that the world has changed sufficiently to warrant preemptive government action whenever possible. Clearly, Attorney General John Ashcroft believed that it was his duty to act as thoroughly and ubiquitously as possible to forestall terrorist attacks. Have Islamic fundamentalist beliefs and technological progress changed the playing field for constitutional doctrine and ethically sound public policy? Does an organization such as al-Qaeda pose such an immediate and massive threat to Americans that its existence justifies the actions taken against the Lackawanna Six?

One might suppose that this case would pose no problems for utilitarians, and that they would agree with the government that the Lackawanna Six ought to be prosecuted. If they were rule utilitarians, however, they might wonder whether the vague language of the USA PATRIOT Act and the failure of the government to show that the defendants actually intended to commit terrorist acts against the United States might dangerously threaten civil liberties in a time of national fear. Such utilitarians would have to decide whether the greatest social good would result from protecting civil liberties by dismissing the charges or by prosecuting them because of the omnipresent threat of al-Qaeda, even though this action might increase the risk of vigilante attitudes developing in the public.

Deontologists, concerned about individual rights and ever sensitive to the danger of a violation of civil rights by governmental authority, would have protested the prosecution and would probably have denounced the USA PATRIOT Act as well. They would be concerned that the Lackawanna Six had been denied equal justice, especially in view of the law's problematical status. Do universal rights hold when a nation is either under attack or perceives itself to be so? Prudent pragmatists would find themselves in a position of having to weigh and balance all the concerns of the utilitarian or deontologist as well. Their decision would be made only after a careful assessment of all the circumstances of the time—especially of whether the government had the time to draft a more careful law, what the public temper and state of mind were, and whether the attendance of the defendants at the training camps constituted a clear and present danger that they would act treasonably. Such pragmatists would no doubt try to draw conclusions about the state of the public mind from the fact that the defendants chose to plead guilty to the charges rather than face a public jury.

USA PATRIOT Act in Broader Perspective

Less noticed among the various concerns raised by the prosecution of terrorists was the fact that the language of the USA PATRIOT Act allowed the Justice Department to prosecute other criminal activities brought to light during intelligence surveillance. Thus, the *New York Times* reported in December 2003 that the Justice Department's "Operation G-String," an investigation into alleged payoffs by a Las Vegas strip club operator to local politicians, utilized investigative tools provided under the money laundering provisions of the USA PATRIOT Act. Senator Harry Reid (D-NV) asserted that he was not aware of the money laundering provisions when he voted for the act. He noted that "he thought the bill was about thwarting terrorists, not, as he put it, 'naked women.'" Representative Shelley Berkeley (D-NV) had similar concerns, stating, "The F.B.I. is flexing its new powers under the

PATRIOT Act to go after garden-variety political corruption. . . . I have a real problem with that" (Broder 2003, A21).

For civil libertarians, generally, the real difficulty posed by the mixing of criminal prosecution and intelligence gathering is the dilution of the Fourth Amendment protections that the courts have laboriously constructed over the past century. The constitutional standards for a solely criminal search and seizure require solid "probable cause" either for a warrant or a warrantless stop and frisk. That threshold is not required for searches and surveillance authorized by the special FISA courts acting under the new criteria provided by the USA PATRIOT Act. Under these guidelines, federal agents have only to show that there is a possible connection to foreign agents or terrorist activities.

From the perspective of the policy analyst, the questions of how technically to protect against terrorism had to be framed within Americans' continuing insistence on the importance of individual privacy and freedom of expression and association. Technical proficiency necessarily requires normative tempering. In the words of one knowledgeable student of the national security policy, "the real assessment of whether Congress acted prudently in passing the USA PATRIOT Act must be drawn by observing how the Administration uses its new powers and how Congress and the courts react to any abuses" (McCarthy 2002, 452). Undoubtedly, continuing national dialogue over the USA PATRIOT Act and the most appropriate and effective means for fighting terrorism will result in incremental tempering of administrative, legislative, and judicial policies.

The direction of these changes may be more consistent if consideration of broader cultural and philosophical issues can be brought into play. Indeed, we would argue that the critical issues engendered by terrorist threats to the United States require reexamination of the normative position of national security in our hierarchy of values. One thinker who has grappled with this issue has been the Harvard philosopher Ronald Dworkin, who has been an especially articulate defender of the American tradition of individual rights. Dworkin is concerned that in a context of crisis Americans have replaced their usual multiform and balanced system of values with a single-value absolutism. Instead of moving values about in a fluid repositioning of national security into a more prominent position, Americans have moved it into an omnipotent position that is insulated from criticism. In Dworkin's view our leaders are following "a strategy of putting American safety not only first but absolutely first," a strategy that "recommends any measure that improves American security against terrorism even marginally or speculatively . . . without counting the harm or unfairness of that measure to its victims" (Dworkin 2003, 38, 39).

There is a real question whether such an absolutist stance can result in prudent policy decisions. Over time, incremental changes based on the priority of national security, whatever the costs in individual liberties, would be debilitating to democratic processes. Even ensuring the safety of individuals and the nation must be balanced against other costs, and this balance will vary as the circumstances change. The prudent policymaker must recognize these changes and act based on their assessment. Clearly, absolute and sweeping decisions can be far more costly in the long run than careful and deliberate steps that are sensitive to the multifaceted nature of American culture and the continuing dialogue issuing from that diversity.

REFERENCES

Baker, Jr., John S., and Dale E. Bennett. "Measuring the Explosive Growth of Federal Crime Legislation." Washington, DC: The Federalist Society for Law and Public Policy Studies (2004).

Bratton, William. *Turnaround: How America's Top Cop Reversed the Crime Epidemic*. New York: Random House, 1998.

Broder, John M. "New Saga in Legalized Las Vegas Vice." *New York Times* (December 15, 2003), A21.

Brown v. Board of Education, 349 U.S. 294 (1954).

Callahan, Gene, and William Anderson. "The Roots of Racial Profiling." *Reason* (August/September 2001), obtained from *Reasononline*, http://reason.com/0108/fe.gc.the.shtml (accessed 4/8/06).

City of Indianapolis v. Edmond, 531 U.S. 32 (2000).

Clemetson, Lynette. "Homeland Security Given Data on Arab-Americans." *New York Times* (July 30, 2004), Al0.

Cole, David. *Enemy Aliens: Double Standards and Constitutional Freedoms in the War on Terrorism*. New York: The New Press, 2003.

Congressional Record (October 25, 2001): S 11020.

Derbyshire, John. "In Defense of Racial Profiling." *National Review* (February 19, 2001): 38–40.

Doty, Cate. "Gore Criticizes Expanded Terrorism Law." *New York Times* (November 10, 2003), A18.

Dworkin, Ronald. "Terror and the Attack on Civil Liberties." *New York Review of Books 50*, no. 17 (November 6, 2003): 37–41.

Friedman, Lawrence M. *American Law in the 20th Century*. New Haven, CT: Yale University Press, 2002.

Herbeck, Dan. "Sentencing Debate Rages over 'Lackawanna Six.'" *Buffalo News* (December 1, 2003), A1, A6.

———. "10 years for First of Six." *Buffalo News* (December 14, 2003), Al, A16.

Humanitarian Law Project et al. v. U.S. Department of Justice et al., 2003 U.S. App. LEXIS 24305 (December 3, 2003).

Institute on Race and Poverty. "Components of Racial Profiling Legislation," University of Minnesota Law School, Minneapolis, MN, 2001. Obtained at http://www1.umn.edu/irp/publications/racialprofiling.html (accessed 12/09/04).

Kocieniewski, David. "The New Jersey Troopers Avoid Jail in Case That Highlighted Profiling." *New York Times* (January 15, 2002), A1, B6.

Krauthammer, Charles. "The Case for Profiling: Why Random Searches of Airline Travellers Are a Useless Charade." *Time* (March 18, 2002), 104.

Lewis, Neil A. "Rule Created Legal Wall to Sharing Information." *New York Times* (April 14, 2004), A17.

Locy, Toni, and Kevin Johnson. "How U.S. Watches Terrorist Suspects." *USA Today* (February 12, 2003), 1A.

Mansnerus, Laura. "The Wounds Linger on Both Sides." *New York Times* (January 15, 2002), B6.

Mapp v. Ohio, 367 U.S. 643 (1961).

McCarthy, Michael T. "Recent Development: USA PATRIOT Act." *Harvard Journal on Legislation* 39 (Summer 2002), 435–53.

McGraw, Seamus. "Ouster Follows His Remarks on a Racial Issue." *The Record* (March 1, 1999), A1.

Minnesota v. Dickerson, 508 U.S. 366 (1993).

Palmer, Elizabeth A. "House Passes Anti-Terrorism Bill That Tracks White House's Wishes." *CQ Weekly* (October 13, 2001): 2399–400.

———. "Terrorism Bill's Sparse Paper Trail May Cause Legal Vulnerabilities." *CQ Weekly* (October 27, 2001): 2533–35.

Scales, Ann. "Polls Say Blacks Tend to Favor Checks." *Boston Globe* (September 30, 2001), A16.

Schuck, Peter H. *Diversity in America: Keeping Government at a Safe Distance.* Cambridge, MA: Harvard University Press, 2003.

Siegel, Fred. *The Future Once Happened Here.* New York: Free Press, 1997.

Staba, David. "Qaeda Trainee Is Sentenced to 8-Year Term." *New York Times* (December 5, 2003), A29.

State v. Steven J. Carty, 170 N.J. 632 (March 4, 2002).

Taslitz, Andrew E. "Racial Questions and the Fourth Amendment." *Law and Contemporary Problems* 66 (Summer 2003): 221–98.

Terry v. Ohio, 392 U.S. 1 (1968).

Toby, Jackson. "Racial Profiling Doesn't Prove Cops Are Racist." *The Wall Street Journal* (March 11, 1999), A22.

U.S. v. Hudson and Goodwin, 7 Cranch 32 (1812).

U.S. Department of Justice, Office of the Inspector General, Audit Division. "Assets Forfeiture Fund and Seized Asset Deposit Fund, Annual Financial Statement Fiscal Year 2001" (June 2002), obtained at http://www.usdoj.gov/jmd/afp/01programauditreport72002.htm (accessed 08/15/03).

U.S. Department of Justice. "Report from the Field: The USA PATRIOT Act at Work," July 2004, 1–29.

Walker, Samuel. *Popular Justice: A History of American Criminal Justice.* New York: Oxford University Press, 1980.

Whren v. U.S., 517 U.S. 806 (1996).

Wiggins, Ovetta. "Ministers Want Probe of N.J. Police: State Rejects Claim of Racial Profiling." *The Record* (May 28, 1998), A1.

Wilson, James Q., and George Kelling. "Broken Windows." *Atlantic Monthly* (March 1982), 29–38.

CHAPTER 8

Social Welfare Policy in the United States: Conflicting Principles of Distributive Justice

American principles of social justice derive from two of the five value clusters we described in Chapter 2—the politics of interest and the secular version of the politics of conscience. The first centers both on the individual's right to acquire property and on the work ethic as the motor force of acquisition. It eventuates in today's idea of the ownership society, the centerpiece of George W. Bush's vision of the good social order. According to this view, social justice is achieved when everyone has the opportunity to become an owner: of a home, of an adequate retirement account, of a private health insurance policy—in short, when someone achieves an independent and secure position in society. The chief mechanism for distributing values in a just manner to these owners is the system of market exchange.

While the politics of interest stresses individual freedom and independence, the politics of conscience emphasizes equality. When market forces fail to produce adequate sustenance for some members of society, it is the responsibility of the organized community, acting through its government, to see that they are taken care of—through such things as public unemployment insurance, public assistance programs, public housing, public health insurance, and public aid to education.

These two conceptions of social welfare seem to be philosophical opposites. In fact they share the same view of the good society—one made up of independent, liberty-loving people who are enjoying their freedom in a context of middle-class mobility. It is not a society of absolute but of relative equality, one in which few people live at the extremes of wealth and poverty. Its middle-classness is a condition to which all can aspire—if not for themselves, then for their children. It is an open society of opportunity—an opportunity sometimes exercised through the market, other times through government assistance. Political debates often obscure the common ground of these two visions of the good polity. Differences are differences of means, not of ends, so that policy change occurs through peaceful electoral and legislative processes. It is, of course, true that these processes are frequently accompanied by partisan anger and rancor. These disagreements are indeed dangerous if they produce stalemates and obstructions that make necessary change impossible.

THE WELFARE STATE IN EUROPE AND IN AMERICA

The acceptance of a paternalistic state, so characteristic of most European nations, has never gained dominance in the United States. America was founded by those fleeing authoritarian government, and a strong case can be made that the concept of sovereign power, often posited by western political thinkers as an essential attribute of the modern state, has had little support in either American experience or ideology. Paralleling Americans' rejection of powerful government has been the country's reliance on individual initiative. This has, of course, often been attributed to the Puritan ethic, which glorified hard work as critical to one's religious calling. There are other historical factors as well that have contributed to the American cultural acceptance of the linkage of individual endeavor with individual worth. For example, Americans have not had to contend with social stratification stemming from feudalism, and ownership of land has been widespread throughout their history.

These conditions and beliefs have conspired to form a culture fundamentally different from that of any other nation in the world. The values that we described in Chapter 2, often referred to as the American Creed are summed up by Samuel P. Huntington as "liberal, individualistic, democratic, egalitarian, and hence basically antigovernment and antiauthority in character" (1981, 4). Huntington suggests that for Americans these norms have posed a continuing conflict between ideals and reality. We argue also that Americans, especially since the mid-nineteenth century, have faced an ongoing dilemma between their fundamental beliefs and their concern for the plight of others. (See also Skocpol 1995, 24.) Americans have placed high priority on economic achievement, which they have seen as a just reward for individual endeavor. At the same time they have evinced sympathy for the less fortunate in society.

Americans have sometimes been labeled as laggards in the movement toward the provision of social welfare. For example, Germany, with a strong national government and a well-organized socialist movement, enacted extensive government-sponsored welfare programs in the late nineteenth century, and other western European nations soon followed suit. Theda Skocpol has shown that Americans also moved to provide government support for certain sectors of the population in the nineteenth century. There is, however, no question that a universal social welfare program of the extent found in many European nations has never been seriously proposed by major American political leaders.

We are suggesting here that this lack has not been one of courage, but one of vision. The American culture has not been able to produce an ideological justification for state provision of welfare that has overridden the popular belief in individual responsibility. The state has been called on only temporarily to compensate for market failure. Examining the importance of values to government policy, Charles Noble notes, "Societies like Sweden, which have statist and solidaristic traditions, have built larger, more egalitarian welfare states. Societies with more individualistic, antistatist cultures, such as the United States, have less active governments and leave far more to the family, the market, and voluntary associations" (1997, 11). Joel Handler has suggested that the concept of *social citizenship* prevalent in European countries has little meaning in the United States because Americans operate within a contractual paradigm that presupposes only individuals, in equal relationships of exchange. Most Americans are unwilling to accept the legitimacy of a system in which the disadvantaged receive government benefits simply because, as citizens, they are entitled to them (Handler 2004, 76–77). These cultural norms frame government policy.

Some commentators have maintained that the flowering of American individualism occurred during the Jacksonian period of the 1820s,1830s, and 1840s. During these years small farmers and entrepreneurs imbibed the Jacksonian principles of economic enterprise. The values of civic virtue epitomized by founding fathers such as George Washington, who made the public interest a paramount value, faded into distant memories as the clamor of average Americans seeking their fortunes moved to center stage in the arena of public policy. After the Civil War the rhetoric of laissez faire economics and politics served to justify the rapid rise of corporate power with its attendant hardships on many of the less fortunate in society. Perhaps the harshest statement of laissez faire was captured in the social Darwinism of Herbert Spencer, an Englishman who was tremendously influential in America. In his words,

> The poverty of the incapable, the distresses that come upon the imprudent, the starvation of the idle, and those shoulderings aside of the weak by the strong, which leave so many "in shallows and in miseries" are the decrees of a large, far-seeing benevolence. (1954, 289)

Americans have avoided class struggle by deferring to the processes of the market as a means of providing for all fairly. But the effects of the market have often violated Americans' basic sense of fairness and have led to reform movements. In Huntington's words, "Americans have been spared class conflicts in order to have moral convulsions" (op. cit., 11). The abolitionist, women's suffrage, and civil rights movements, for example, cut across class lines in the name of social justice.

By the late nineteenth century it had become increasingly obvious to many that market processes alone carried the seeds of severe injustice for some. The Populist and Progressive movements of the late nineteenth and early twentieth centuries promoted—both successfully and unsuccessfully—state assistance for the less fortunate and for workers. The period of the most expansive government movement into social reform previous to the Great Society of Lyndon Johnson was the New Deal.

During the New Deal the nation faced devastating economic woes, and so President Franklin Delano Roosevelt moved on many fronts to provide government assistance. Roosevelt was, of course, responding to catastrophic economic conditions, but he faced as well an emergent reform movement based on claims of social justice. Chief among these was Louisiana Senator Huey Long's "Share the Wealth" program. Long was building substantial support in the South and the Midwest until his assassination in 1935, and Roosevelt saw the wisdom in providing programs targeted toward the less fortunate. At the end of the 1930s, programs of Social Security, unemployment insurance, and assistance to widows and survivors were in place.

Also of long-term importance was the administration's support of organized labor through its enactment of the National Labor Relations Act. This legislation gave working men and women the means to protect themselves economically through organization. In fact much of what survived from the New Deal could be seen not as government largesse but as programs allowing individuals to provide better for themselves. This was especially true of the form taken by Social Security. This program and unemployment insurance both provided only for those who had been employed, and it excluded farm laborers and domestic help. Additional unemployment programs were left largely to the states. The relief programs that remained—benefiting the aged, blind, and orphaned—were placed in the hands of the states, with supplementary funding from the national government. Thus, at the close of the New Deal, no general or universal relief programs existed.

Franklin D. Roosevelt was first and foremost a pragmatist and a liberal capitalist. He responded to pressures on the left by moving in a limited fashion toward some social welfare programs, and in this respect he may have helped to maintain support for the capitalist system. Less noticed—but perhaps of more influence—was his political need to satisfy the right. As Frances Fox Piven and Richard A. Cloward have noted in *Regulating the Poor* (1971), southerners in Congresses at this time strongly opposed any form of universal welfare. They feared that such programs would provide support for southern blacks, and they worked diligently to limit the recipients of welfare programs and to allow the states wide discretion as to how these programs were to be structured. The New Deal coalition was based on southern racist support and northern working class ethnic voters, politically and ideologically a difficult combination. One way in which Roosevelt successfully straddled these differences was by assuring the white southerners that they would be protected from pervasive social reform. After studying the role of southerners in Congress during the New Deal and after, Ira

Katznelson, Kim Geiger, and Daniel Kryder conclude, "President Roosevelt and congressional leaders tailored New Deal legislation to southern preferences. They reached an implicit modus vivendi: southern civil society would remain intact and southern representatives would support the key elements of the administration's program. . . ." (1993, 297). At this period in the nation's history, social justice foundered on the shoals of southern racism.

The most expansive movement into welfare came during the Great Society administration of Lyndon Johnson. President Johnson launched major domestic programs in many areas, but his War on Poverty was a clear effort to provide welfare support on a scale never before contemplated. In keeping with the American ideology of self-help, Johnson saw this program as a route to empowering the poor. At the same time he addressed directly the racial discrimination that had pervaded earlier welfare programs.

Johnson understood that policy in America results largely from the organized interests populating a pluralistic society. Often these interests do not only initiate new programs. After legislation is enacted, they also monitor its administration and work to reorient its implementation toward their particular needs. Johnson recognized as well that the poor in America lacked the organizational base and skills to compete effectively with the politically articulate. To a great extent ghetto areas in America were deprived of basic governmental services, while more prosperous and politically active sectors drained off resources originally intended for the poor. In the competition that pervades the process of making pluralist social policy, the poor were predestined losers.

Three major initiatives constituted the core of Johnson's assault on this problem. All revolved around the goal of creating politically articulate constituencies of the poor and disadvantaged. National policymakers believed that the nation would reject massive aid specifically for the poor, so through managerial politics directed from the White House, they worked to organize poor areas with the goal of forcing the orientation of welfare programs at the local levels toward the poor. Thus, the War on Poverty programs circumvented established governmental agencies by directing money to neighborhood groups through specifically targeted categorical grants-in-aid. Second, community action boards established to administer federal programs in an area were required to have local representation. Third, on a national scale, the Johnson administration enacted civil rights legislation that finally gave effective protection to black rights. The Voting Rights Act of 1965 meshed especially well with the administration's efforts to stimulate local activism by the poor. By providing for supervision of black voter registration and voting in the South, this legislation ensured a political voice for blacks in this region.

Although massive in its total impact, the Great Society program continued an incremental approach toward providing assistance to the poor and disadvantaged. By removing racial barriers, it contributed greatly to the integration of blacks into the political process. By trying to organize the poor generally, it attempted to move this sector of the population, with mixed results, into the policy process, a movement that has been inherently incremental in nature. Throughout this period, claims of universal entitlement were voiced by some of the more radical activists, but influential political leaders continued to think and act within the basic individualistic assumptions of the American culture. Government benefits were couched in terms of enabling the disadvantaged to have an equal opportunity to provide for themselves, not in terms of universal entitlements.

The basic norms of American culture resurfaced with considerable political play in the 1980s and 1990s. In their seminal work, *Regulating the Poor*, which was published in 1971, Piven and Cloward had predicted just such a turn of events. Despite their sympathy for radical reform, they recognized the constraining effects of the American work ethic. In their words, "[t]here is always pressure to abolish large-scale work relief, for it strains against the market ethos and interferes with the untrammeled operation of the marketplace" (347).

After examining the welfare efforts of both the New Deal and the Great Society, Cloward and Piven concluded that once a semblance of stability returns to the economy and to society, Americans push welfare programs to the side and leave all but the most-in-need to the vicissitudes of the market. This came to pass with the advent of the Reagan administration and the subsequent capture of Congress by the Republicans in 1994.

Even many Democrats, whose party had historically led the movement to expanded welfare and assistance programs, sensed the need for reform. Then-governor of Arkansas, Bill Clinton, became a prime mover in the Democratic Leadership Conference, which was a group of governors and other Democratic leaders who sought a more moderate image for the Democrats. In practical policy terms Governor Clinton was a key player in the National Governors' Association's proposals for welfare reform that were enacted by Congress as the Family Support Act of 1988 (Rovner 1988, 17–21). In his first run for the presidency, Clinton advocated "ending welfare as we know it," and with the Republican gains in Congress in 1994, the push for more extensive welfare reform intensified (Tanner 1996, 59–62).

After the Republican capture of the House of Representatives, President Clinton in his 1996 State of the Union speech declared that "the era of big government is over." Determined to be viewed as a moderate, Clinton agreed to congressional reductions in the Food Stamp program and in benefits to immigrants (Graubard 2004, 518–19). Perhaps his largest step toward the ideological center was his act of signing congressionally initiated welfare reform legislation. Given the Republican gains in Congress, the president understood that his party was ideologically vulnerable because of its past support of expansive public assistance programs. Basic American values linking economic endeavor and self-worth had found an important place on the conservative agenda, and he was not going to allow his party to be marginalized on this issue.

Devolution of assistance programs to the states became the word of the day, and in 1996 the vast categorical Aid to Families with Dependent Children (AFDC), dating from the New Deal, was transformed into a block grant-in-aid that gave wide discretion to the states as to how they were to provide for the poor. The limits imposed by Congress allowed no more than two years on welfare at any one time and no more than a total of five years. Additionally, states were given financial incentives to offer work programs to move the poor and unemployed back into the labor force.

AMERICA'S RESPONSE TO IMMIGRATION: ILLEGALS AND WELFARE

At first glance immigration policy in America might seem somewhat removed from the issues involved in resolving questions of social welfare. Immigration to America has for the most part been undertaken by those seeking greater freedom and opportunity. Greater government assistance has not been the goal of immigrants. Moreover, for much of the twentieth century, immigration policy was determined by the 1924 Johnson-Reed Immigration Act, which set rigid quotas that favored western European nations but placed no restrictions on immigration from the western hemisphere. The quotas for those to be admitted to the United States were based on "national origins," meaning that the percentages allowed were based on the percentage of Americans from that nation in the United States in 1890. As a result of this formula, immigrants from Ireland, Great Britain, and Germany constituted almost 70 percent of the total, and those applying from Asia were almost completely excluded. The McCarran-Walter Act of 1952, which was passed over President Harry Truman's veto, increased slightly the allotment for Asians but retained the basic national origins formula.

The major change in immigration policy in the twentieth century occurred with the Immigration Act of 1965 (technically the Immigration and Nationality Act Amendments of 1965, P.L. 89-236), signed by President Lyndon Johnson at the foot of the Statue of Liberty. This act has been labeled the "most powerful engine of ethno-racial diversification in the history of any nation" by Peter H. Schuck, who sees it as "one of the great turning points of American history" (2003, 75–76). In this legislation Congress phased out the national origins formula over a period of three years and established totals for regions of the world that emphasized, among other criteria, skills needed in the American labor market and prominent scientific, artistic, or other professional status. Many thought that this approach was inherently more equitable than the national origins standard, which carried fairly transparent racial undertones. For the first time, however, the law placed a limit on immigration from Central and South America.

As Steven M. Gillon (2000) has shown, however, the Immigration Act of 1965 established a set of preferences that have rendered subsequent immigration policy almost uncontrollable and have contributed to a dramatic rise in immigration numbers, both legal and illegal. The bombshell lying among the priorities to be applied by immigration officials was the family preference criterion. Unforeseen by Congress and the administration at the time, this qualification had the potential to expand exponentially—which is exactly what it did. An Asian student could enter America on a student visa, obtain a degree, and take a job that allowed him or her legal resident status. A male student could, for example, bring his wife into the country—and, later, his or her parents, who were exempt from any quota ceilings. In turn brothers and sisters would receive preference, until within a decade the original visa granted could generate literally dozens of additional immigrants. This phenomenon, along with the blanket granting of political refugee status to those from troubled nations such as Cuba and Vietnam, contributed in a major way to skyrocketing immigration numbers.

Instead of reducing immigration, the 1965 Immigration Act opened the door to what has been described as a "veritable stampede" of immigrants. Moreover, this wave of immigration has differed fundamentally in at least three ways from previous influxes of immigrants. First, recent immigration has been heavily from developing countries, and, in particular, from Mexico. These immigrants enter the United States because they are very poor and in most cases the jobs that they fill in this country keep them at or below the poverty level. Second, the revolution in technology, in both transportation and communications, means that immigrants never have to break their ties with their homelands. They locate in communities of their countrymen, as did most immigrants in the past, but they also continue almost daily contact with their families in their native lands. This means that learning to speak English and integrating into American culture and society are less pressing for them than for immigrants in the early twentieth century, when the last large wave of immigration occurred. Third, by placing a quota on immigrants from south of the border, the 1965 Immigration Act created an entirely new class of illegal immigrants.

Prior to the 1965 act, Mexican workers simply walked across the border into the United States. Basically, all that they had to show the immigration authorities was an indication that they had a job awaiting them. In particular, the bracero program, which Congress ended in 1964, had allowed Mexican workers to enter the United States for seasonal work in huge numbers. With the enactment of the Immigration Act, many of these workers who remained in the United States feared, justifiably, that they would not be able to return if they left (Schuck, op. cit., 88). Also, because immigration from Mexico was now restricted, huge numbers of Mexicans simply began entering the United States illegally.

The result of the legal and illegal immigration from Mexico and other Spanish speaking countries of the western hemisphere has been that large Hispanic communities have emerged in the Southwest and in Florida. As of 2003, Hispanics had replaced African Americans as the nation's largest minority, and Schuck points out that by that time Texas and California had nonwhite majorities (92). Not only have these communities begun to flex political muscle, but in California and the other states of the Southwest, they have also become a significant drain on social service expenditures.

Although there is much unhappiness among the taxpaying citizenry of the areas, there appears to be no way politically to control immigration into the Southwest. Support for unrestricted immigration crosses ideological boundaries, with American unions anticipating an opportunity to increase union membership, and agribusiness and the service industries needing cheap labor. When Congress has revisited the immigration issue, it has basically legitimized illegal immigration, as in 1986, when in the Immigration Reform and Control Act, it granted amnesty to approximately three million undocumented aliens in the United States (Geyer 1996, 161–62). President George W. Bush followed this approach, as well, when in 2004 he proposed giving legal worker's status to illegal immigrants for up to six years. This status would be accompanied by all the benefits to which legal immigrants were entitled.

Unfortunately in some areas, the immigrant inflow has created a heavy burden on state budgets for welfare expenditures. California, in particular, has been hit severely. A study by the National Academy of Sciences estimated that in the mid-1990s welfare expenses for immigrants cost California native households an average of $1,174 in state and local taxes annually (Borjas 1999, 122, 239, n. 35). This figure resulted from the large number of poor Mexican immigrants entering California and from that state's generous welfare benefits. The major ethical question is this: Should immigrants be entitled to the benefits of a welfare network financed by American taxpayers? And perhaps in more starkly human terms, should illegal immigrants be entitled to welfare benefits? One might agree that newly admitted immigrants need a helping hand to get on their feet financially. But are they also entitled to the longer-range benefits that American citizens receive?

It does appear that the longer that they are in the country, the more likely immigrants are to begin using welfare benefits. This may be because they become more knowledgeable about the social services process, but it may also reflect their decision to remain in this country when they lose employment. In this latter instance, high welfare benefits may actually impede the return migration of immigrant workers, who can see that they can live much better on welfare in America than they can as employees in their native lands. Congress attempted to address the concerns of states carrying heavy immigrant welfare burdens in its 1996 reform of the welfare system. In the words of George J. Borjas, "the welfare reform legislation embodied the idea that the problem with immigrant use of welfare lies in welfare policy, not in immigration policy" (op. cit., 120). The new legislation denied immigrants entering the country after August 22, 1996, most welfare benefits, and it established stricter income level standards for those benefits for which they could still be eligible. Also, those immigrants already in the country were to be removed over the next year from food stamp eligibility and from the Supplemental Security Income (SSI) rolls (ibid., 119). The states were skeptical of these changes because they feared that they would have to pick up those dropped from federal support.

In 1997 Congress repealed the removal from food stamps eligibility and from SSI of immigrants already in this country, and Borjas notes that most of the rest of the 1996 welfare reform legislation penalizing immigrants has not been enforced (120). He suggests that denial of basic assistance to immigrants would have serious—and probably more costly—effects than the expense of providing, for example, housing and healthcare. In any case the political will to act in a niggardly fashion toward immigrants is clearly not a congressional attribute. Thus, the question of how to deal with welfare and immigration remains. It appears that the conjunction of these two issues has created a policy tangle that is not easily amenable to control at the national level. Despite Milton Friedman's injunction that "[i]t's just obvious that you can't have free immigration and a welfare state" (quoted in Borjas, op. cit., 1999, 114), American policy continues in its muddling fashion to move in this direction.

WELFARE AND ILLEGAL ALIENS: THE CASE OF CALIFORNIA

The impact of increased immigration has hit the southwestern states the hardest, and among these, California has attracted the most immigrants. Schuck cites estimates, based on the 2000 census, of 8–9 million undocumented immigrants in the United States, of which 4.5–5 million are from Mexico (op. cit., 89). Thus, it is not surprising that California has seen a large influx of illegal, or undocumented, aliens. These are individuals who have either crossed into the United States illegally or who have entered on temporary permits and simply remained after their permits expired. This population has placed a considerable drain on social services in that state.

It is important at the outset to understand that the benefits that illegal immigrants receive are derived primarily from their children who have been born in the United States. Under Section 1 of the Fourteenth Amendment, anyone born in the United States is automatically a citizen of the United States and of the state in which they reside. Legally, U.S. citizens cannot be denied welfare entitlement benefits. In a 1997 report to Congress, the General Accounting Office (GAO) found that instances of outright fraud on the part of illegal immigrants were no more numerous than those perpetrated by native Californians. The issue in terms of welfare costs occurs when a child is receiving benefits that are administered by his or her parents, one or both of whom are illegal immigrants. Additionally, some of the siblings might also be illegals.

In its 1997 study the GAO concluded that in 1995 "about $1.1 billion in Aid to Families with Dependent Children (AFDC) and Food Stamp benefits were provided to households with an illegal alien parent for the use of his or her citizen child" (U.S. General Accounting Office 1997, 3). Of this total, California alone accounted for $720 million. Additionally, Medicaid payments to undocumented mothers for births in California constituted 14 percent of all births there in 1995. Although expenses for illegal aliens comprised about 10 percent of California's AFDC costs, separate studies on Orange and Los Angeles counties indicated that in those areas, up to 20 percent of the caseloads were citizen-children of undocumented immigrants. Thus, California has been impacted heavily by illegal immigrant costs, and its most populous counties have been hit even harder (9). The transformation of AFDC into Temporary Assistance for Needy Families in the 1996 welfare reform act did not change the eligibility of citizen children for welfare benefits.

As a result of the large percentage of immigrants in California and the budget constraints imposed on that state both by constitutional limits on property taxes and by increasing demands for public services, a sustained effort to limit social service expenditures for illegal aliens emerged in the 1990s. In 1994 the citizens of California were successful in placing on the ballot Proposition 187, an initiative to deny state payments to illegal aliens. In its "Findings and Declaration" the initiative measure, among other grievances, declared, "The People of California find and declare as follows: That they have suffered and are suffering economic hardship caused by the presence of illegal aliens in this state . . ." The initiative then proceeded to deny "public social services," "health care services from a publicly-funded health care facility," and admission to public elementary and secondary schools, as well as to public postsecondary educational institutions to any person not a citizen or lawfully in the United States.

This initiative was popular among California voters and was strongly supported by Governor Pete Wilson. On November 8, 1994, it passed with 59 percent of the vote. Unfortunately for the measure's supporters, debate on it began to assume strongly anti-immigrant tones. Governor Wilson's widely quoted statement—"It's time to send Jose home"—at a time when Jose had replaced Michael as the most widely chosen name for new male babies, was impolitic at best. Indeed the question became whether Proposition 187 was a welfare reform measure or an attempt to limit immigration—or both.

The backlash from immigrant and Hispanic groups was severe. Georgie Anne Geyer reports that in October 1994, Hispanic groups took to the streets of Los Angeles promoting heavily racist messages. Signs and slogans urged, "GO BACK TO EUROPE . . . PILGRIMS GO HOME." Others labeled the proposition's supporters "YANKEE GRINGO RACISTS." These signs were accompanied by an effigy of Governor Wilson, which was beaten, "killed," and placed in a coffin (Geyer 1996, 308–9). In response to lawsuits filed by advocacy groups immediately after passage of the initiative, a federal judge, Marianna Pfaelzer, issued an injunction preventing its enforcement.

Judge Pfaelzer relied heavily on the Supreme Court's decision in *Plyler v. Doe*, 457 U.S. 202 (1982). In that decision the Court considered a Texas statute that denied free public education to "illegal alien children." Speaking for the Court, Justice William J. Brennan asserted that the equal protection clause extends to all who live within a state's boundaries and are subject to the jurisdiction of a state's laws. He held, however, that a state may distinguish between lawful residents and those who are within the state because of their intentional unlawful actions. In this instance the Court could find no legitimate state goal for penalizing children who were in this country through no fault of their own. Moreover, congressional immigration policy made no provision for such action by the states. In Judge Pfaelzer's opinion California could not extend its discrimination against undocumented aliens and their children beyond what Texas had unsuccessfully attempted. Following Brennan, she also held that federal law was dominant in the field of immigration and that California's initiative was incompatible with federal policy in this area.

Attorney General Dan Lungren's notice of appeal to the Ninth Circuit Court of Appeals never moved beyond that stage. Political backlash against Proposition 187 gained tremendous impetus, and most elected officials in California began to see merit in backing off on enforcement of the initiative. In 1998 Gray Davis, who had strongly opposed Proposition 187, was elected governor, and the steam went out of the legal efforts to have the initiative declared constitutional. Instead, the government suggested mediation to the district court, with the result that California agreed not to enforce its provisions denying state benefits to illegal aliens. Thus, in one sense, the clear will of the voters was effectively thwarted. In another sense the activation of Hispanic voters made actions against immigrants—legal or illegal—hazardous. The election of Gray Davis and of other Democrats statewide was widely attributed to voter reaction against the heavy-handedness of proponents—largely Republicans—of Proposition 187.

The political and economic fallout from Proposition 187 carried over for years in California politics and emerged prominently again in the recall election campaign against Governor Davis in 2003. In September 2003, the governor signed legislation (SB 60) that would have enabled illegal aliens more easily to obtain California drivers' licenses, a proposal that he had previously vetoed in 2002 (Schuck op. cit., 361–62, n. 49). Governor Davis argued that illegals were driving anyway and that with drivers' licenses they would be able to drive legally to work, to school, or to the hospital. His opponent, Arnold Schwarzenegger, criticized the governor's action, and almost immediately after Davis was defeated, the legislature repealed SB 60, an action that was quickly signed by Governor Schwarzenegger.

The driver's license issue reopened many of the previous arguments about the treatment of undocumented immigrants. SB 60 did not actually grant illegal aliens the right to a driver's license. It simply made it easier for these people to apply for a license by requiring much less in terms of identification. Governor Davis argued that many undocumented immigrants were driving anyway. This law, he believed, would encourage illegal aliens to be more responsible for their actions. To obtain a license, they would need insurance and would have to pass a driver's test. They would be on record and more easily traceable. This latter point was in response to the belief that the increase in hit-and-run accidents was due to the likelihood that illegal immigrants, who were unlicensed, were fleeing the scenes of accidents. In his book *Mexifornia*, Victor Davis Hanson noted "the growing number of immigrants who do not always drive well and rarely do so under legal conditions, but are nevertheless on our freeways in enormous clunkers that sometimes engage in an ethnic version of demolition derby" (2003, 65). On the other side of the argument was the concern that a driver's license would open the doors to increased social service support and would allow undocumented immigrants the right to vote (ibid., pp. 65–66).

Ethical Analysis of the Case

Before raising the question of ethical principles for immigration policy into California, we should clarify the principal values that are at stake in the current controversy. Unvoiced, but clearly prominent in the background of this case, is the fact that poor Mexicans and other Central Americans wish to emigrate to California because they find jobs there that are lacking at home. This means that California farmers and other business people have a need for the abundant cheap labor the immigrants represent. Another value lies in the costs to the taxpayer of social welfare programs that are designed to meet the needs of these people. The cost of a much stricter enforcement of immigration laws and the successful prevention of illegal entry would also have to be assessed. The value of having safe drivers in the population is also clearly an important one.

Utilitarian legislators would probably focus their attention on a cost-benefit analysis of the expense of social welfare benefits for the illegal immigrants and their children vis-à-vis the value of their labor to California business. If the costs were found to be less than the benefits, then it would seem appropriate simply to add the illegals to the welfare rolls without more ado—and, in addition, to be sure to issue them drivers' licenses after having them qualify to drive. If costs exceeded benefits, the utilitarian would probably vote to deny them. Would this adequately encompass all the ethical issues involved?

Deontologists would be concerned with insuring basic human rights for the immigrants. They might have difficulty, however, in specifying exactly what these are. Would they think illegals entitled to the same rights as citizens? Would deontologists vote for driver's licenses for illegals? Would they accept results of a cost-benefit analysis that called for repatriation of illegal immigrants?

The prudent pragmatist in looking at the situation might advise that the farmers and business people who profit from the use of illegal labor bear the welfare burden for their workers through taxes devised for this purpose. This would no doubt meet with extreme opposition unless the authors of the legislation also engaged in a strenuous effort to educate the public about the comparative values involved. If it proved to be the case that illegal labor was diffused throughout the economy and that no particular groups of employers benefited from it in a special way, then the legislators would have to educate the public about the need to be willing to pay for the value received. The proposal in 2004 of President George Bush that illegal workers in the United States in general should receive a six-year amnesty before being denied welfare benefits adds evidence that the labor of these people has considerable social value—and that this value should be recognized. Additionally, rather than have to deal with the problems that necessarily derive from the secretiveness and lawbreaking of illegals, legislation should be passed to ensure the legal admission of aliens from the south in numbers adequate to the economic needs of California.

As a postscript, consider the impact of 9-11 on this issue. Congressional action in the cause of increased homeland security appeared destined to remove the issue of drivers' licenses from the immigration agenda in California. In October 2004, Congress enacted legislation to encourage strongly a nationwide system of standards for the issuance of drivers' licenses by the states and a national data center for information on drivers so licensed (Wald 2004).

HEALTHCARE FOR THE POOR

The Social Security Amendments of 1965 (P.L. 89-97) established healthcare for the poor through the Medicaid program. Unlike Medicare, Medicaid covers the poor (as defined by a specified income level) regardless of age, is funded directly through tax dollars, and offers a wide range of medical assistance (e.g., prescription drugs, nursing home care, etc.). The costs of Medicaid are shared between the states and the federal government, with a state's share based on a formula using that state's per capita income over a three-year period. Americans may make distinctions between deserving and undeserving poor with regard to welfare assistance, but there seems to be general agreement that the poor—whatever their orientation toward life—are entitled to basic healthcare.

The Medicaid program is another example of the incremental movement of policy in the American political system. Typically, Congress has expanded Medicaid coverage by first permitting states to broaden coverage in particular areas or by granting waivers for specified population groups. After several years this discretion at the state level is often replaced with federally mandated requirements that apply nationwide (Gruber 2003, 20). The elderly and the young have been the primary beneficiaries of these halting steps toward wider healthcare coverage, and advocacy groups and organizations representing those who provide care for these segments of the population have become important constituencies for Medicaid.

Somewhat surprisingly, the states have also become important supporters of the Medicaid program because they have discovered that it can provide a measure of fiscal relief for their budgetary problems. In 2004 Medicaid expenditures from state funds for the first time exceeded those for K-12 education (21.9 percent to 21.5 percent), making these expenditures the highest cost area in state budgets (Richard 2004). However, many states, through creative budgeting practices, have been able to supplement these expenditures with federal funding. The Kaiser Commission on Medicaid Facts reported that for 2002 Medicaid accounted for 43 percent of all federal grants to the states, making it the largest source of federal funding to the states. Although the federal/state funding formula was originally to be 50/50, many states have found ways to increase their eligibility for federal funds to the point that in FY 2004 some states were able to obtain up to 77 percent in federal support (Kaiser 2004).

Another trend in the Medicaid program has been its gradual disassociation from poverty income levels as the criterion for eligibility. Critics have argued that such a standard stigmatizes those receiving Medicaid, and in its welfare reform package of 1996, in which the AFDC program was replaced with block grants-in-aid to the states, Congress ended the requirement that eligibility for Medicaid first require eligibility for welfare. Later, in 1997, Congress expanded Medicaid coverage to disabled workers with incomes up to 250 percent of the federal poverty level and to uninsured children whose parents were low-income but above the income level required by Medicaid. This latter program—the State Children's Health Insurance Program (SCHIP)—strove to provide healthcare to all low-income children. Then in 2000—moving completely away from any income threshold—Congress allowed states to extend Medicaid to any uninsured woman, regardless of assets or income level, if through Centers for Disease Control screening she was found to need treatment for breast or cervical cancer.

The chronology of Medicaid changes reflects both an effort to improve healthcare for the poor and the influence of organized special interests. Increased assistance to the disabled is obviously an incentive to keep these people at work and off the welfare rolls. On the other hand the assistance to women with cervical or breast cancer, while certainly praiseworthy, intentionally has no relationship to poverty at all. In terms of the welfare of the poor, the inclusion under Medicaid or related public financing of health conditions simply because they are important to special interests has the potential to crowd the indigent off the public health agenda, insofar as these people have been and remain notoriously inarticulate politically. At the same time, removing public healthcare from dependence on income level does move the nation closer to universal healthcare, albeit haphazardly.

In addition to their concerns that the income requirements stigmatize recipients, critics have noted that the Medicaid program and its progeny, such as SCHIP, are highly vulnerable to economic conditions. When states face fiscal problems, their legislators naturally look to pare areas of large expenditure. In the field of healthcare, these cuts can take a variety of forms. States can limit or reduce coverage. They can increase co-payments for certain programs and can change eligibility requirements (e.g., move from a threshold of 150 percent of the poverty line to 100 percent). Many states are currently moving to restrict eligibility for individuals seeking to enter nursing homes as Medicaid patients. On the reimbursement side states can lower payments to hospitals, nursing homes, and doctors. The last can be especially onerous for the poor, insofar as some doctors simply refuse service to Medicaid patients because of the reimbursement rate, slow payments, and the mountains of paperwork involved.

Thus, during the economic hard times of 2000–2002 and the years immediately following, many states moved to limit expenditures under Medicaid and SCHIP. The Kaiser Commission reported that in December 2003, forty-nine states planned some form of Medicaid reductions to provide budgetary relief for FY 2004. The SCHIP program also suffered from these poor economic conditions. From June 2003 to December 2003, enrollment in SCHIP declined for the first time. Hardest hit was Texas, where the legislature specifically targeted SCHIP enrollment. Using a number of the techniques identified earlier, Texas authorities lowered SCHIP enrollment by about 75,000 children from June to December 2003.

The current funding structure for healthcare for the poor places the poor at the mercy of institutional factors that have no relationship whatsoever to their needs or to any concept of social justice. The incremental approach that has been used to advance healthcare for the poor can be a vicious two-edged sword. Without a consensual commitment to fundamental principles of fairness, state legislators under fiscal duress can find cutting back on healthcare for the poor to be an attractive—and relatively painless—alternative to large tax increases.

MEDICAID AND THE POOR IN ALLEGANY COUNTY: A CASE STUDY

The effects of depressed economic conditions in combination with increased fiscal demands impacted the poor of Allegany County, New York, in rather grim fashion in 2004. Allegany County is a lightly populated, rural county in western New York, a region that in 2004 had been economically depressed for at least a decade. It has a large area of 1,035 square miles (approximately the size of Rhode Island) but a declining population of less than 50,000. It has the second poorest per capita income in New York State and almost no industrial base. The largest employer in the county is the county government, which has approximately 600 employees. With such a meager tax base, Allegany County has one of the highest property tax rates and the highest sales taxes in the region.

In New York the state government has been of little assistance to economically strapped counties like Allegany, and, in fact, it has made their fiscal burdens even heavier. In contrast to other states, New York has shifted half of its Medicaid costs down to the county governments, which are, of course, the legal creations of the state and subject to whatever demands it wishes to impose on them. Thus, the counties in New York State pay 25 percent of Medicaid costs that finance a healthcare program that in 2002 was more expensive than those of California and Texas combined. This is a tremendous burden on all county budgets, which are based heavily on property taxes. In 2003 and 2004, in some counties in western New York, the Medicaid share of their budgets exceeded the amounts raised from property taxes, and other forms of revenue, such as the sales tax, had to be tapped to pay mandated Medicaid expenses. The fiscal demands on counties had been greatly exacerbated in 2002, when the state expanded Medicaid to provide health insurance for all uninsured below certain income levels. The counties were forced to shoulder 25 percent of the additional costs for these insurance premiums at a time when the state, as a whole, was facing economic stagnation, if not an actual downturn.

Because of the fiscal pressures imposed by the state on counties, Allegany County in FY2004 was forced to raise property taxes an average of 22 percent, possibly the largest such increase in county history. With the county legislators asking for more cost-saving measures from their agency heads, the Commissioner of Social Services turned to examining the costs of burying the poor. Until 2004, the county had paid a rate of $500 for stillborns and for the deaths of all infants up to the age of one year; it paid $1,750 thereafter for the burials of indigents or those on Medicaid or welfare. Medicaid, however, reimbursed at rates of $500 and $1,100, respectively, leaving the county to pick up $650 for burial of those past one year of age.

As a cost-savings measure, the Commissioner of Social Services recommended that the county reduce its reimbursement to $1,100, the amount fully funded by Medicaid. This would, she estimated, save the county approximately $31,200, which at that time translated into about a 0.2 percent savings on the property tax levy. The county legislature unanimously passed the commissioner's recommendation on March 8, 2004.

The county's action meant that the only choice for those without additional funds was cremation, and the county's morticians were quick to protest. Obviously, the county's new reimbursement policy put them in an awkward position. Any expenses beyond the cost of a minimal cremation urn were now someone else's burden. Without private funds the deceased would be denied funeral rites, burial, and a headstone, among other benefits that those with sufficient funds would normally receive. The funeral directors understandably raised questions about denying the poor and their families the dignity of a proper burial. As one director put the matter, "The traditional funeral gives the family the opportunity to gather with friends, say goodbye and begin the grieving process. This is especially important following an unexpected or tragic death" (Embser 2004). Funeral directors could expect families to be asking for something more than ashes in a plain urn, and they would be the individuals dealing with often distraught family members about this issue.

The more basic moral issue, however, is the question of the right to dignity in death. Obviously, the county's new policy did not deny a family the costs of basic disposal of their loved one's remains, but it may have made a dignified disposition impossible for some.

Another way of looking at Allegany County's action might be to stress the generous healthcare coverage provided for the living poor in New York State. Indigents in that state have better health benefits than those provided in most private health insurance programs. In New York, the poor have dental, eye, and a broad variety of other healthcare needs paid for by the state and counties, with 50 percent of these costs assumed by the federal government.

Probably because Allegany County is predominately Christian in population, the issue of religious belief did not arise during the debate over reducing county support for burial of the poor. However, some religions prohibit cremation as a sacrilegious desecration of the body or for other reasons related to their beliefs. These religions include Islam, Conservative and Orthodox Judaism, and the Greek Orthodox Church. Until 1963, the Catholic Church also forbade cremation, and this may explain Allegany County's previous willingness to provide county tax dollars to enable the poor to avoid cremation. From another perspective, cremation remains the choice of a minority of Americans, whatever their religious beliefs or lack thereof. In recent years only about 25 percent have chosen cremation, indicating that most Americans prefer burial with all of the traditional rituals and trimmings. (See "Cremation vs. Burial: Jewish & Christian Beliefs" 2004.)

Also absent in the discussion of burial costs for the poor was any organized constituency that could speak on its behalf. Clearly, the Department of Social Services, which serves the poor in many capacities, could not take up the cudgels for them. In a larger, more diverse, more urban county, protests from advocacy groups for the less fortunate would undoubtedly have been forthcoming. But in small rural counties, wherever they are located in the nation, such organization and activism remain rare.

Ethical Analysis of the Case

A utilitarian would probably find it easy to dispose of the ethical questions in this case. The greater social good would quite clearly lie in keeping taxes down for the many and reducing burial benefits for the small number of the very poor. This would be the case unless the ethicist thought that the intensity of suffering by those deprived of the subsidy would offset the intensity of the pleasure of those experiencing tax relief. But there does not seem to be any device for measuring the comparative pains and pleasures.

Deontologists always sensitive to the value of equality, would no doubt opt for higher taxes and a retention of the burial subsidy at its present figure. They would also emphasize the plight of those whose religious beliefs forbid cremation. Would forcing the poor to this expedient be equitable? Is this an issue of equal treatment or of religious belief?

Prudent pragmatists would find themselves faced with the need to weigh and balance the value of the subsidy for the very poor (i.e., the disvalue of the cremation alternative) and the value of tax relief for those bearing the cost. Would the premier healthcare provided to the living poor somehow offset the shabbier treatment at their death for the prudent pragmatist? Also to be weighed in the balance is the question of the suffering of those whose religious beliefs prohibit cremation.

Would the ethically concerned feel morally called upon to engage in political action that might obtain more generous funeral allowances for the poor without increasing the tax burden of the county? What action might be useful? If you were a county legislator representing the citizens of Allegany, would you accept an ethical obligation to do something about the funeral subsidies for the poor among your constituents? Do you think a prudent pragmatist would differ from utilitarians and deontologists in his or her approach to the question?

Whatever the ethical issues posed by the specific decision made by the Allegany County legislature, broader questions about the position of the poor in American society remain. Incremental expansion of assistance to the poor has enabled the American policy process to provide greater health coverage for the poor. But it has left a large portion of the population uncovered, and this portion appears to be at greater risk of death because of lack of health insurance and also tends to suffer poorer health generally. (See National Academy of Science, Institute of Medicine 2002.)

Equally important, the current approach to healthcare for the poor lacks stabilizing core values. States vary not only in their coverage. They also remain poised to alter this coverage in response to changing economic and political demands. Is a basic reform of the Medicaid system needed to remedy this problem? What would a prudent pragmatist suggest as the political as well as the ethical principles that should inform such an overhaul?

REFERENCES

Borjas, George J. *Heaven's Door*. Princeton, NJ: Princeton University Press, 1999.

"Cremation vs. Burial: Jewish & Christian Beliefs," at www.religioustolerance.org/crematio.htm (accessed 8/18/04).

Embser, John W. Letter to Ronald Truax, Chair, Human Services Committee, Allegany County Legislature, Allegany County, NY (May 12, 2004).

Geyer, Georgie Anne. *Americans No More*. New York: Atlantic Monthly Press, 1996.

Gillon, Steven M. *That's Not What We Meant To Do*. New York: W.W. Norton, 2000.

Graubard, Stephen. *Command of Office*. New York: Basic Books, 2004.

Gruber, Jonathan. "Medicaid." In *Means-Tested Transfer Programs in the United States*, ed. Robert A. Moffitt, 15–77. Chicago: University of Chicago Press, 2003.

Handler, Joel. *Social Citizenship and Workfare in the United States and Western Europe*. New York: Cambridge University Press, 2004.

Hanson, Victor Davis. *Mexifornia*. San Francisco: Encounter Books, 2003.

Huntington, Samuel P. *American Politics*. Cambridge, MA: Harvard University Press, 1981.

Kaiser Commission on Medicaid Facts. "State Fiscal Conditions and Medicaid" (April 2004), at www.kff.org/kcmu (accessed 04/02/06).

Katznelson, Ira, Kim Geiger, and Daniel Kryder. "Limiting Liberalism: The Southern Veto in Congress, 1933–1950." *Political Science Quarterly* 108 (Summer 1993): 283–306.

National Academy of Science, Institute of Medicine. "Care without Coverage: Too Little, Too Late" (2002), at www.iom.edu (accessed 05/19/06).

Noble, Charles. *Welfare as We Knew It*. New York: Oxford University Press, 1997.

Piven, Frances Fox, and Richard A. Cloward. *Regulating the Poor*. New York: Vintage Books, 1971.

Plyler v. Doe, 457 U.S. 202 (1982).

Richard, Alan. "Medicaid Threatens K-12 Share of State Budgets," *Education Week* (October 20, 2004), 20.

Rovner, Julie. "Welfare Reform: The Issue That Bubbled up from the States to Capitol Hill." *Governing* (December 1988), 17–21.

Schuck, Peter H. *Diversity in America*. Cambridge, MA: Harvard University Press, 2003.

Skocpol, Theda. *Social Policy in the United States*. Princeton, NJ: Princeton University Press, 1995.

Spencer, Herbert. *Social Statics*. New York: Robert Schalkenbach Foundation, 1954 [Reprint of second edition, 1877].

Tanner, Michael. *The End of Welfare*. Washington, DC: Cato Institute, 1996.

U.S. General Accounting Office. "Illegal Aliens: Extent of Welfare Benefits Received on Behalf of U.S. Citizen Children" (November 1997), GAO/HEHS-98-30.

Wald, Matthew L. "U.S. to Specify Documents Needed for Driver's Licenses." *New York Times* (December 9, 2004): A27.

CHAPTER 9

Biotechnology and Humanity

Perhaps the most urgent ethical dilemmas that beset American policymakers today derive from the ceaseless technological revolution in which we live. Our mastery of the physical world and our technical ability to manipulate things has reached a point at which we have begun to question whether there is any given reality in the world that can be labeled "human nature"—or "nature" in general. Where are the barriers that limit our power to control the world? The usual processes of human birth can now be bypassed with the resources of in vitro fertilization (IVF), a person's sex can be changed from male to female or vice versa by newly invented surgical procedures. We have learned to extend human life greatly through the wizardry of medicine, and we stand on the verge of developing an ability to clone human life quite independently of any sexual process—to create parentless men and women. New strains of crops of all kinds and new breeds of animals have been created for our use, along with a million mechanical and electronic devices for making life easier and more pleasurable. Nothing seems to be given anymore. Nature is no longer defined for us. We create it anew daily as we innovate technologically.

Those who have been raised in the culture of scientific progress—such as Nobel Laureates in genetics Sir John Eccles, Sir Macfarlane Burnett, Walter Gilbert, or James Watson—celebrate our growing control over nature. The processes of nature they see as blind and unpredictable. We must take control of the future and bend it to our purposes. As Richard M. Zaner has put it, nature must be "finessed" (2003, 14). According to these scientists, those who oppose this approach are obscurantist and irrational. On the other hand, there are those who regard this view as naively rationalist. In this view such rationalists are unaware of the darker side of human life and are not regardful of human pride, the fatal flaw the Greeks called *hubris*. This view is represented by such people as Leon Kass, appointed by George W. Bush as chairman of the National Bioethics Commission (NBAC). These scholars celebrate a traditional view of nature, which they see not as blind process, but as full of divine purposes.

Whichever group is to prevail, we know that there will be policies enacted to regulate developing biotechnologies—either by laying down stringent limits to what scientists seek to accomplish or by giving them their head. Therefore, since our desires and our fantasies of what is desirable are limitless, a whole realm of decisions about the good and the bad, about what we ought to do, which used to be settled by our concept of "nature," must be recanvassed because of our new capabilities, and boundaries must be set to what we ought to do. For the ideas of law and right have always signified limit and constraint. Desires are boundless, and the boundless is chaos. No one would argue that we ought to do whatever we can do, since it is obvious that such an idea would cause the destruction of the human race and the world as a whole. We must set new limits for ourselves through the exercise of reason, as embodied in law—a law that we give to ourselves. But how ought we to frame this law, or these laws? What does prudence dictate about how to move from traditional standards to new ones? Of one thing we can be sure: that our leaders will legislate limits. Whether those limits will be ethical is the question before us. We begin our reflection on these large problems with a review of the story of biotechnological advance and with the specific moral questions that this advance has raised. We will then turn to case studies of the more interesting and salient dilemmas that have appeared.

THE BIOTECHNOLOGY REVOLUTION

The beginning of concern about ethical boundaries to scientific research dates from the medical experimentation with human subjects by doctors and scientists in Nazi Germany, whose doctors killed and maimed many subjects. These experiments were especially shocking because they were conducted with the sanction of the government. To prevent any future behavior of this sort, the War Crimes Tribunal at Nuremberg developed a set of ten principles to govern future conduct of research with human subjects: the Nuremberg Code. This code set forth the conditions necessary to guarantee that in the future, participation in such experiments would rest only on informed consent of the subjects, made in the absence of any coercion. Investigators were made responsible for informing subjects of risks to be undertaken and for obtaining their consent, as well as for the scientific qualifications of those performing the experiments, the credibility and safety of the experiments, and termination of the experiment when threats of injury or death developed.

The adoption of this code occurred at the threshold of the decade of the 1950s, a time that was to be unprecedented in the remarkable growth of biomedical research. The new research was welcomed by the American government, which proceeded to fund scientific projects at an increasing rate through the National Institutes of Health (NIH). This was followed during the 1960s both with the development of procedures for obtaining the informed consent of the subjects of the burgeoning research and also with the establishment of Institutional Review Boards to oversee these procedures.

With the 1970s there developed among elites the concern that the extraordinary growth of scientific knowledge was beginning to affect the direction of social development, especially after Watson and Crick had described the structure of DNA and after the discovery of recombinant DNA. One writer reports, for example, that Raymond Aron wondered whether democracy could function in this situation. "How" he asked, "could legislators, politicians, or the electorate evaluate the complex facets of social problems when the most basic knowledge about them increasingly fell into the domain of the scientific expert?" (Reiser, in Bulger 1993, 3). The problem took on new dimensions in the 1980s, when big business developed an interest in the biological sciences because of the profits to be realized on the new frontier. By 1984, almost a quarter of the external support for biotechnological research in the university was supplied by industry (ibid., 7). In the NIH Guides for Contracts and Grants, there began to appear requirements of programs to guarantee scientific integrity, professional standards, codes of conduct, rules of responsible authorship, and other restrictive devices. Ethical issues would have to be incorporated in scientific training. This development was capped first with the creation of the Office of Scientific Integrity in 1989 and later, in 1995, with the establishment of the National Bioethics Advisory Commission. The role of the latter is to advise the National Science and Technology Council and other government entities regarding "bioethical issues arising from research on human biology and behavior" (Eiseman 2003, iii).

What is typical of the moral issues that have emerged from the biotechnological revolution is their unprecedented character. In the fields of social justice, foreign policy, criminal justice, and civil rights, there exist a tradition of moral precedents and principles for citizens and decision makers to draw upon. But in biotechnology the capabilities that we need to regulate are new. In the field of genetics, for example, does the ability to diagnose the genetic roots of numerous diseases (such as cystic fibrosis, hemophilia, thalassemia B, or Huntington's disease) bring the right—either to parents or society—to destroy affected fetuses by abortion? George Annas, an American professor of health law, suggests that parents might muse to themselves, "This embryo is going to cost a lot of money to raise, and we don't know how to fix it yet, so why don't we just try for another one instead?" (Leo 1989, 59).

Does genetic knowledge give insurance companies the right to require applicants for health or life insurance to submit to genetic screening—and to deny coverage to those who might someday develop genetically based diseases? (Questions of autonomy and equity are involved here.) Does it give employers a right to screen prospective employees for defective genes?

Do new ways of using DNA to establish identity—"genetic fingerprints"—make these devices automatically available for use in parenting suits or in criminal prosecutions? (Questions of individual right to privacy versus the interests of society are involved.)

There is little controversy about using our new abilities to manipulate genes to rid existing individuals of dread diseases such as Huntington's or Parkinson's. But vexing problems attach to germline therapy (therapy directed to sperm and ovaries that will affect future generations). Implicit are a possible new eugenics to shape future populations according to the ideas of an elite who might think that blond hair and blue eyes are desirable traits—or who might like to insure the intelligence of the future by selecting against inferior genes. Should individuals who can afford such therapy be empowered to design their own children? If such things are allowed, the very idea of any natural "givens" would disappear.

PUBLIC CONTROL OF SCIENTIFIC RESEARCH

What norms have been established by public enactment for the conduct of research scientists in the various fields of biotechnology? Working from the Nuremberg Code it was relatively easy to establish agreed-upon rules and principles in this area early on. In 1975 the National Advisory Health Council recommended to the Surgeon General that public health support of clinical research should be given only if the appropriateness of research methods has been established for work involving human beings—and only after informed consent has been obtained from the subjects of research. The year prior, the Helsinki Declaration was adopted by the World Medical Assembly, which contained guidelines for physicians involved in research with human and animal subjects, and these guidelines have been amended three times since, the last time in 1989. The NIHealth has published a requirement for programs on the responsible conduct of research for all recipients of its awards. Despite all this effort, studies have shown that the safeguards established are not foolproof. Subjects, misunderstanding the underlying scientific methodology of experiments in which they are involved, will often misinterpret the risk-benefit ratio of their participation. (See Part VI, "Research with Human Subjects," in Bulger 1993.) But by comparison with other areas of concern, this one has been relatively unproblematical.

STEM CELL RESEARCH

In November 1998 two research teams reported a breakthrough in the culturing of human stem cells, a development that had revolutionary implications for the treatment of heart disease, Alzheimer's disease, pancreatic cancer, and diabetes. People suffering from these illnesses would no longer have to find replacements for specific kinds of cell tissue, but they could instead have recourse to undifferentiated stem cells, which are capable of being developed into every kind of cell possessed by the human body. The new findings could not be immediately exploited, however, as they posed substantial ethical problems. Since the cells were extracted from human embryos and fetuses, which had the potential of developing into complete human beings, the new science presented the prospect of embryos produced for the purpose of harvesting them for their parts. New human beings would be sacrificed to save the lives of others. Would this be tantamount to murder?

Embryonic stem cells appear about five to seven days after the fertilization of an egg in a round ball structure called a blastocyst. They are undifferentiated at this point, but they will eventually divide and develop into the various parts of a human person. The beginning of differentiation is the division of the cells into ectoderm, mesoderm, and endoderm. From the first of these cells, emerge skin, eyes, and nervous system. From the second, bone, blood, and muscle tissues form. And from the third come the lungs, liver, and gut. These cells are termed *pluripotent* or *totipotent*, since they contain all that is required for a complete human being.

The ethical sensitivity of embryo research was recognized as far back as 1978, when the federal government banned the use of federal funds for research with human embryos. In 1994, however, the Human Embryo Research Panel reported to the NIH that human embryonic research might be acceptable if embryos were not created for the specific purpose of such research. It was also legal at that time for private funds to be used for embryo research. It was with private funds that the breakthrough of 1998 was accomplished. Material used consisted of embryos left over from IVF work. The couples who produced these embryos were required to give their informed consent for this to be done.

Stem cells can also be harvested in other ways. One is by collecting germ cells from embryos produced by abortion, which can be cultivated in vitro to produce stem cells.

The blood from the umbilical cord of a newborn child can also be used as a source of stem cells. Yet another way is by transferring the nucleus of an adult somatic cell to an enucleated ovum by cloning. Such a process produces a human blastocyst, just as in research with stem cells otherwise harvested. The procedure, however, has not been fully worked out as yet. One advantage of this method would be using somatic cells from the person needing help. Stem cells thus produced would not be rejected by the patient's autoimmune system as might those from other donors. Cloning research has been carried on by Advanced Cell Technology, a biotech firm based in Massachusetts. Neither ES (embryonic stem) cells nor EG (embryonic germ) cells are themselves embryos or whole organisms, nor can they be made into such. But once produced, they can be propagated indefinitely as stem cell lines.

The Federal Regulation of Research

Following the legalization of abortion by *Roe v. Wade* (1973), the U.S. Congress became concerned that the right use be made of aborted fetuses. One result was the declaration of a moratorium on the funding of research with such fetuses by the Department of Health, Education, and Welfare (DHEW). At the same time Congress set up a National Commission for the Protection of Human Subjects of Biomedical and Behavioral Research. It assigned the commission responsibility for developing guidelines for human fetal and embryo research, and it required the commission to establish standards for funding such research.

The statutory moratorium was lifted when the commission issued its report in 1975. In the report the commission called for a National Ethics Advisory Board to be created to prepare standards and research protocols for the federal funding of embryo research. In doing so, it was envisaging the possible use of embryos left over from IVF research. The board was set up and was mandated to provide advice about the ethical acceptability of such research. The report was published in 1979, and it gave qualified approval to this kind of research, although it made no recommendation at this time for funding it. After the charter of the board expired in 1980, a de facto ban on funding remained in place throughout the 1980s.

In 1994 Congress created a Human Embryo Research Panel, which recommended that some areas of embryo research be deemed eligible for federal funding, and it also approved funding of research with human embryos created with the intention of using them for research. President Clinton thereupon overruled the latter stipulation and ordered that such research not be funded. He did, however, permit the NIH to consider funding research with embryos left over from IVF research. But Congress overruled him and prohibited funding for any research which involved the destruction of or damage to human embryos—the Dickey Amendment. This ban left free, however, the conduct of such research through private funding. The Dickey Amendment has been reenacted every year since.

THE BUSH PROHIBITION: A CASE STUDY

On August 9, 2001, the Bush Administration put the 1994 regulations on hold. President Bush said both that federally funded research could use only stem cells already available as leftovers from IVF research and also that no further destruction of embryos would be permitted.

The moral grounds of this policy continue to be hotly debated. Many scientists, physicians, and advocacy groups for patients claim that the policy is hindering growth in a vital research area. In May 2004, an editorial article in the *Los Angeles Times* reported the plea of former First Lady Nancy Reagan for more federally funded stem cell research, a plea prompted by the condition of her husband, who lay ill for years with Alzheimer's disease

("New Allies For Cell Research," May 12, 2004, B12). The editorial pointed out the moral schizophrenia of our nation. On the one hand we deem ethical those attempts by infertile couples to have children through in vitro fertilization. But on the other, apart from cell lines already developed before August 2001, we deny funding for research with the millions of embryos left over from these attempts. The editorial went on to say that allowing private funding—while forbidding public funding—may well lead to moral chaos in the research, because of the "anything goes" attitude of private enterprise. To allow federal funding would, on the other hand, provide needed rules for the conduct of research as well as ways of monitoring it.

Arguments such as these have led delegations of members of Congress to meet with presidential advisers to urge a policy change. And in June 2004, fifty-eight senators, including fifteen Republicans, sent a letter to President Bush requesting that he loosen restrictions on stem cell research. "This issue is especially poignant," said Senator Dianne Feinstein (D-CA), given President Reagan's passing. "Embryonic stem cell research might hold the key to a cure for Alzheimer's and other terrible diseases" (Weiss 2004, A3).

On the other hand there are those who believe the current restrictions are too liberal and that they reward those who have destroyed incipient human life. In brief, "some ethicists argue that there is a moral imperative to remove all restrictions upon potentially life-saving research, other ethicists argue that there is a moral imperative to protect the lives of human beings in their earliest and most vulnerable stages" (President's Council on Bioethics 2004, Ch. 3). The clearest and most adamant argument against stem cell research is made by those who also oppose abortion. Such groups include the hierarchy of the Roman Catholic Church and other "pro-lifers"—evangelical congregations and fundamentalist Christians in particular. Their argument rests on the simple proposition that every embryo is a human person from the moment of its conception and is, therefore, due all the rights and protections enjoyed by those who have been born. This view rejects a developmental conception of personhood, one which distinguishes between the nonsentient embryo and the fetus after it has acquired both feeling and the basis of cognition (i.e., a brain and nervous system). It shares the deontological conception of Kantians, who declare a human person to be an end in him- or herself, never to be used as a means to another's well-being. (However, not all Kantians are ready to attribute this status to the unimplanted embryo.)

This all-or-nothing view has not always been the official position of the Catholic Church. Thomas Aquinas, a doctor of the church who lived in the thirteenth century, did not find "personhood" in the fertilized embryo, but he understood that this "status" developed only at a much later stage in the process of procreation. In fact, even as late as the early 1980s, there were different Catholic opinions on the matter. One held for a qualitative difference between the "pre-embryo" less than fourteen days old following fertilization and those later phases of development that constituted the "embryo proper."

The distinction seemed to rest on the fact that the brain and nervous system are not in evidence until after two weeks of development—and that these are what identify the person. But church authorities, relying on what they termed "recent findings of biological science," decided that the moment of conception is the crucial moment. A Vatican *Instruction* of 1987 states that "in the zygote (the cell produced when the nuclei of two gametes have fused) resulting from fertilization the biological identity of a new human individual is already constituted" (quoted in Doerflinger 1999, 137). The term *pre-embryo* has been abandoned.

A counterargument to this view holds that during the first fourteen days after conception, the zygote remains capable of twinning—that is, it can become two babies instead of one. In a 1999 essay presenting the Catholic viewpoint on the matter, Richard Doerflinger dismisses this argument by writing that this happens only occasionally and that "the vast majority of embryos, from the outset, do not have the property of producing twins spontaneously" (ibid., 137–38). It is true that with manipulation, a cell can be *made* to divide and produce twins, but this is not a natural process. This would be like cloning, in which adult cells are made to reproduce themselves. "Each new finding has underscored the Catholic view of human life as a continuum from the one-cell stage onward" (ibid.).

Doerflinger goes on to argue that attempting to establish boundaries between a "nonperson" and "person" in the developmental process is arbitrary. He also remarks that the various panels set up by the federal government to deal with the question of funding stem cell research have attempted to separate out the moral responsibility of researchers from that of the people providing the embryos. In 1993, when Congress allowed federal funding for the use of fetal tissue from induced abortions, it tried to distinguish the actions of the researchers—and their intentions as well—from those of the people who had produced the abortion. This came to be called the issue of complicity, and the ethical problem was to free researchers from culpability for the deaths of fetuses. Defenders of this approach try to establish an analogy between using aborted fetuses in research and using those produced by accident and homicide victims. But Doerflinger, who says that such arguments are unconvincing, insists that induced abortion cannot be considered an accident and that consent to use the organs of homicide victims is not obtained from their killers (ibid., 140).

At the opposite pole from the official position of the Catholic Church is that of two authoritative secular ethicists, Glen McGee and Arthur Caplan, who are both on the faculty of the University of Pennsylvania. They approve unreservedly of stem cell research and think its continuation important for the relief of painful disease. Writing in the *Kennedy Institute of Ethics Journal* in 1999, these authors attempt to ascertain what it is that is unique and of continuing significance in the preimplantation embryo—that is, what is it that transcends the destruction of the embryo when stem cells are removed? The answer to this question? What persists is the embryo's recombined DNA. One cannot argue, they claim, that the cytoplasm, egg wall, and mitochondria, which are destroyed with the removal of the stem cells, are the essence of the embryo. But it is clear to them that the DNA is. "The personifying feature of the 100-cell blastocyst is its DNA," they write (155). Putting it this way, they seem to be saying that if you want to talk about "personhood," it is this that is not killed; it is this that is preserved in the destruction of the embryo used for stem cell research, thus turning the Doerflinger argument upside down. It is alive and "has a much greater chance of continuing to exist through many years than does the DNA of a frozen embryo (which in most cases already will have been slated for destruction by the IVF clinic that facilitated the donation" (ibid.). "It is not the same as the sacrifice of an adult because the life of a 100-cell blastocyst is contained in its cells' nuclear material" (ibid.). The writers dismiss the complicity issue, because the idea of complicity implies that something wrong has been done. They don't believe it has. With this argument, McGee and Caplan have presented an entirely new moral framework for assessing the morality of stem cell research.

A third position, which has many different nuances, is taken by a very large number of ethicists who favor stem cell research but who agree with the Catholic position that destroying embryos entails the sacrifice of something human. The central characteristic of this view is that while an embryo does not have rights and interests, such as a human person has, it nevertheless should not be treated like any other piece of human tissue. They think that it should be accorded special respect, because, if implanted in a uterus, it has the potential of becoming a human being. Even without such implantation, this respect is due because of the life symbolism that attaches to the embryo. (See Robertson 1999, 118.) One proponent of this view writes,

> Under this normative approach, embryo research has been deemed acceptable when necessary to pursue a legitimate scientific end that cannot be pursued by other means, when there has been local or national review, . . . and when the embryos have been donated for research with [the] informed consent of the providing couple, and additional procedural safeguards. (ibid.)

Those involved in the decision would have to weigh and balance the importance of the research vis-à-vis what is due to the embryo. For example, using stem cells for toxicology testing of cosmetics would not be acceptable (ibid.). If, however, a decision is made in favor of the research for a truly worthy project, the killing of the embryo would then be looked upon as a justified sacrifice. Whether this would mean not according the embryo the special respect that is due it, however, is not clear. Perhaps the fact of engaging in a weighing and balancing would constitute according the embryo its due respect. ES stem cell research, employing leftover IVF embryos, would on the face of it constitute a legitimate use of them. Advisory commissions both in the United States and in Great Britain have used the principle of special respect in their reports.

Another view implies that special respect is shown in the use to which the cells are put. Here is an example: "It would be wrong for a woman to intentionally become pregnant and abort her fetus to harvest its stem cells for her own use" (Juengst and Fossel 2000, 1). (See also Bruce 2002.) There has not been agreement among people who hold for this standard on whether creation of embryos for research would be acceptable procedure. In fact, some who hold with the McGee and Caplan view of the embryo and say that it is essentially its recombined DNA do not accept the legitimacy of creating embryos for research—on the grounds that this view would create a slippery slope leading to the cheapening of the value of embryos.

Among those who do not find problematical the research use of surplus embryos, the principle of subsidiarity is used to decide at what point ES cells should be employed. It is a principle that is also found in European legislation on the subject. The principle rank-orders the sources of research material, with animal material specified as the first resource to be employed. After this, adult stem cells should be used; next, affected or at-risk embryos should be taken before healthy ones. (This, however, one might think would compromise the research being done.) Lastly, surplus embryos should be used before embryos are created by therapeutic cloning (Pennings and Van Steirteghem 2004, 1060).

There is yet another way of looking at the problem. All of the views we have examined accept the idea that there is a natural trajectory from fertilization of an egg to the emergence of a fully formed human life. They differ in their conceptions of what is due this being at the various stages of emergence. But one might object that there is, in fact, no such natural trajectory. Stem cells in the blastocyst are capable of being developed in a large variety of directions. There is no "natural end" to be achieved. There is only a manipulable process that is given as "nature." (See Lauritzen 2005.) Looked at this way, the moral dilemma of harvesting stem cells from embryos disappears. The very idea of natural ends as fulfillments is lost, and the scientific way is open for us to employ the cells for whatever "ends in view" (as John Dewey would have put it) we happen to have.

Ethical Analysis of the Case

The central issue in this case is whether the federal government ought to fund embryonic stem cell research. In the background is also the question of whether it would be important to regulate private research in order to establish some ethical parameters for that work. Utilitarians, if convinced that benefits would outweigh costs, would probably urge funding of stem cell research, though it is not clear what position they would take on the issue of regulating private work. It is also not clear what measures of cost and benefit would be appropriate.

The deontological position on the funding question would vary with its position on the status of the embryo from which the stem cells were to be taken. If deontologists were to see the embryo as being already a human being, they would probably oppose opening up more lines of stem cell DNA for research. If they do not think the embryo is a person but still deserves some sort of special respect, they will call for action with those parameters in mind.

A prudent pragmatist would want to emphasize that rational discussion of a profound moral issue, discussion that might possibly lead to some resolution of differences, was important. It is vital for meaningful ethical argument that all participants in the discussion agree on the definitions of basic terms. And this is not the case here. As in the abortion controversy, rational discussion is impeded by radical differences about the meaning and status of the term *human person*, and the question of at what stage in gestation "personhood" appears. Insofar as these definitions depend on theological presuppositions—and that these, in turn, rest on faith rather than on reason—it would seem impossible for Roman Catholics and evangelical Christians to engage in a meaningful discussion of these issues with non-believers. Roman Catholic opinion as to when personhood appears has changed in the past, however, as we noted earlier, in light of scientific findings about the zygote. Would the prudent pragmatist, therefore, think it useful that those holding the official Roman Catholic view respond to the McGee and Caplan argument that in destroying an embryo for stem cell research, personhood is preserved in the salvaged DNA rather than in the parts of the blastocyst that are destroyed? Might the fact that the living DNA is used to improve the life of a fully developed person rather than to become an independent person in its own right be a problem?

What weight would prudent pragmatists give to the informed consent of parents of multiple embryos left over from in vitro fertilization procedures, a consent that allowed the use of the excess embryos in stem cell research? Would pragmatists think there was a moral difference between allowing research on the existing thirty-two lines of DNA (as federal law now allows) and using new ones from the supply of frozen embryos?

Casuistry, a forerunner of prudent pragmatism, developed, as we saw in Chapter 4 of this book, out of the ethical speculations of Catholic theologians. From what we have written here, does the Roman Catholic viewpoint on stem cell research still seem to have a casuist character, or is it more deontological in flavor? If we were to assume away the question of varying definitions of basic terms by interlocutors, what weight would a prudent pragmatist give to the argument that the use of spare embryos, left over from IVF, for stem cell research is ethically preferable to their destruction?

What would the prudent pragmatist answer to the person who is ready to argue the question from the standpoint of the scientist who denies the existence of a natural trajectory from conception to birth that we outlined earlier? Since moral chaos is implied in the idea that there is no such natural fulfillment, he or she would have to find some substitute for the unfettered will of the researcher who plans to manipulate stem cells. Since morality is a set of norms shared by society, perhaps the most plausible starting point would be the moral tradition. Whatever the end in view, it would have to fit in with what has gone before—if it is not identical with it. Without working out from the tradition, by analogy, no guidelines at all would be available. But this leads us back to our earlier frame of reference and to the questions we have canvassed earlier.

Assume now another position—that of a Roman Catholic or of a member of an evangelical church, who is a U.S. Congressman or Congresswoman. In voting on legislation to fund or prohibit the funding of embryonic stem cell research, should his or her position be determined by a personal theological commitment or by the person's role as a democratic representative charged with serving the common good of a pluralistic society? (See Cuomo positions discussed in Chapter 6.)

In the fall of 2005 two new ways of obtaining embryonic stem cells were reported in the journal *Nature*; the research was done with mice. The first involved creating an embryo that had been genetically disabled, so that it was unable to attach to the uterus. In the second case, researchers plucked a single cell from an eight-cell embryo, leaving the rest of the embryo intact and capable of being implanted. Bioethicist Jonathan Moreno, of the University of Virginia, thinks that neither method solves the ethical problem. He questions whether it is ethical to create a disabled embryo, using the first method.

As to the second, one might well consider a single cell of an embryo to be itself an embryo. Moreno is quoted as having remarked, "I don't think you can technologically fix your way out of ethical issues" (Hostetler 2005). Tadeusz Pacholczyk, a Catholic ethicist commenting on the second method, said that taking the single cell would constitute a violation of the embryo. He also agreed with Moreno that the lone cell could be regarded as itself an embryo and that its destruction would constitute taking a human life (Cook 2005). The ethical problems canvassed in our case, therefore, remain.

Therapeutic Cloning of Stem Cells

While it has not been difficult to find consensus across the globe that reproductive human cloning is not acceptable and should be legally banned, therapeutic cloning of embryos for research is another matter. Here we find a marked division among those who are prepared to recommend use of normally engendered embryos for stem cell research.

As that research advances, it will become important to isolate tissue that is compatible with the immune systems of prospective patients. Thus, one writer tells us that "the ability to develop a large library of ES cell genotypes that encode different transplantation antigens so that cell replacement therapies would be available for a large range of the population, likely would depend on the creation of embryos expressly for that purpose." In some cases it might be necessary to create by nuclear transfer cloning from a prospective patient's own cells if there are to be on hand histocompatible ES cells for that patient (Robertson 1999, 122).

Opponents of cloning embryos through nuclear transfer processes may assert either deontologic (symbolic) concerns about respect for human life or consequentialist ones—namely, that there would be bad social results. Those in the former category see cloning of stem cells as an inherently disrespectful attitude toward human life, since the embryo in this case has only instrumental value. Others disagree. Some find an inconsistency in this position, however, since those in this category hold that the preimplantation embryo is too little developed to be considered to have rights or interests. Furthermore, one writer argues also that the deontologic constraint against creating embryos for research can be overridden by the specially compelling considerations of human need. He does this by claiming there is an analogy with breaking a promise in order to deal with a crisis. Admittedly, the action remains morally problematic in either case. "In the promise breaking case, an apology will normally be in order, and sometimes even some sort of compensation" (Fitzpatrick 2003, 29). In the case of creating embryos for research, "we should not allow ourselves to grow too comfortable" with the action. And we should accept that one cannot justify destroying cloned embryos expressly created for research by asserting that the destruction is foreseen, but not intended, as in the case of bringing embryos for IVF into being (ibid.). One should always be on the lookout for alternative procedures.

Consequentialists fear that permitting cloning may in the future lead to the commodification and commercialization of embryos—or to their production for trivial uses. Ethicists such as Arthur Caplan, whom we spoke of earlier, combine both deontologic and consequentialist concerns. Some writers think these concerns are not well founded, however, since, given the controversial nature of the project, cloned embryos would be created for only the most compelling reasons (see Robertson, op. cit., 124). One tells us that "it seems deeply inconsistent for us to be so repulsed by the exploitation involved in cloning as to oppose it despite its plausible promise of benefits to countless patients, while at the same time holding the exploited entities in low enough regard as to find IVF practices unexceptionable" (Fitzpatrick, op. cit., 29).

Other Dilemmas

The moral problems implicit in the idea of stem cell research extend in all directions. Were we to overcome objections both to using "spare" embryos and to creating others by cloning, we should still not be out of the woods. Consider what would happen if Alzheimer's disease, Parkinson's disease, and other similar killers were successfully treated by the implantation of healthy stem cells. There would be vast changes in the structure of society. Such successes might push life expectancy, in the western world at least, up past 100 or even to 120. Old age might be moved backward by twenty to forty years, creating a new class of people who are in good, if not robust health. If the working life did not grow longer accordingly, where would the resources come from to sustain this population? And how would these people occupy themselves? (Bruce, op. cit.) The regeneration of vital tissues through ES cell technology might eventually even affect our conception of personal identity. And consider the burden that would be placed on our systems of medical care and social security (Robertson, op. cit., 110).

In the face of such a range of moral puzzles, how should we proceed to face these challenges in a responsible way? That policies will be adopted, there is no doubt. But how can we be certain that they will be rational? This is surely not a matter to be debated only in the halls of Congress, by policy analysts, or by bioethicists. As one writer has put it, "these are developments that call for a new type of contract between science and society . . . [for a dialogue between experts and rulers and] civil society" (Bruce, op. cit.). As we wrote in Chapter 5, the ideas of scientists and ethicists must be set forth in public fora and thoroughly debated and digested there. The revolutionary achievements in biotechnology challenge the many levels of our democratic society to engage one another in a detailed, informed, and rational discussion of ends and means. "People from all walks of life—scientists, lawyers, ethicists, clergy and the general public—should be involved in making the decision" (Wright 1999). Our complex and omnipresent technology of communication needs to be brought systematically into play if we are to find our way out of the ethical tangle confronting us.

As a society, we need first to rank-order the values involved in the issue of stem cell research. Are we ready to accord to preimplantation embryos the status of human beings, with all the rights and interests of those who have been born? If so, we must give up on the project of embryonic stem cell research. If this position is espoused only by a minority, what status should the majority accord to the embryo that is understood as only a symbol of human life? What respect is due to it, and how should it be registered? Perhaps showing respect will consist in being sure that the uses to which we put our projected research are of the highest priority for the cure of diseases for which there are no alternative resources. Here we are in a combined deontologic and consequentialist framework—or a prudent-pragmatic one, which embraces both.

What about cloning cells for research? What is the danger of sliding down a slippery slope that will coarsen national attitudes toward human life? Is it feasible to ban reproductive cloning (for the purpose of producing babies), while permitting therapeutic cloning (for the purpose of deriving stem cells for use in cures)?

There are other purely consequentialist concerns that must be weighed and balanced. How many of our scarce monetary resources are we willing to budget for stem cell research in comparison with other public health needs? This will be a question first for policy analysts at the NIH, then for Congress and the administration. The latter must also calculate the total sum to be directed to improving the national health through scientific advance and how much through social change and through creating greater equality of well-being, especially for children. Detailed data must be collected both on the state of the national health in comparison with that of other postindustrial countries and on the comparative access of all groups in our society to the primary goods. The condition of the environment must also be factored in. The upshot is that rationally to answer certain questions—for example, "Shall there be embryonic stem cell research?" and, if so, "How much federal funding should it get?"—can only be answered after a large-scale comparison of values has been made at all possible levels of our democratic society. Anything short of such a large-scale cooperative social effort will be entirely inadequate.

ORGAN TRANSPLANTATION AND ORGAN DONATION

Over the four decades since 1960, the technical capability for successfully transplanting human organs has developed remarkably. We are now able to transplant kidneys, livers, pancreases, hearts, and lungs from both live and cadaveric donors. This development has been largely due to the discovery of new immunosuppressive drugs that prevent organ rejection. In 1999 it was possible to provide 22,000 successful transplants, both for the relief of suffering and the prolongation of life. With the new ability has gone a vast increase in the demand for such organs, witnessed in the increasing length of waiting lists for transplant surgery. In the year 2003 this amounted to some 80,000 people, with ten to twelve people dying each day for lack of a new organ. In 2004, 10,603 people donated organs, but 87,292 had requested one. Demand thus continually outstrips supply.

Naturally, this has sparked lots of discussion about how the supply of organs might be increased, and a variety of proposals have been put forward to accomplish this end. First and foremost, to promote efficiency and honesty in organ procurement, there was a need for a national system for procurement and allocation. The first legislation to emerge from the ensuing political activity was the National Organ Transplantation Act of 1984 (NOTA). In addition to setting up a national clearing-house, this act provided that no transfer of organs could be done for a "valuable consideration." This act was designed to head off the development of a commercial market in organs, though its actual effect was to drive the market underground. The procurement system has operated with the donation of living organs, from relatives and friends of the persons in need, or with cadaveric organs obtained similarly through donations by relatives of the deceased. The ban on commercial sales flowed directly from the Kantian strain in our political culture that demands that human persons be considered always as ends in themselves, not only as means. It was thought by those who drafted the legislation that selling one's parts was a kind of prostitution, making oneself into a mere object. It was also believed that, as a practical matter, the potential harms outweighed potential benefits.

Despite NOTA, ethical controversy has continued, with proposals for various kinds of sale mechanisms vying with more moderate schemes for "gifted giving" short of pure commercial transactions. A considerable journal literature has accumulated, setting forth the entire spectrum of argument. Those who embrace the most extreme individualistic position in the debate have been the libertarians, with ethicists Michael B. Gill and Robert M. Sade authoring one of the clearest and most detailed statements on behalf of the sales approach.

They call not for an open market, but rather for the right of donors to give organs for a monetary consideration. No one, however, would be allowed to buy in the open market. Procurement would be, as now, by a single central buyer, who would also handle allocation according to need, a monopsonistic arrangement. These authors argue for the ethicality of their proposal by the prudent-pragmatic device of analogy, claiming that the sale of organs is analogous to the uncontested right of people to sell blood. They also note that members of the procurement agency, doctors involved in transplant operations, other medical staff, and hospitals now receive pay for their services—and that the supply of needed material should not have a different moral status. Since giving is legal, they do not see why addition of the motive of self-interest should be a barrier. (To the libertarian, it is, after all, the motive of self-interest that is the prime mover in human affairs.) In addition these writers claim that there is no empirical evidence that parting with one of two kidneys would create a substantial risk to the donor, nor that the selling of kidneys would diminish the supply of those who donate without financial incentive. They do not apply this argument to hearts and livers for live donors, of course. The demand for kidneys is one of the highest.

They try to meet head-on the Kantian objection that selling organs is treating oneself as a means. The law, they argue, is not generally used to enforce duties to the self. Selling a kidney, they further claim, is not analogous to either suicide or slavery. Our kidneys do not constitute our humanity. The seller retains control of his or her destiny. The true Kantian standpoint in this matter, the writers claim, is the requirement of informed consent. This is what guarantees our autonomy. They also do not think that selling kidneys produces social inequality, since due to the regulatory system employed, the poor would have an equal chance with the rich to receive a needed kidney. Only medical criteria would be used for allocation.

To the argument that only the poor would sell, out of desperation, and that this development would constitute exploitation, Gill and Sade reply that, analogously, only the poor will pick fruit and vegetables, or clean toilets. Therefore, unless we are ready to claim that capitalism as a system is exploitative, we should not consider kidney sales to be so. The committed

Marxist would, of course, accept that capitalism is inherently exploitative, but our political culture, preeminently a capitalist culture, rejects this idea. Gill and Sade also claim that there is no danger of a slippery slope leading to the sale of hearts by living donors. This is too manifestly different. (See Gill and Sade 2002.)

Cynthia Cohen, writing in the same issue of the *Kennedy Institute* journal as Gill and Sade, denies their claim of an analogy between kidneys and blood. Blood, she writes, is continuously renewed, whereas kidneys are fixed and always the same. Also, losing a pint of blood is not inimical to body function, but losing a kidney is. The second kidney is a backup, which in certain circumstances can be vital. Unlike the donation of blood, the sale of a kidney calls for intrusive surgery. (See Cohen 2002.)

Other writers have argued for a version of the sale schema that is less extreme than the one proposed by Gill and Sade. Abdallah Daar, for example, suggests a system of remuneration that stops short of monetary payments. A donation might be recompensed by time off from work, or by the supply of child care to the donor, or by the payment of medical expenses. The American Medical Association has moved even further toward the commodification of organs by endorsing a futures market in cadaveric organs as an expression of individual autonomy. (See Daar 1998.)

Francis Delmonico and two coauthors (2002) open an essay on gifted donation by noting that the legal gate to paid transplants has already been opened by giving free passage home to patients who go abroad for operations that involve organ purchase. They also think that the processing and sale for profit of bone and tissue, which can be stored, has already circumvented the intention of the National Organ Transplantation Act. And they point to the introduction in state legislatures of bills to permit compensation for donors' travel and subsistence. They therefore urge the legalization of still other measures of gifted donation.

One measure would be the institution of a donor medal of honor. Another would be a federal act reimbursing deceased donors' families or estates for funeral expenses. This might be enacted on an experimental basis to see whether one might measure a comparative increase in the supply of donated organs. Still another suggestion is the creation of an organ exchange program. A family member who is willing to donate an organ but whose blood is incompatible with that of the intended recipient could place his or her kidney in an exchange program and receive from it one that is compatible with that of the relative he or she wished to benefit. Yet another device to encourage donations would be medical leave for organ donation. This would, of course, require the cooperation of business firms. Income tax deductions and estate tax exclusions have also been suggested. There is also a proposal for a system of insurance, in which potential donors pledge their organs at death against the benefit of receiving one in the event of a future disability. In all these suggestions the writers believe that the symbol of altruism has been preserved and that this is important for maintaining the kind of society in which we live. A purely commercial approach, they believe, would foster the development of class distinctions—and ultimately infringe on the values of life and liberty that are central to our way of life (Delmonico et al., 2002).

Public opinion, at least in its elite echelons, has gradually been moving away from the 1984 legislative ban on organ sales. Donald Joraleman (2001) notes that in 1996 there was a call to reconsider the NOTA ban at the annual meeting of the U.S. Department of Health and Human Services Division of Transplantation. Somewhat later, we find the Council on Ethical and Judicial Affairs of the AMA proposing a futures market in cadaveric organs. According to this proposal, people would contract to have their organs harvested at death, with the stipulation that a named third party receive money if the organs are used. This was followed by a call from the International Forum for Transplant Ethics for a reconsideration of the ban on the sale of kidneys by living donors. Opinion surveys show an even split in the mind of the general public on the question of organ sales, with citizens under thirty-five more ready to entertain the idea. Introduction of the concept of rewarded giving, an effort to retain an altruistic note in a commercial transaction, has been changing the terms of the debate as well.

This development is helped along by an effort to substitute ethically neutral terms into the language of the discussion. The groups in favor of change have not yet engaged in much public relations activity, but this effort is beginning (Joraleman 2001).

The ethical dilemma in the controversy about organ sales lies in a conflict between the value of supplying human need and the value of altruistic action. If we place a supply of vital organs in the marketplace, are we thereby eroding human fellow-feeling and generosity? Is self-interest already so strong a motive in American political culture that we endanger the social bond by encouraging it even more? If so, we are faced with the paradox that a policy designed to serve an important human need might involve diminishing communal sentiment. Would this be the case?

If we look at other societies' experience, we find in some cases that a market in kidneys has hampered the development of cadaver and liver-related donor programs. In India, for example, 60 percent of kidney donations are paid. (This is the case even though sales have been outlawed and criminalized.) The practice, according to a pair of Indian scholars, has resulted in an increase in the stark inequalities that have traditionally marked Indian society. Should we expect the same result in more equal, developed societies such as our own? (Phadke and Anandh 2002)

The short supply of available organs in comparison with the large demand has raised other ethical questions, not just the one discussed earlier. At present, organs are allocated according to an assessment of medical need, and waiting lists are established on this same principle. Should our society introduce other criteria for preferment in allocation? Looked at from a utilitarian standpoint, some kinds of people are of more value than others for increasing the overall social good. Should scientists whose skills contribute heavily to technological advances from which we all profit receive priority status? What about people whose skills contribute heavily to national security? What of artists who raise the level of high culture?

Should a society in which equality of opportunity is a leading value get involved in aristocratic discriminations of this kind? Should our utilitarian side give way to our Kantian in this case? Or should we move in the other direction? Minorities are heavily represented in the ranks of those awaiting organ donations. Should they be given priority over white middle and upper class people because of this disproportionate burden of illness? Or would this infringe on the preeminent value that our culture places on every human life?

ENHANCING THE ORGAN SUPPLY BY CHANGING THE MORAL CULTURE: A CASE STUDY

We have seen that the patient demand for donated organs continues, from year to year, to outstrip the supply. What might be the most effective and most ethical way to bring the two into equilibrium, a goal which is an undisputed social good?

That something needs to be done is evidenced by the story of Todd Krampitz, a thirty-two-year-old Texan who was beset by cancer and needed a liver. He and his wife bought advertising space in newspapers, had ads posted on billboards around Houston, and appeared on nationally broadcast TV news shows to publicize his plight. Their primary intention was not to encourage Americans to donate more organs, but to persuade a family to donate a liver to Krampitz directly. Their quest succeeded.

Arthur Caplan, a well-known bioethicist, in an online article in MSNBC News, deplored Krampitz' action as an unethical undermining of the national distribution system, and he called on Congress, the secretary of Health and Human Services, and the president to close the loophole in the law "so that individual self-interest cannot destroy the common good" (MSNBC Newsonline, 8-25-04). (See also Caplan and Coelho 1998.) The United Network for Organ Sharing, a quasi-public agency supported by a Health and Human Services grant, maintains a list of people in the United States who are waiting for liver transplants. At the time that Krampitz found a donor, there were more than 17,000 people on the list. "The system," writes Caplan,

> which has worked well for almost 20 years, uses a complex set of formulas, including blood type, tissue type, size of donor, medical urgency and likelihood of survival, to distribute organs. Krampitz would not have gotten a liver using the current formula. He was not as near death as others were on the day of his operation. And his cancer is so advanced that it may be impossible to make a transplant work for him. (ibid.)

Caplan may overstate the case when he writes that "someone else who could not afford to take out ads died because Krampitz was not told to wait his turn" (ibid.). The liver that Krampitz received would in all probability not have been available to those on the national waiting list. It would not have been donated at all had it not been for the advertising. But the case does raise issues of fairness and equality that can be resolved only by substantially increasing the supply of organs. What is the optimal ethical way to do this?

We observed earlier that despite historical reservations about the ethicality of a commodification approach, public opinion seems to be moving in that direction. Witness the greater willingness of younger respondents in opinion polls to sanction the use of the market principle in this area. Leading institutions such as the AMA have also embraced the individualist approach with their proposal for a futures market in cadaveric organs. Amitai Etzioni, a leading figure in the communitarian movement that we discussed in Chapter 2, has proposed in a recent essay a communitarian alternative to this individualist, market initiative (Etzioni 2003). Etzioni presents his argument as a challenge to the assumptions of neoclassical economics, which underlie the view that commodification is the best way to increase the supply of donor organs. Commodification assumes that people's preferences are fixed and that to change them—to bring people to do something they otherwise would fail to do—financial incentives must be offered. Etzioni, in contrast, holds for a psychology that assumes that preferences can be changed by moral suasion. People will change their preferences and be willing to do things they otherwise would not, "not because they are compensated, but because they have come to believe that these things are right" (ibid.).

In this case Etzioni sees the problem as one of changing the moral culture—of establishing in the public mind the view that organ donation is an act that people perform "because they consider it their social responsibility, something a good person does akin to volunteering." Most people "could be swayed relatively readily, if the moral culture around them changed" (ibid.), since polls have shown that 85 percent of Americans already support the idea of organ donation. In his essay Etzioni outlines a program of cultural dialogue akin to those that have taken place in recent decades about obligations to the environment, about race relations (affirmative action), about the death penalty, and about gay marriage. He thinks it is clear that these dialogues have significantly changed the moral opinions of a large number of Americans.

To trigger a nationwide moral dialogue about organ donation, Etzioni proposes a number of catalysts. One would be a new donation sign-up form in which the act of donating is described as a moral duty. (By contrast, standard cards presently in use advance no moral argument, but only provide an opportunity to donate.) Another would be the composition of brochures to accompany donor cards, such as the Donate Life initiative of the Department of Health and Human Services, one in which donation would be represented as a moral duty, not merely an option. Typically, these appeals "do not bring into the picture the expectations of one's fellow community members, . . . and [they] are relatively 'cool' in tone," Etzioni writes (ibid.). He thinks it would also be useful to multiply the opportunities to commit to donating. To do this, the "said form [should] be handed out in each doctor's office, clinic, and hospital" with the other forms one usually fills out on medical visits. Even if thousands of forms have to be handed out before a single new donor is recruited—and whether or not people are persuaded to donate—the massive dissemination of the forms, he thinks, would help change the moral culture. Creating an electronic book of donors might also help. This would give community recognition to donors and would "put mild social pressure on those who have not yet stepped forward" (ibid.). Etzioni adds to these measures the proposal that each state enact a law to make signing a donor card a binding commitment. At present, though legally entitled to proceed to harvest organs on a donor's death, medical personnel often consult family members about it and may be prevented by them from proceeding with the harvesting. Etzioni contrasts this approach of the responsive communitarian to increasing organ donations with that of the authoritarian communitarian. The first seeks "a careful balance between autonomy and the common good" whereas the latter assumes that the "common good should trump individual rights" (ibid.).

Ethical Analysis of the Case: Communitarianism vs. Commodification

How do we increase the supply of organs available for transplantation? Utilitarians, who share the psychological hedonist assumptions of the libertarian, would no doubt opt for commodification and would be pleased to accept the arguments of Gill and Sade about the capitalist approach. The most efficient way of maximizing the goal value would be the utilitarian rule of thumb in deciding. Utilitarians would agree with William Anderson that scarce goods must be rationed and that the market accomplishes this admirably. "A free market price" he writes, "is not an arbitrary designation. . . It reflects the relative scarcity of [a] good relative to the demand for it" (Anderson 2003).

The deontologist would have qualms about people selling off parts of themselves. Donation is one thing, and the deontologist would have no problems with unselfish giving. But selling an organ would imply both financial need and a kind of coercion which the deontologist would find deplorable. A person is an end in him- or herself and should always be treated so by self as by others.

The prudent pragmatist would keep in mind both the efficiency norm of the utilitarian and the equity norm of the deontologist. Might commodification have a corrosive effect on American moral culture? How broadly should market incentives operate in public life? Would pragmatists be able to state a criterion for making distinctions? How would they appraise Etzioni's communitarian approach—changing the moral culture? Since he envisages using state law to make donation commitments legally binding, is Etzioni's method purely one of encouraging dialogue, or does it involve an element of coercion? A prudent pragmatist would not find coercion in itself unacceptable; it would be a question of what kind and under what circumstances. The communitarian way of encouraging organ donations frankly accepts the legitimacy of developing social pressures on citizens to "do their moral duty." Is this kind of coercion acceptable to the prudent pragmatist under the circumstances? If you were a state legislator or a federal member of Congress or the Senate, how might you use the force of law to promote the goal of increasing organ donations?

REFERENCES

Anderson, William. "Communitarianism and Commodification" (2003), Mises Institute online, at http://www.mises.org/fullstory.aspx?control=1174 (accessed 12/29/04).

Bruce, Donald M. "Stem Cells, Embryos and Cloning—Unravelling the Ethics of a Knotty Debate." *Journal of Molecular Biology* (June 17, 2002), http://www.sciencedirect.com/science?_ob=ArticleURL&_udi=B6WK7-462733v-B&_cover . . . (accessed 6/18/04).

Bulger, Ruth E. et al. *Ethical Dimensions of the Biological Sciences*. Cambridge, England, and New York: Cambridge University Press, 1993.

Caplan, Arthur, and Daniel H. Coelho. *The Ethics of Organ Transplantation*. New York: Prometheus Books, 1998.

———. "Cutting in Line for Organ Transplants," MSNBC News (August 24, 2004), http://www.bioethics.net/articles.php?viewCat=2&articled=67. . .   (accessed 3/3/05).

Cohen, Cynthia. "Public Policy and the Sale of Human Organs." *Kennedy Institute of Ethics Journal* 12, no. 1 (March 2002): 47–64.

Cook, Gareth. "New Approach Reported in Stem Cell Creation." *Boston Globe* (October 17, 2005), http://web.lexis.com/universe/document?_m=30182fb33c6lbdc315d637a6ea2dcd6l . . . (accessed 10/19/05).

Daar, Abdallah S. "Paid Organ Donation—The Gray Basket Concept." *Journal of Medical Ethics* 24, no. 6 (December 1998): 365–68.

Delmonico, Francis L. et al. "Ethical Incentives—Not Payment—for Organ Donation." *New England Journal of Medicine* 346, no. 25 (June 20, 2002): 2002–5.

Doerflinger, Richard M. "The Ethics of Funding Embryonic Stem Cell Research: A Catholic Viewpoint." *Kennedy Institute of Ethics Journal* 9, no. 2 (1999): 137–50.

Editorial. "New Allies for Cell Research." *Los Angeles Times* (May 12, 2004), B12.

Eiseman, Elisa, National Bioethics Advisory Commission. *Contributing to Public Policy*. Rand Institute, 2003.

Etzioni, Amitai. "Organ Donation: A Communitarian Approach." *The Communitarian Network*, at http://www2.gwu.edu/~ccps/organ_donation.pdf (accessed March 16, 2003).

Fitzpatrick, William. "Surplus Embryos, Nonreproductive Cloning, and the Intend/Foresee Distinction." *The Hastings Center Report* 33, no. 3 (May/June 2003): 29.

Gill, Michael B., and Robert M. Sade. "Paying for Kidneys: The Case Against Prohibition." *Kennedy Institute of Ethics Journal* 12, no. 1 (March 2002): 17–45.

Hostetler, A.J. "An Answer to Stem-Cell Morality?" *Richmond Times Dispatch* (October 17, 2005), http://web.lexis-nexis.com/universe/document?_m=d4323178fcaa6f53b6ad2cd50bd0f5f3&. . . (accessed 10/19/05).

Joraleman, Donald. "Shifting Ethics: Debating the Incentive Question in Organ Transplantation." *Journal of Medical Ethics* 27 no. 1 (February 2001): 30–35.

Juengst, Eric, and Michael Fossel. "The Ethics of Embryonic Stem Cell Research." *Journal of the American Medical Association* (December 27, 2000): 1–5.

Lauritzen, Paul. "Stem Cells, Biotechnology, and Human Rights: Implications for a Posthuman Future." *Hastings Center Report* 35, no. 2 (March 4, 2005): 25–33.

Leo, John. "Genetic Advances, Ethical Risks." *U.S. News and World Report* (September 25, 1989), 59.

McGee, Glenn, and Arthur Caplan. "The Ethics and Politics of Small Sacrifice in Stem Cell Research." *Kennedy Institute of Ethics Journal* 9, no. 2 (1999): 151–58.

Pennings, Guido, and Andre van Steirteghem. "The Subsidiarity Principle in the Context of Embryonic Stem Cell Research." *Human Reproduction* 19, no. 5 (2004): 1060–64.

President's Council on Bioethics, *Monitoring Stem Cell Research*, Washington, D.C. 2004, ohttp://pool-access.qfo.gov/GPO/LPS 46139. . . (accessed 4/26/06).

Phadke, Risore D., and Urmila Anandh. "Ethics of Paid Organ Donation." *Pediatric Nephrology* 17, no. 5 (May 2002): 309–11.

Robertson, John A. "Ethics and Policy in Embryonic Stem Cell Research." *Kennedy Institute of Ethics Journal* 9, no. 2 (1999): 109–36.

Weiss, Rick. "58 Senators Seek Easing of Rules for Stem Cells." *The Washington Post* (June 8, 2004), A3.

Wright, Shirley. "Human Embryonic Stem-Cell Research: Science and Ethics." *American Scientist* (July/August 1999), http://proquest.umi.com/pqdweb?index=o&did=000000042564368&SuchMode=1&sid=8&F. . . (accessed 6/14/04).

Zaner, Richard M. "Finessing Nature." *Philosophy and Public Policy Quarterly* 23, no. 3 (Summer 2003): 14–18.

CHAPTER 10

The Natural Environment and Human Well-Being

In the United States, concern for protecting the natural environment through government action gained prominence only in the latter third of the twentieth century. Driven by a capitalist ideology that drew on the value of utilizing nature's resources to the fullest extent possible and faced with seemingly limitless natural resources, Americans for the first several centuries of their residence in North America focused almost entirely on industrial development and agricultural production. There were, of course, those who sought to protect America's natural environment even in the late nineteenth century, and they found a twentieth-century champion in Theodore Roosevelt, who stands as the first president to place protection of the natural environment on the national agenda. In this, Roosevelt was strongly supported by his friend Gifford Pinchot, whom he appointed head of the newly named Forest Service and who has been widely recognized as the leading conservationist of the Progressive Era. Following Roosevelt's administration, Americans were distracted by two world wars and the economic ups and downs of the Roaring Twenties and the Great Depression, respectively. During the New Deal, the Civilian Conservation Corps is salient as a program that contributed to improving the environment, although the case can be made that sending young people into rural areas to work in the fields and forests was designed primarily to provide them some kind of gainful employment. Also during the New Deal the harnessing of America's rivers for hydroelectric dam projects to foster economic development, to control flood damage, and to lower unemployment became important.

ENVIRONMENTAL POLICY—A MAJOR CONCERN

By the 1960s, however, the progress of American industrialization had reached a stage at which its threats to the natural environment began to attract widespread attention. Prominent among those concerned about damage to the environment was Rachel Carson, whose book *Silent Spring* (1962) rapidly became a bestseller. Carson publicized the threats posed by the widespread use of pesticides, and, as with many of the works describing dangers to the environment, she tended to be graphic in her portraits of impending environmental disaster. To their credit, publicists like Carson recognized that technological progress carried an environmental dark side. These concerns were reinforced in the 1980s when thousands died because of an industrial accident at Bhopal, India, in December 1984. Later, in November 1986, at Chernobyl in the Ukraine, the worst nuclear power plant accident in history spread radioactive fallout across Europe. Clearly, the American government had some obligation to protect against such disasters.

Others were fearful that unrestrained industrial development would damage the environment's capacity to provide for the human race. Perhaps the clearest theoretical statement of this position was made by Garrett Hardin in his essay "The Tragedy of the Commons," published in *Science* in 1968. Hardin hypothesized conditions in a village in which the local folk had communal access to a common pasture to graze their flocks. The long-term public good would dictate a coordinated, planned use of the commons to preserve it for generations to come. But without such oversight each herder would look toward the immediate advantage to his or her own flock, with the tragic result that the commons would eventually be overgrazed and ruined as a source of free forage. Hardin was primarily concerned about the effects of uncontrolled population growth and the possibility that such growth would overreach Earth's capacity to sustain a large population increase. But his homily also served as a metaphor for the effects of private enterprise on common goods, such as water and air in the modern era. He wrote,

> In a reverse way, the tragedy of the commons reappears in the problems of pollution. Here it is not a question of taking something out of the commons, but of putting something in. . . . The calculations of utility are much the same as before. The rational man finds that his share of the cost of the wastes he discharges into the commons is less than the cost of purifying his wastes before releasing them. (ibid., 1245)

The concerns of Carson and Hardin were quickly reinforced by many others, with the result that protection of the environment soon became a major priority for Americans. As Mary Graham points out, in 1965 the environment was not considered a major issue by most Americans; by 1970 it ranked second only to crime as something that Americans thought needed action (1999, 3). On April 22 of that year, Americans turned out by the millions to participate in the nation's first Earth Day. This event has been described as the "nation's largest environmental demonstration ever" (ibid., 2). By 1970 political leaders from both parties were vying with each other to project the most environmentally friendly image to the American public.

The years from 1969 to 1973 stand out as especially significant for governmental environmental action. During this period eight major statutes dealing with various aspects of environmental policy were passed. In 1970 President Richard M. Nixon established the Environmental Protection Agency (EPA) through his executive reorganization authority. The EPA quickly became the major regulatory agency at the national level, and it remains the primary initiator of environmental policy today. These governmental moves were strongly backed by an increase in the number of environmental activist groups and by an explosion of citizen involvement in such groups. In 1960 these groups could claim a membership of about 124,000. By 1972 this figure had mushroomed to over 1,000,000 members (ibid., 37).

While these actions were evidence of important moves by the national government into the area of environmental policy, their fragmented nature reflected the uniquely American approach toward dealing with major issues. The establishment of the EPA itself was basically a reassembling of fifteen existing programs from the Department of Health, Education, and Welfare; the Department of Interior; the Department of Agriculture; and other noncabinet-level agencies. Moreover, a number of environmentally significant programs remained under the aegis of other agencies. Congress compounded the fragmentary nature of national environmental policy by dribbling out regulatory authority through a series of major statutes during the 1970s. In the words of Daniel J. Fiorino, each of these laws "specifies different goals, requires different approaches to balancing risks and benefits, and relies on different implementation strategies" (1998, 204). The power of the EPA to act was further diluted by the demands of a federal system that allocated discretion and authority to the states as well.

Added to the diffuse nature of environmental policy has been its permeability to judicial action by various interests. While environmental groups were proliferating in number and growing in membership, the Supreme Court was increasing their opportunities for influencing public policy. Prior to the 1970s, these groups focused their activities on elected officials and the electoral process. Their access to the courts at the federal level was limited by the Supreme Court's restrictive interpretation of the Administrative Procedure Act of 1946. Under the Court's interpretation of standing, a party had to show tangible injury to be able to obtain a judicial hearing. However, through a sequence of cases, the Supreme Court gradually made intangible injury claims a basis for standing to sue. In particular, groups claiming to represent neighborhoods, tourists, or sports enthusiasts, could claim that government action or development by private enterprise threatened their aesthetic enjoyment of the natural world. Broadening the standing requirement in this direction was tailor-made for environmental groups wanting to use the courts to further their causes. The result has been that "[i]nterest groups that represent a range of views on environmental matters—from regulated companies, to trade associations, to nonprofit environmental and citizens' groups—participate actively in legislative, executive, and judicial arenas to influence policy" (ibid., 204).

As environmental issues gained access across the public agenda, public discourse evolved to accommodate a more sympathetic view of the need to act to protect the environment. Dryzek points out that what were once seen as swamps are now labeled wetlands. Unsettled areas described as part of the American frontier are now called wilderness, with the accompanying understanding that these areas should be protected (1997, 3–4). Dryzek also notes that Weyerhauser, one of the nation's largest timber companies, promotes itself as the "tree growing company" (ibid., 99). The reader can undoubtedly come up with other examples of the movement of American discourse toward a more environmentally friendly tone. This evolution of dialogue reflects changed public assumptions about the environment, which have also heavily influenced how policymakers have approached perceived environmental problems.

Command and Control

Graham suggests that in 1970 Americans believed that urgent government action was needed to deal with what they perceived as an environmental crisis. They assumed that government could, in fact, fashion effective remedies. Thus, the legislation enacted between 1969 and 1973 was characterized by the "command-and-control" model, meaning that the national government would set standards, requirements, and deadlines, and all others—private industry, local governments—were expected to fall into line. As described by Fiorino, the actions required by the EPA have had a strong tendency to create an "adversarial" relationship with those regulated. "Often the laws and regulations that implement them [EPA decisions] are detailed and prescriptive; they give industry little discretion for deciding how to achieve environmental goals most effectively" (op. cit., 207).

Michael E. Porter, a student of American management practices, has echoed Fiorino's views. In Porter's opinion environmental regulation has too often deterred necessary innovation that could both spur industrial productivity and lessen pollution emissions (1998, 354). At the same time, instead of instinctively "digging in their heels" (ibid., 369), industrial leaders would be better served by recognizing that pollution is a system inefficiency that is costly to them. Pollution byproducts require disposal expenses and incur fines and other sanctions from government. Improving resource productivity could make American industry much more competitive in European nations that have more rigorous pollution standards than the United States, and such productivity improvements could maximize their resource use. Porter argues that government regulation should be fashioned to stimulate product innovation and to maintain a level playing field so that those companies working to lessen pollution are not competitively disadvantaged by those who do nothing (ibid., 363). However, the policy of command-and-control "has spawned an industry of litigators and consultants that drains resources away from real solutions" (ibid., 354).

Major improvements in the environment were achieved during the decades following 1970, but as the 1990s neared, American concerns about a robust federal system, the rights of private entrepreneurs, and the importance of individual initiative began to reassert themselves (Fiorino, op. cit., 208). Graham contends that strong ideological positions were being articulated at the national level, but that entrepreneurs and local government officials were turning toward pragmatic adjustments to deal with individual and local problems. In 1984 R. Shep Melnick had also recognized the disjunction between nationally articulated goals and the practical implementation of environmental policy with the comment that "our symbols are more in need of reform than our practices" (1984, 134).

As early as the 1970s, the EPA began to experience some of the inherent difficulties in a command-and-control approach to protecting the environment. This approach was made even more onerous by Congress's turn to "technology forcing" as a means of achieving a cleaner environment. Basically, Congress began to insist on deadlines by which certain standards had to be met. Immersed in the pluralism of the American economy and political apparatus, such a rigid, draconian approach met a predictable fate. Few deadlines were met, although progress was made in all areas. As an alternative, EPA administrators moved to enlist the dynamics of the market system in their attempts to control pollution. Chief among these efforts was the use of offsets to pollution that industry could use to build new plants or allow expansion in an area. These offsets, sometimes called tradable discharge permits, allowed an industry to purchase from industries closing or reducing activity the rights to their pollution emissions as long as the result was a net overall gain in improved quality. The long-term effect was an improvement in pollution control while allowing continued economic growth. Additionally, the opportunity to sell their shares of pollution may have made plant closure of some of the dirtier, older plants more attractive.

A More Flexible Approach

There is no question that the younger Bush administration's environmental policies marked a major shift in orientation. The Clinton administration had prided itself on its environmental activism. However, Republican capture of the House of Representatives slowed any major strides in environmental policy, leading environmental scholar Walter A. Rosenbaum to conclude "In the end the Clinton administration was distinguished more by its ambition than its accomplishments" (Rosenbaum 2005, 8). Nonetheless, through executive orders, the appointment of aggressively environmentalist administrators, and litigation, the Clinton administration continued to push command-and-control environmental efforts. These efforts, Rosenbaum suggests, led to a "hardening" of the "mood of discontent with the existing regulatory regime" (ibid., 9) by the end of the Clinton presidency. The ensuing Bush administration insisted on a much more flexible approach toward environmental policy, which was evidenced by lowering standards and abbreviating procedures. Thus, the restrictions on developing wetlands areas were weakened (Marquis 2002), environmental reviews required for certain types of logging on federal lands were removed (Brinkley 2004), the determination that mercury emissions are hazardous was rescinded (ibid.), and large livestock farms were offered an amnesty from prosecution for air pollution emissions if they joined a data monitoring program for two years (Janofsky, January 22, 2005).

These changes by the Bush administration were part of a much more massive effort to roll back the burdens of government regulation generally, and by August 2004, the *New York Times* could report that the costs of regulation imposed on private industry and state and local governments were the lowest of any period since 1987, when such data were first collected. This shift in policy orientation motivated at least one long-time EPA administrator, Eric V. Schaeffer, to resign in protest. In stepping down, Mr. Schaeffer argued that the Bush approach undermined his ability to use litigation to force industry compliance (Seelye 2002, A15). Many environmental groups were also critical of the more lenient treatment of industry, and in 2003 three more top enforcement officials at the EPA resigned (Drew and Oppel 2004). These criticisms reflected unhappiness over obvious policy changes. Whether the Bush administration's new policy direction would be as effective as or more effective than previous efforts remained to be seen. By January 2005, the administration, for example, could claim that 55 percent of the oil refining industry had been brought into compliance with clean air standards. The utilities industry, however, remained stubbornly resistant to reaching settlements with the EPA (Janofsky, January 28, 2005).

It is questionable whether centralized command and control can ever be effective for any length of time in a nation as institutionally and socially diverse as the United States. A more effective, pragmatic approach needs to recognize the recurring conjunction of diversity and incrementalism in American culture and politics, and in the area of environmental policy, this combination dictated more flexible, localized ways of dealing with environmental issues in the 1990s.

CLEAN AIR

In the words of Melnick, a careful student of environmental policy, "[a]ir pollution presents a classic example of a market externality or spillover. . . . In the absence of government action, air pollution imposes costs on society in the form of adverse health effects, harm to vegetation and materials, and reduced visibility" (1984, 25). Historically, given the opportunity, industry has simply taken its impact on the atmosphere as a spinoff for which it need bear neither cost nor responsibility. This began to change in the 1960s, when minimal legislation monitoring air quality was enacted at the national level.

The first statutes by Congress dealing with air pollution were tentative. The 1955 Air Pollution Act authorized federal grants for research in this area, and the 1963 Clean Air Act provided grants to state and local pollution control agencies and also for research. The 1965 and 1967 acts targeted auto pollution, with the latter statute authorizing the EPA to set new source performance standards that the states were required to help enforce.

The 1970 Clean Air Act Amendments however, are prominent as the first major comprehensive effort to control air pollution. Melnick asserts that "[t]he year 1970 was a political watershed for pollution control" (op.cit. 1983, 28). The 1970 legislation rested on the premise that the optimal method of pollution control, the command-and-control approach, was through central direction from the national government. Following this assumption, Congress adopted the concept of technology forcing that set deadlines by which certain air or emissions standards had to be met. The act also instituted the use of a national ambient air quality standard (NAAQS) as a guide for levels of allowable pollution. Especially important for environmental groups was the provision—Section 304—that allowed citizen suits against polluters. This was the first federal environmental legislation to authorize such litigation, and by the use of *shall* throughout the statute, it provided specific targets for citizen suits. In other words environmental activists were now in a position to argue in court that Congress had required action. These suits could be brought not only against violators of the act, but also against the EPA itself. These policy innovations soon became models for regulating pollution in other areas.

The surge in regulatory activity in the early 1970s was the consequence of a policy window opened by propitious political events. In particular both President Richard M. Nixon and his potential presidential rival, Senator Edmund Muskie (D-ME), jockeyed vigorously to exploit the sudden increase in popular support for environmental action. After this initial period of action, industrial forces and state and local governments reacted against regulation by attempting to weaken and delay its implementation. Although these obstructive tactics were constantly present in the halls of Congress, the basic premises of the 1970 act remained intact. In this respect Melnick notes; "While it is always good fun to ridicule the glacial speed with which Congress proceeds, the legislative branch's proclivity for slow, painstaking deliberation is one of its chief virtues. Its many veto points allow large numbers of interests to be heard and in some way accommodated" (op. cit. 1984, 130). By the 1980s liberals supporting the environment realized that swift congressional action might easily be detrimental to their cause. Writing in 1999, Graham could conclude about environmental policy generally that "a sense of national crisis had been replaced by an enduring public commitment" (op. cit., 88–89).

The greatest problem stemming from the 1970 Clean Air Act Amendments was the command-and-control stance that they assumed. The regulatory structure itself tended to founder on the policy mazes posed by federalism and the opportunities for delay provided by the policy process at the national level. Thus, the 1977 reauthorization of the act postponed deadlines and offered new standards of air quality, and the EPA turned to a process of ongoing informal negotiation with governmental and private polluters.

In the next major environmental legislation, enacted in 1990 during the administration of George H.W. Bush, Congress accepted the utility of emissions trading in addition to utilizing grants and tax incentives to improve air quality. Emissions trading marked an important step toward allowing market forces to play a greater role in abating the kind of air pollution that contributed to acid rain conditions in the Northeast. In 2002 the White House could declare that the "acid rain cap and trade program created by Congress in 1990 reduced more pollution in the last decade than all other Clean Air Act command-and-control programs combined"—and at less cost than those programs (White House 2002, 1).

Commentators on America's clean air policy initiatives over the past three decades agree that significant decreases in air pollutants have occurred. Obviously, the command-and-control orientation of much congressional legislation has had some effect, although there is considerable evidence that progress has been the result of EPA negotiation and flexibility within the framework provided by more rigid congressional standards.

Bush's Office of Management and Budget (OMB) published a report in September 2004 showing that clean air regulations produce between $101 billion and $119 billion in benefits each year, including fewer hospitalizations and lost workdays from pollution-caused illness. Compared with this progress, company costs for antipollution technology amounted to only between $8 billion and $8.8 billion. Thus, the ratio of regulation benefits to costs was in the area of between 10 and 15 to 1 (Adams 2004, 4). The Bush administration has argued, however, that industry compliance with a cap-and-trade program, as evidenced by the results with regard to acid rain pollutants, would be much more widespread and thus progress toward federally promulgated standards would be swifter and less costly than other methods.

THE CLEAR SKIES INITIATIVE: A CASE STUDY

On February 14, 2002, President George W. Bush announced his "Clear Skies Initiative." This proposal built on the experience of the previous three decades and moved dramatically from a command-and-control approach to a reliance on market mechanisms. The White House declared that "[a]fter 30 years of experience in regulating air pollution, America has proved that there is a better way to accomplish our clean air goals" (op. cit., 2).

President Bush proposed placing emissions caps on sulfur dioxide, nitrogen oxides, and mercury that would reduce these pollutants by approximately 70 percent by 2018. These caps would rely on market dynamics that would provide incentives for creating sources to curtail emissions. Each emitting source would be given an allowance for the tonnage of a pollutant that could be emitted. These allowances would be tradable. Thus, if a plant cut its emissions below its allowance, it could trade or market its excess allowances to an expanding plant or one that was having greater difficulty cutting back on polluting emissions. Plants would also be encouraged to cut emissions as deeply and as soon as possible in order to save emissions allowances for later in the plant's life, when EPA standards became more stringent. Likewise, corporations would have a greater incentive to close older, less efficient plants and to use the allowances gained from such closures for expansion elsewhere or on the market.

With the exception of coal producers and coal powered utilities, industry, generally, responded positively to the Bush approach. The coal producers and coal powered utilities believed that the mercury ceilings proposed were unrealistic, insofar as mercury is currently difficult to remove from coal induced emissions. Other industries, however, saw Bush's proposal as enabling them to seek the most cost-effective way to reduce emissions. Just as important, it provided them with certainty as to their pollution requirements. Under the command-and-control orientation of other pollution abatement efforts, industry and state and local governments were continually at the mercy of activist lawsuits that were costly both in terms of litigation expenses and in terms of the uncertainty created by these suits. The Clear Skies Initiative offered industry the kind of stability that allowed long-range planning with the attendant cost savings.

The Bush administration, of course, found reliance on a market-based approach compatible with its ideological assumptions about the proper role of government. From its viewpoint the Clear Skies Initiative allowed business to solve its problems with a minimum of government interference. Moreover, the variation in industrial technologies made nationally imposed uniform methods of enforcement less effective than a policy that allowed industry variation to be worked into the overall strategy of pollution reduction. Under the Clear Skies Initiative, industries could adjust according to both their technological differences and the regional differences in air quality needs. The Bush administration also saw the initiative as requiring many fewer environmental employees than a command-and-control policy, thus reducing bureaucratic growth and saving taxpayer dollars.

Critics of the Clear Skies Initiative have focused on what they have seen as gaps in its coverage and have advocated continuation of a command-and-control policy. In an overall critique of Bush administration environmental initiatives, Robert S. Devine argues that the Clear Skies approach does not include many important air polluters, such as oil refining plants. Devine also believes that carbon dioxide emissions should have been covered by Bush's proposal. Additionally, Devine finds fault with Clear Skies because it moves away from what he and other critics see as more rigorous regulation under the Clean Air Act. The latter allowed states to enact more stringent pollution standards than those established by the EPA, whereas the Clear Skies Initiative would set nationally determined pollution caps, and these would presumably preempt any conflicting state regulations.

Going to the heart of the Bush administration's ideological assumptions, Devine has declared, "[M]arket-based mechanisms . . . often do not work as well as advertised" (2004, 151). Many critics have echoed Devine's lack of faith in reliance on market mechanisms to produce significant reductions in pollution emissions. While opponents of Bush's proposal concede that it would produce some reduction in air pollution, they continue to insist that the Clean Air Act's regulatory approach would result in greater reductions. Again, Devine is willing to grant that uncertainty of enforcement and of litigation is a problem for industry, but he argues a "unified front" by the administration and energetic enforcement would reduce both the number of lawsuits and the uncertainty within the industries affected (ibid., 153). Conservationists remain skeptical of the cap-and-trade approach. Nitrogen oxide and mercury impacts are largely near emissions sources so that trading between adjacent areas under these circumstances accomplishes nothing. In fact, "if you wind up with a pollution trading program, that puts communities immediately downwind from [dirtier power plants] at higher risk," Nat Mund, a clean air expert with the Sierra Club said (Whipple 2003).

These differences of opinion about how to proceed in reducing air pollution reflect a fundamental ideological and normative cleavage in American political culture. The Bush administration bases its proposal on a market dynamic that has been tremendously productive throughout history. Moreover, it appeals to the profit motives imbedded in that dynamic, while restricting government interference. On its behalf the White House points to the dramatic reductions in emissions contributing to acid rain that were the result of a similar approach. Those on the other side of the dialogue place their confidence in government regulation and the setting of goals to be met. As a result, Congress historically has extended the time limits allowed or has simply ignored the failures of industries to meet their deadlines. From the perspective of advocacy groups, governmentally imposed standards provide the materials for continual litigation. A deadline and a standard are specified in legislation; industry fails in many cases to meet them; consequently, environmental groups are then positioned to sue industry, and often government, for failing to be more rigorous in enforcement. Such suits can serve the dual purpose of attempting to improve the environment and at the same time rallying the membership to the cause.

Also of special interest among the criticisms of the Clear Skies Initiative was the outrage at the administration's failure to include carbon dioxide among the emissions to be regulated. As events transpired, this omission was one of the vulnerable points which critics attacked in Congress in 2004 and

2005. Republican Senator John McCain and Democrat Joseph Lieberman have introduced legislation of their own to reduce carbon dioxide emissions by capping overall greenhouse emissions from the generation of electricity, transportation, and commercial and industrial sectors.

Certainly a number of opponents of the Clear Skies Initiative have shown that the Clean Air Act achieved laudable results and that command-and-control policy implementation proved its worth. As Gregg Easterbrook has noted, "over the past two decades most federal regulations have significantly reduced pollution without any harm to economic growth" (2002, 17). EPA data for 2001–2002 indicated that since 1970 nitrogen oxide emissions were down by 17 percent, sulfur dioxide emissions by 49 percent, lead emissions by 98 percent, carbon monoxide emissions by 41 percent, and emissions from combustion by 82 percent (Fay 2004, 36).

There have been complaints that the business of law enforcement has been hampered by political interference with the enforcers. Eric Schaeffer, who had directed EPA's Office of Regulatory Enforcement, resigned in 2002 in protest against the Bush administration's efforts to weaken enforcement of the Clean Air Act. He now heads a public interest group called the Environmental Integrity Project, which is dedicated to developing support for a more vigorous policy of environmental protection (Schaeffer 2004, 37).

Religious groups have also lined up to protest the Bush administration's Clear Skies Initiative. In a letter of April 22, 2004, one hundred Christian leaders issued an Earth Day rebuke to Mr. Bush for failing to set reduction standards for power plant carbon dioxide emissions. They claimed that "powerful corporate interests have had [a] disproportionate influence" in framing environmental policy. "We believe," the letter reads, "that the Administration's energy, clean air and climate change programs prolong our dependence on fossil fuels which is depleting Earth's resources, poisoning its climate, punishing the poor, constricting sustainable economic growth and jeopardizing global security and peace" (RNS 2004, 15).

There is also a conflict between the Clear Skies Initiative and other administration goals. President Bush had promised to clear the air in national parks of haze, but the Clear Skies plan threatens to make the haze problem worse. Thomas Kiernan, in an article in the journal *National Parks*, claims that this will happen at the Shenandoah National Park, one of the nation's five most polluted parks, where a power plant has been proposed five miles outside the park. Elimination of a program called "New Source Review" will silence the voice of the Park Service on the pollution effects of the proposed plant (Kiernan 2004, 4).

In a report of late May 2000, "Clear the Air," a national public education campaign designed to reduce coal-fired power plant emissions, claimed that power plant pollution is linked to 24,000 annual deaths, including 2,800 from lung cases. The underlying analysis, done by EPA consultants, also linked power plant pollution to 38,000 annual heart attacks and claimed that this pollution cuts fourteen years from a person's life (*Nation's Health* 2004, 7).

In any case the Bush administration's Clear Skies proposal foundered on the opposition of those concerned about mercury standards, the omission of carbon dioxide limits, and skepticism about the program's contribution to reducing acid rain. The latter point, in particular, united northeastern Republicans in opposition, although a number of moderate Republicans across the country also opposed the Bush administration on this issue (Jalonick 2004). The Clear Skies Initiative was renewed in 2005, but at this writing it has not yet cleared the necessary legislative hurdles.

What is clear from the perspective of the student of public policy is that the introduction of the carbon dioxide issue into the debate moves clean air policy from a focus on health-debilitating pollutants to a question of more cosmic proportions—that of global warming. No one claims that carbon dioxide emissions directly affect the personal health of America's elderly and young. The advocates for regulating carbon dioxide emissions in addition to pollutants that directly threaten public health have moved beyond the immediate and tangible issues impinging on individual health. In a subtle but very real sense, they appear to be seeking to move the United States under the scope of the Kyoto Treaty protocols regulating greenhouse emissions, which the U.S. Senate has refused to even consider. As of early 2005, the Senate remained deeply divided on the issue of carbon dioxide emissions, with Senator James M. Inhof (R-OK), chair of the powerful Environment and Public Works Committee, declaring that global warming was "the greatest hoax ever perpetrated on the American people" (Janofsky, January 27, 2005).

Government attempts to control air pollutants provide a number of lessons and raise important ethical issues for the student of policy. In the first instance, government policy in this area is an excellent example of how interaction between government policies and basic cultural values work changes in both. Delving into what for American policymakers was largely uncharted territory, the nation's leaders in the 1970s moved to improve air quality in the nation. Although these early efforts were inherently fragmented and incremental, they were based on a sense of crisis and a belief in directive control. As this sense of crisis dissipated and directive control morphed into informal negotiation and resolution, policymakers began to refashion their assumptions of what was needed and how it could be best achieved.

Some have argued that the Clear Skies Initiative moves government policy and its implementation into tune with basic cultural norms in America. Garrett Hardin began his essay on the tragedy of the commons with the assertion that an "implicit and almost universal assumption of discussions published in professional and semipopular scientific journals is that the problem under discussion has a technical solution" (op. cit., 1243). But he declared that the issue posed by the commons cannot be solved by the techniques of modern science or organization theory. The problem of the commons requires changing "human values or ideas of morality" (ibid.), and "morality is system-sensitive" (ibid., 1245). Hardin urged an approach that avoided heavy bureaucratic regulation and relied on "mutual coercion mutually agreed upon." Under this system citizens would "institute and (grumblingly) support taxes and other coercive devices to escape the horror of the commons" (ibid., 9). Others have agreed with Hardin about the essential importance of value modification. Writing in 1994, after examining the role of activist environmental groups, Christopher J. Bosso concluded, "What will matter most are the percolating actions of countless citizens, moderated as always by the coalition-forcing system itself. This process will be messy, incremental, ideologically fractious, often parochial, and always frustrating. But this is the process of new values being expressed and put to everyday use" (ibid., 48).

There is little question that industry, left to its own devices in the market, tends to emulate the tragedy of the commons. But today, even profit-motivated, bottom-line industries have seen the value of projecting an environmentally friendly image and the economic advantages of improved pollution control. At the same time government officials have recognized the difficulties and costs of unilaterally imposing standards and deadlines on American entrepreneurs and state and local government polluters. They are attempting instead to have enlightened self-interest work the necessary changes in economic behavior.

Ethical Analysis of the Case

Protection of the natural environment as a policy area differs from all others in that it includes all future national values. The results of environmental policy are more far-reaching and more inclusive for the welfare of the whole society than other policy sectors. For this reason utilitarianism is less well-suited to serve as an adequate tool of ethical analysis for environmental issues than other systematic methods because of its focus on present tastes and preferences as the standard of value, and because its exponents explicitly discount the future. Efficiency is measured in the short run; the long run is too complex and subject to a host of unknowable causes, and it must therefore be discounted. Since utilitarianism focuses its analysis on costs and benefits, monetarily measured, it must focus on present costs and benefits.

With this limitation noted, we might nevertheless suppose it worthwhile to perform a cost-benefit analysis of pollution control policies employed by the federal government. In the foregoing case we have noted that such analyses have already been done, and they seem to show that the benefits of command-and-control policies have thus far outweighed the costs to industry in terms of lives saved and health preserved—purely contemporary values.

Nevertheless, the cap-and-trade policies favored by the Bush administration have the virtue of being noncoercive and of allowing the market to determine the balance of costs and benefits. The market provides an automatic measurement, which does not have the problems of error inherent in cost-benefit policy analyses.

The central concern of deontologists with questions of equity would no doubt demand a comparison of present with future values. While the utilitarian's concerns are for society as a whole, as presently structured and with value understood to mean present value, the deontologist focuses on the individual, understood as *every* individual, present and future, as an absolute value. Some varieties of deontological ethics, in fact, extend concern for rights from human persons to animals, plants, and the whole of natural reality. Such schools of thought reject out of hand the primacy of present economic values and of an ever-expanding economy in favor of theories of sustainable growth. There are also schools of global ethics, working with what their exponents consider to be universal values, which must be globally embraced and enforced. These schools reject utilitarianism, in the form of mainstream modern economics, and opt instead for theories of stewardship, which deny any absolute property right, such as that asserted by both liberal and conservative thought. Stewardship economics is biocentric and is embraced by people attracted to the green parties of Europe or to movements like that of Ralph Nader in the United States. These parties and movements stand squarely within the liberal tradition and celebrate as founding heroes philosophers such as John Locke. But they reject out of hand the hedonist individualism of the liberal mainstream. (For a leading example, see Brown 2001.) We must ask, however, whether there is a place for industrialization in such theories. If not, where does this leave the less developed societies?

The prudent pragmatist, in facing the myriad and opposed values represented in the health of the environment, would recognize as the central problem the need to reconcile the value of economic growth with the sustenance of healthful air, water, and nonrenewable resources. For the prudent pragmatist environmental issues represent a classic version of weighing and balancing values in tension, with a careful investigation of circumstances as the determining factor. Prudent pragmatists would, of course, recognize with the deontologist the need to give appropriate weight to future circumstances, so far as we can envisage them today. They would give close scrutiny to studies showing the comparative costs and benefits of command-and-control versus cap-and-trade policies, and they would attempt to divorce themselves from any ideological predilections. Insofar as prudent pragmatism seems to be especially favorable toward incremental policy solutions—and to the rejection of grand and comprehensive schemes of change—its adherents will have to ask themselves whether in this instance incrementalism is adequate to the task before us. Drastic measures may at some point be called for if disaster is to be avoided. Environmental integrity may well become compromised beyond recovery, and the whole future of the world made forfeit to misguided policy.

To clarify the facts, the total nature of the circumstances with which we are faced, prudent pragmatists will invoke the resources of deliberative and discursive democracy. They will exercise their faith in the power of both reason and free discussion to lay bare the pattern of facts required for prudent judgment as well as to overcome the oversimplifications produced by undue reliance on abstract ideology. Something like this, in fact, seems to be happening to the Bush administration's Clear Skies Initiative as it makes its way once more through the network of environmental agencies, both public and private, and the halls of the U.S. Congress.

THE HARNESSING OF AMERICA'S RIVERS

Although the usefulness of damming America's rivers had been apparent from the nation's beginnings, its value increased immensely with the harnessing of electricity and the means to transmit it over long distances. At the close of the nineteenth century, private industry had begun to capitalize on hydropower from rivers such as the Niagara; as a result, Buffalo, New York, became known as the City of Light. The immensity of extensive hydroelectric projects, however, required investment capital most easily provided by government sources.

Both Republicans and Democrats saw the potential of hydroelectric power. President Herbert Hoover began plans for harnessing the Colorado River with the Hoover Dam in 1928. In Hoover's view, "[e]very drop of water that runs to the sea without yielding its full commercial return to the nation is an economic waste" (quoted in Blaine Hardin 1996, 99). The Hoover Dam was completed under the New Deal, and it was during the Roosevelt administration that the government moved in grand fashion into utilizing America's rivers.

By far the largest jewel in the Roosevelt administration's hydroelectric crown was the Tennessee Valley Authority (TVA). Damming the Tennessee Valley was one of Roosevelt's earliest New Deal proposals. The largest project of this sort undertaken to that time, the effort produced sixteen new dams and the reconstruction of five others in the decade following its initiation in 1933 (Watkins 1990, 380). In the short term, Roosevelt saw that building dams would relieve the unemployment rolls, but the long-term benefits were even more substantial. The dams controlled the flooding of the Tennessee River and freed hundreds of thousands of acres for farming, and the hydroelectric power produced low cost energy to a badly depressed economic area. Also important for Roosevelt and his advisers was the opportunity for planning provided by the big dam projects. In many cases, such as the Hoover Dam and the Grand Coulee, the sheer scale of construction awed and impressed Americans. These projects were tangible demonstrations of America's technological prowess and can-do spirit. In his dedication of the 727-foot-high Hoover Dam, for example, Roosevelt took great pride in pointing out that it had created the largest man-made lake in the world, with enough water to cover the entire state of Connecticut to a depth of ten feet (Black 2003, 367–68).

Of interest for the policy analyst was the appearance at this time of formal cost-benefit analysis in the policy process in this area. The Army Corps of Engineers became especially adept at justifying projects based on its accounting of the costs and benefits to be derived from those projects. Over the years it built an especially comfortable relationship with the relevant congressional committees and the National Rivers and Harbors Congress, an association of contractors and local government officials. This policy "iron triangle" provided political clout to back up the Corps' analyses. In 1977, a student of interest group power, Carol S. Greenwood, could declare that this relationship was

> an awesome combination of technical knowledge and political strength shared by the Army Corps of Engineers, congressmen on the public works committees, and the National Rivers and Harbors Congress, an interest group that includes legislators, corps members, and local interests such as local and state governments, building contractors, unions, water transportation companies, and so forth. (Greenwood 1977, 226)

In this context cost-benefit analysis worked well because everyone agreed on what constituted costs and benefits. Difficulties developed, however, as other interests began to intrude on this cozy relationship. This intrusion became especially influential after the 1970s as environmental interest groups became more numerous and gained easier access to the courts. Additionally, environmental concerns received new institutional support with the creation of the EPA and of environmental committees in Congress. Environmentalists insisted that their values be calculated in the cost-benefit formulas, and they used the courts to challenge environmental impact statements that were required under the 1969 National Environmental Policy Act (ibid., 227). Damage to the natural environment, damage to wildlife, and damage to water quality were now offered as costs that needed to be considered. Values accepted almost without question in the 1930s, 1940s, and 1950s were being challenged and modified as environmental concerns moved onto the public agenda.

PROBLEMS AND CONTRADICTIONS IN THE DAM COMPLEX: A CASE STUDY

Because of the power that proponents of dams such as the TVA, the Army Corps of Engineers, and the Bureau of Reclamation in the Department of Interior had accumulated, the construction of new dam facilities continued into the 1970s. Today, many believe that the point of diminishing returns has been reached. Former Secretary of Interior under President Bill Clinton, Bruce Babbitt, has been one of these critics. In 2004 Babbitt pointed out that America had approximately 75,000 dams, and he argued that it was time to "undedicate" some of these structures. Babbitt himself had participated in tearing down several dams on the East Coast, and he noted that a dozen dams had been removed in recent years. These dams, however, were small structures that had far outlived their usefulness. The serious questions for students of public policy are posed by the major dams that environmental groups also want destroyed.

The arguments of the environmental groups run along similar lines whatever dam is being targeted. Dams slow water flow and create aquatic conditions less habitable for some fish species. In the Northwest, in particular, dams along the Columbia-Snake River complex have greatly reduced the number of salmon because the fish have to swim upstream past the dams to spawn, and devices to enable them to bypass the dams have not been very successful. Environmentalists are also concerned about losing the natural beauty of freely flowing rivers, which are submerged under artificially created lakes. Two areas that have received particular attention from environmental groups have been the Glen Canyon Dam forming Lake Powell on the Colorado River and four fairly recent dams along the Snake River in southeastern Washington State.

The claims of animal rights activists appear to have played a minor role in the attacks on America's dams. In fact many of those promoting the freer flow of rivers and expressing concern about the fish populations are sportspeople of various pursuits. Some have been avid hunters, and obviously trout and salmon fishermen have an interest in promoting better fishing opportunities. In a more general sense environmentalists are worried about the threats that dams pose to biodiversity. These criticisms focus on the species that may be depleted in an area by a dam. Finally, the argument, noted earlier, for maintaining the pristine, natural beauty of an area, has also been prominent. The one point on which those advocating for the ethical treatment of animals and those promoting a more numerous and healthier salmon population would appear to agree is the normative importance of treating any living being humanely.

As Elizabeth Grossman points out in her book *Watershed: The Undamming of America* (2002), the four Snake River dams—Ice Harbor, Lower Monumental, Little Goose, and Lower Granite, built in 1962, 1969, 1970, and 1975, respectively—are among the last of an era of dam building that began in the 1930s. Of course, these dams have created strong vested interests since their construction. They contribute 4–5 percent of the hydroelectric power generated in the area, and while this is not a large percentage, the electric power grid blackouts threatening California have made every kilowatt of electricity crucial. The Snake River dams have also been touted as the means for making the city of Lewiston, Idaho, an inland port. With their completion Lewiston became the innermost port on the west coast, and it was able to sustain barge transportation to the Pacific Ocean 500 miles away, with an estimated economic benefit of $34 million annually.

Since the building of the last dam in 1975, the salmon and steelhead population has declined to the point that they are listed as endangered species in the Snake River. The battle between environmentalist groups and local industry and elected officials has been ongoing. Environmental groups want the dams breached, which in this instance would mean building river beds around them to allow the water to flow freely. During the 2000 presidential race, the Clinton administration deferred a decision on breaching the dams, offering instead the possibility of alternative steps to encourage an increase in the fish population (Jehl 2000, A1). At that time, candidate George W. Bush opposed breaching the dams. The confrontations among the various interests continued until December 2004, when the Bush administration released a decision based on a study by the fisheries division of the National Oceanographic and Atmospheric Administration declaring that the dams had become "an immutable part of the salmon's environment" and that federal agencies had no "discretion" to remove them (Barringer 2004, A1). The federal government insisted that it was concerned about the survival of the Snake River species and suggested a program of carrying fish around the dams and the use of a new type of weir, or water slide, that would facilitate movement downstream past the dams.

The story of the Glen Canyon dam, which was completed in 1963 along the Colorado-Arizona border, differs in important ways from that of the Snake River dams. The Glen Canyon dam, for example, has had a huge regional economic impact. Some 20 million people use its water, and it supplies electrical power to about 400,000 households (Grossman, op. cit., 168). Tourists, seeking water recreation of all sorts, spend an estimated $500 million annually in the area. Additionally, Lake Powell has developed a new ecosystem that features peregrine falcons, bald eagles, the Kanab ambersnail, carp, and catfish (ibid., 56). Some native species appear to have suffered from the dam, such as the southwest willow flycatcher, razorback sucker, pikeminnow, and the bony tail (ibid., 95).

In 1996 the Sierra Club proposed draining the lake to restore the natural grandeur of the canyons that had been flooded by the dam. The Sierra Club's proposal gained a tremendous amount of publicity, even leading to congressional hearings on the subject. Some claimed that targeting the Glen Canyon Dam was primarily an effort to reinvigorate club membership. Whatever the purpose, opponents argued that draining the lake would do little to restore the pristine beauty of the canyons because these walls have now been coated with sediment of all kinds. One commentator has suggested that draining the lake could leave the area looking like "the world's largest bathtub ring" (Zengerle 1997, 22).

It seems clear that, fueled by environmental activism, changed public views about the environment, and diminishing returns from new dams, the era of dam building in America has drawn to a close. The questions raised by the foregoing cases concern to what extent the construction projects of the past should be rolled back. Does, for example, the new ecosystem created by Lake Powell stand lower on the natural order of things than the ecosystem and natural beauty existing before 1963? Or with regard to the Snake River, how far should the needs of salmon and steelhead be pushed in the face of tangible economic losses?

Ethical Analysis of the Case

While the values at stake in the dam issue are quite clear and well defined, a utilitarian approach to the resolution of the dilemma this case presents does not seem to be the most useful. It might well be that summing individual preferences about the dams would still produce a majority opinion in their favor, given the large number of consumers of the water and the relatively small number of environmentalists. But the newly appreciated values we have discussed here and the political activity they have spawned clearly indicate that the greatest good of society cannot be arrived at simply by counting noses. It is subtler and more complicated than that. Adding into the utilitarian equation a consideration of intensity, duration, and other qualitative features might help. But we have no agreed-upon way to give numbers to these qualitative factors.

The deontological approach also seems to be wanting in this case. It is not at all clear what a standard of equity would be. The values at stake are in fundamental tension. Clearly, a position advocating free and unfettered river flow stands at one extreme. But still within the environmental purview is the potential for clean and renewable energy from dams. At the other extreme is the autonomous drive toward profit, using whatever technology is available.

Prudent pragmatism offers some possibilities in this policy area. In Maine, for example, environmental groups, government, and a power company reached an agreement whereby the environmental groups agreed to reimburse the power company approximately $25 million to tear down two of its dams on the Penobscot River and to decommission another. In addition, the power company will be allowed to increase power output at its six other dams as recompense for nearly 90 percent of the power production lost from the three dams covered by the negotiated settlement. This agreement was lauded by all concerned and was expected to increase dramatically the salmon population on the Penobscot River (Belluck 2003, A1, A25). At other dams, government, conservation groups, and private industry are working on techniques to allow fish to circumvent the obstacles posed by dams. In some instances, the government has allowed periods of increased flows from dams in order to flush out sediment and cleanse the banks downstream.

In a pluralist society with an incremental approach to problems, it seems that resolutions of differences are usually possible. Often this requires modifications in public values and certainly a willingness to be flexible and candid on the part of the protagonists. Does, for example, the Sierra Club's position on the Glen Canyon Dam represent a concern for the environment or rather a means for activating group membership into more radical positions?

Are those environmentalists attacking the Snake River dams willing to concede that removing the dams may not be sufficient to increase the salmon population in light of overfishing and the threats posed by pesticides and other toxins in the water? Do environmental groups recognize that hydroelectric power generates far less pollution than the coal powered generation of electricity? What is the proper balance among these concerns?

REFERENCES

Adams, John K. "Illogical Extremes." *On Earth* 25, no. 4 (Winter 2004): 4.

Barringer, Felicity. "U.S. Rules Out Dam Removal To Aid Salmon." *New York Times* (December 1, 2004), A1, A26.

Belluck, Pam. "Agreement in Maine Will Remove Dams For Salmon's Sake." *New York Times* (October 7, 2003), A1, A25.

Black, Conrad. *Franklin Delano Roosevelt: Champion of Freedom*. New York: Public Affairs, 2003.

Brinkley, Joel. "Out of Spotlight, Bush Overhauls U.S. Regulations." *New York Times* (August 14, 2004), A1, A10.

Brown, Peter G. *The Commonwealth of Life: A Treatise on Stewardship Economics*. New York: Black Rose Books, 2001.

Carson, Rachel. *Silent Spring*. Boston: Houghton Mifflin, 1962.

Devine, Robert S. *Bush versus the Environment*. New York: Anchor Books, 2004.

Drew, Christopher, and Richard A. Oppel Jr. "How Industry Won the Battle of Pollution Control at E.P.A."*New York Times* (March 6, 2004), A1, A10.

Dryzek, John S. *The Politics of the Earth*. New York: Oxford University Press, 1997.

Easterbrook, Gregg. "Bush, Pollution, and Hysteria." *The New Republic* (July 1, 2002), 16–18.

Fay, William D. "A Striking Difference." *Electrical Perspectives* 29, no. 6 (November/ December 2004): 36–42, 45.

Fiorino, Daniel J. "Environmental Protection Agency." In *Historical Guide to the U.S. Government*, ed. George T. Kurian, 203–8. New York: Oxford University Press, 1998.

Graham, Mary. *The Morning After Earth Day*. Washington, DC: Brookings Institution Press, 1999.

Greenwood, Carol S. *Group Power*. New York: Praeger Publishers, 1977.

Grossman, Elizabeth. *Watershed: The Undamming of America*. New York: Counterpoint, 2002.

Hardin, Blaine. *A River Lost: The Life and Death of the Columbia*. New York: W.W. Norton, 1996.

Hardin, Garrett. "The Tragedy of the Commons." *Science* (1968): 1243–48.

Jalonick, Mary Clare. "Northeasterners Just Say No To Bush Environmental Agenda." *CQ Weekly* (January 3, 2004): 43–46.

Janofsky, Michael. "Big Refiner Is Fined and Will Spend $525 Million to Improve Air." *New York Times* (January 28, 2005) A17.

———. "Climate Debate Threatens Republican Clean-Air Bill." *New York Times* (January 27, 2005), A21.

———. "E.P.A. Offers an Amnesty If Big Farms Are Monitored." *New York Times* (January 22, 2005), A8.

Jehl, Douglas. "White House to Delay a Decision on Breaching Dams in Northwest." *New York Times* (July 20, 2000), A1, A20.

Kiernan, Thomas C. "Clearing the Air." *National Parks* 78, nos. 1/2 (January/February 2004): 4.

Marquis, Christopher. "Bush Administration Rolls Back Clinton Rules for Wetlands." *New York Times* (January 15, 2002), A16.

Melnick, R. Shep. *Regulation and the Courts*. Washington, DC: The Brookings Institution, 1983.

———. "Pollution Deadlines and the Coalition for Failure." *The Public Interest* (Spring 1984): 123–34.

Porter, Michael E. *On Competition*. Boston: Harvard Business School Publishing, 1998.

RNS. "Church Leaders: Bush's Clean-Air Policy Foul." *Christian Century* 121 (May 18, 2004): 15.

Rosenbaum, Walter A. *Environmental Politics and Policy*, 6th ed. Washington, DC: CQ Press, 2005.

Schaeffer, Eric. Interview in *Multinational Monitor* 25, nos. 5/6 (May/June 2004): 37–40.

Seelye, Katharine Q., "Top EPA Official Quits, Criticizing Bush's Policies." *New York Times* (March 1, 2002), A15.

Watkins, T.H. *Righteous Pilgrim: The Life and Times of Harold L. Ickes, 1874–1952*. New York: Henry Holt and Company, 1990.

Whipple, Dan. "Bush Environment: Pushing 'Clear Skies,' " at http://web-lexis-town/universe/documenty_m=919e8d9+b5693110+911aa95a41e93de_. . . (accessed 1/10/2003).

White House, The. "Executive Summary—The Clear Skies Initiative" (February 14, 2002), at www.whitehouse.gov/news/releases/2002/02/print/clearskies.html (accessed 12/05/2004).

Zengerle, Jason. "Water Over the Dam." *The New Republic* (November 24, 1997): 20–22.

CHAPTER 11

Ethical Defense

AMERICA IN THE WORLD: LEADER OR HEGEMON?

No one can deny the gradual but consistent trajectory by which the United States emerged from the position of a second-rate military power at the beginning of the twentieth century to the sole superpower by its end. For the current era, World War II certainly stands as a major watershed on America's journey toward world dominance. That conflict depleted the power of most of the world's major industrialized nations, leaving the United States relatively unscathed.

Following World War II, the world entered the period of the cold war, which was a major and prolonged confrontation between the United States and its allies on one side and the Soviet Union and its supporters on the other side. Although this was a period of continual tension and occasional outbreaks of armed conflict, it was also characterized by an element of stability and predictability lacking in today's world. The United States knew who and where its enemies were, and both sides in the struggle retained a rational sense of how far each could be pushed or antagonized. The United States, for its part, seemed generally to follow the containment strategy first articulated publicly by George Kennan in his essay in the July 1947 issue of *Foreign Affairs*. Kennan argued that the United States should follow a policy of patience that encompassed military, economic, and political initiatives to hold Soviet aggression in check.

The fall of the Berlin Wall in 1989 and the ensuing disintegration of the Soviet Union left the United States in a position of dominance on the world scene but without any definitive sense of what that position should entail. Without the looming threat of the Soviet bloc, Western European nations moved to work more closely together and to distance themselves from U.S. influence. At the same time, Eastern European nations looked toward the United States for both leadership and assistance. In the Far East Japan remained a close ally of the United States, and China began to demonstrate renewed economic vigor. During this time the United States, although prospering enormously economically, found itself involved in numerous foreign enterprises militarily that seemed bereft of any consistent policy assumptions.

In 1993 Samuel P. Huntington stepped into this void with his controversial "clash of civilizations" thesis. Published first in *Foreign Affairs* and later as a book, Huntington's argument depicted as naïve the idea that it was only a matter of time until liberal democratic ideas and institutions spread throughout the world. There are, Huntington asserted, important regions of the world that culturally differ fundamentally from Western democratic ideals and practices. Since the cold war, the world had become "divided between a Western one [civilization] and a non-Western many" (Huntington 1996, 36). Although nation-states would remain important in Huntington's opinion, he regarded "the greatest dangers for stability" as those "between states or groups from different civilizations" (ibid.). In particular, he placed special emphasis on the Islamic world and the basic divergences from Western thought that exist therein. There was, he stated, no reason to believe that the adherents to Islam would voluntarily relinquish beliefs and practices that many Westerners found to be repugnant. There were, on the other hand, important reasons to believe that these differences could lead to conflict with the West.

The terrorist attacks on September 11, 2001, changed dramatically America's sense of its role in the world and seemed to confirm important elements of Huntington's argument. For the first time, all Americans could see that there were forces in the world bitterly opposed to their ideals and, moreover, willing to attack them on their home territory. For better or worse, America's response to Islamic fundamentalism was overwhelmingly military, and it was amazingly successful within the criteria of military doctrine. With but a handful of troops, the United States and its allies routed the Taliban in Afghanistan and installed a sympathetic government within a matter of months. A short time later, the American military, again with allies, attacked and subdued Iraq. What these efforts confirmed for the rest of the world was the virtual invincibility of the American military prowess. What was less clear was how successful the United States could be in installing and nurturing thriving democratic governments in areas that had never, or rarely, experienced the Western concept of democracy. Still lacking, years after September 11, was a clear sense of how America planned to conduct itself on the world stage. In particular, its reliance on military prowess was beginning to make even its long-time allies nervous—and in some instances increasingly hostile.

Of particular concern to observers was the growing influence of the American military in the formulation and negotiation of foreign policy. Andrew J. Bacevich describes the influence of "a new class of military viceroys" who have emerged as a result of the Goldwater-Nichols Department of Defense Reorganization Act of 1986 (2002, 173). At the beginning of the twenty-first century, the United States had divided the world into military regions headed by commanders-in-chief (CINCs), who have been likened to proconsuls of the Roman Empire. The four most important of these CINCs commanded the European, the Middle Eastern, the Pacific, and the Central and South American regions. Bacevich argues that these commanders and their military advisers have become increasingly powerful because of a perceived ineffectiveness of civilian agencies, especially the State Department (Bacevich 2002, 174–80). Whatever the cause of their rise to importance, CINCs now take an active role in areas such as controlling drug trafficking and nation-building.

Commentators on the phenomenon of American dominance unleashed by the events of September 11 were divided in their appraisals of what they saw. Some argued that America throughout the twentieth century had been bent on a mission of imposing its values on the rest of the world. This development, they argued, could be seen by America's military actions and the increasing ubiquity of its economic power. This school of thought seemed to see America as playing out its nineteenth century mission of Manifest Destiny in the world at large. (See, for example, Mearsheimer 2003.) In contrast other pundits and scholars contended that in the world of the early twenty-first century, the United States had an obligation to step forward and impose some form of *pax Americana* on the world. The British historian Niall Ferguson has argued that the alternative to a unipolar world led by the United States is not necessarily a stable multipolar world. It could instead be an apolar world that would "turn out to mean an anarchic new Dark Age" (Ferguson 2004, 34). The neoconservative thinkers and policy wonks who were important in the first term of the younger Bush's administration also acted on the assumption that American power, whether it was welcome or not, should be used to better the world.

At the beginning of the twenty-first century, Americans looked out upon a chaotic and threatening world without a clear understanding of how or why they found themselves in the quandary facing them. Many Americans believed that through no fault of their own and acting with the best of intentions, they were being cast as the bully of the international community. Some saw this development as an inevitable consequence of becoming the most powerful economic and military force in the world. Others argued that through their international adventures and insensitivity to other cultures, Americans had brought world opprobrium upon themselves. The essential question for those trying to make ethical sense out of American foreign policy was whether the emergence of Islamic terrorism and the events of September 11 had so refashioned the world that previous assumptions about moral behavior and acceptable foreign policy were no longer either valid or viable.

America's responses to the September 11 attacks inevitably raised questions about what constituted a just war against terrorists and those who supported them. Ian Clark points out that just-war doctrines can be separated into those justifying war and those specifying how war should be waged. He notes that these doctrines derive from church doctrines of the Middle Ages, and they assume reasonable cultural homogeneity among combatants such as nation-states or established principalities of some sort. After a period of dormancy of several centuries, questions about the ethics of war resurfaced during the twentieth century because of the huge human costs of modern wars (more recently including the threat of nuclear weapons) and because of Marxist-Leninist claims as to the virtue of wars of liberation (Clark 1990, 34–35, 45–48). Michael Walzer has also written extensively on the ethics of war and contends that preemptive war may be justified when there is "a manifest intent to injure, a degree of preparation that makes that intent a positive danger, and a general situation in which waiting . . . greatly magnifies the risk" (Walzer 1977, 81). Walzer also argues that other forms of intervention—in cases of secession or civil war—may be justified, but these are rarely clear-cut situations. He is stronger on humanitarian intervention in instances in which a government is encouraging or engaging in mass slaughter. He notes, however, that from his study of intervention, he has found that governments rarely intervene for purely humanitarian purposes (ibid., 101–8). More recently, Walzer has concluded that concerns about a war being just have had some impact on military policy. He is concerned, however, that just-war theory "has been taken over by the generals and is being used to justify and explain those [military] actions" (Walzer 2004, 13). Understandably, he believes that the application of moral standards to the launching of military action requires judgment by someone more neutral than those initiating such action.

AMERICA AT WAR

Although most Americans may look back to the end of World War II as the beginning of an era of peace, in fact much of the period since 1945 has been one of armed conflict—a fact that David Halberstam has captured with the title of his book *War in a Time of Peace*. Some of these conflicts have been prolonged, bitter, and costly in terms of human lives. The Korean conflict lasted from 1950 to 1953 and cost America 33,651 dead. The Vietnamese conflict lasted longer and was even more costly in terms of human life, with 58,168 Americans losing their lives from combat and related causes. Fortunately, most of the military actions taken by the United States during this period have been both of shorter duration and much less costly in terms of human lives. John Mueller argues that these engagements have constituted "the remnants of war." They are minor skirmishes in a world that has accepted that war is no longer a useful form of international interaction (Mueller 2004). Nonetheless, these military actions have often resulted in the loss of life and far too often have carried the possibility of breaking out into broader, more devastating conflicts.

For many Americans it has been difficult to discern any pattern to American military initiatives. During the cold war, military operations were often characterized as attempts to halt communist aggression. But in the post-cold war era this common rationale has not been available. Thus, Americans have witnessed military action to stabilize the Middle East, to suppress drug activities in Panama, to thwart Castro in Grenada, to provide humanitarian aid in Somalia and the Balkans, and to repel Iraqi aggression in Kuwait. After the Vietnam War, Caspar Weinberger articulated the Weinberger Doctrine (which evolved into the Powell Doctrine, after Colin Powell, a disciple of Weinberger) to provide some guidance as to when the military should or should not be committed to a conflict. Weinberger declared that American troops should not be committed unless there is a threat to American vital interests, there are clear and attainable goals, there is popular and congressional support, sufficient force is available to win, and armed force is a last resort. Powell later added the requirements that there be an acceptable exit strategy and that overwhelming force be available for deployment (Halberstam 2001, 390; Bacevich 2002, 48, 51).

Although these parameters seemed reasonable, presidents soon found themselves committing troops in violation of these guidelines. In Somalia, for example, what began as a humanitarian mission to assist with widespread famine became a military effort to capture a tribal warlord, Mohammed Farah Aidid, an effort which failed and ultimately led to an ignoble American withdrawal. The American intervention in the Balkans also fell short of the Weinberger/Powell guidelines, but it achieved stability in the region without costing American lives. While American troops were intervening in Somalia and the Balkans, they were not committed until very late in Rwanda, where the Hutus, in a mass genocide, slaughtered over 800,000 of their traditional enemies, the Tutsis. There seemed little rhyme or reason as to when the American military might be brought into play. For presidents and their foreign policy advisers, the world had become too complex to enable coherent, consistent action.

One rather muscular approach toward a new paradigm for American foreign policy was presented by the neoconservatives, who in 1997 offered a statement under the auspices of what they labeled The Project for the New American Century. The adherents to The Project for the New American Century were scholarly policy wonks and holdovers from the first Bush administration. In their view American foreign policy should be guided in aggressive fashion by whatever action was necessary to protect American interests. If these interests are threatened, the American military should be brought into play, preemptively if necessary. The project's "Statement of Principles" declares, "If we shirk our responsibilities, we invite challenges to our fundamental interests." It concludes by urging the United States "to build on the successes of this past century . . . to ensure our security and greatness in the next" (Project for a New American Century). Several of the signatories to this statement—Dick Cheney,

I. Lewis Libby, Donald Rumsfeld, and Paul Wolfowitz—moved into the second Bush administration and were widely considered in the first term of that administration to be guiding policy despite the reluctance of the career military and Secretary of State Colin Powell to deploy military power readily.

The hubris of American strategists is understandable in view of both the unmatched technical superiority of American weaponry and the distribution of American forces around the globe. As noted earlier, by the beginning of the second Bush administration, the American military had divided the world into regions of military command, with commanders expected to represent the United States in a wide range of policy matters. Thus, as that administration moved into the White House in early 2001, American military might could be deployed to considerable effect within a few hours in almost any part of the world. Still lacking, however, were coherent strategies or comprehensive goals to guide the deployment of American military power.

In an important sense, the September 11 attacks changed the confused nature of American foreign policy. Now Americans had a definable, if elusive, enemy. In a dramatic and historic speech to Congress following those attacks, President Bush identified the al-Qaeda terrorist network as the perpetrators. As he spoke, American forces were already on the ground in and around Afghanistan, moving against the Taliban government that had protected the terrorist network. Here the U.S. public and most of the rest of world offered moral and material support. The Taliban were an especially noxious form of theocratic government, and it was clear that they had aided and abetted Osama bin Laden and his al-Qaeda followers. The issues of morality and rational policy choice became more confused with regard to those countries that President Bush labeled "The Axis of Evil"— Iraq, Iran, and North Korea. Was the United States justified in taking military action against these nations as well?

Americans have almost always believed that deployment of American forces into combat must have a clear moral purpose. Often Americans have been convinced that the enemy had attacked first, with the Japanese attack on Pearl Harbor serving as the clearest example of this rationale for military action. During the cold war Americans increasingly witnessed the deployment of troops to thwart communist aggression or communist efforts to destabilize governments friendly to the United States. Sometimes these governments were reasonably representative of their populace; many times, they were not. With the advent of the first Bush administration, Americans found themselves called upon to intervene militarily for humanitarian purposes. This was offered as the justification for action in Somalia, the aborted initiative in Haiti, and the cooperation with NATO in the Balkans. At what point humanitarian intervention was justified remained murky, however, with the United States essentially an onlooker to the horrific slaughter that occurred in Rwanda during the Clinton administration. Was there then somewhere among the previous justifications and precedents for military action a basis for preemptive action against the members of the Axis of Evil, none of whom seemed to pose a near-term military threat against the United States?

PREEMPTIVE WAR

THE DECISION TO INVADE IRAQ: A CASE STUDY

The American action to repel the Iraqi invasion of Kuwait in the Gulf War of 1991 received wide support among the world community and the American public. It was a response to blatant aggression by a nation ruled by an oppressive leader who had not hesitated in the past to slaughter thousands of his countrymen. The military action was conducted by a broad-based coalition of nations that contributed troops, material, and financial support. And finally, the allied coalition employed overwhelming force to achieve total victory in a short time and with minimal civilian casualties.

Despite these facts the war left an unsettled situation in that area of the Middle East. Saddam Hussein remained in power, and Iraq constituted an important locus of anti-American sentiment in a highly volatile region. Hussein exacerbated this volatility by expelling U.N. arms inspectors, who were charged with detecting any indication of attempts by the defeated Iraqis to produce and stockpile weapons of mass destruction (WMD). President George W. Bush's suspicion of Hussein was further heightened by his belief that Hussein had masterminded an assassination plot against his father in 1993 (Woodward 2004, 187).

During the Clinton administration, members of the The Project for a New American Century lobbied vigorously for aggressive action against Iraq. In an open letter of January 26, 1998, they urged the Clinton administration to acknowledge that overthrowing Hussein should be a goal of American foreign policy. A number of signatories to this letter were to become major foreign policy players in the ensuing Bush administration.

For the second Bush administration, Iraq became a focus of attention shortly after the September 11 attacks. The administration was clearly uneasy that a Middle Eastern state totally hostile to the United States and of proven unpredictability in foreign adventures continued to exist. In his comments on the day after the September 11 attacks, President Bush declared that nations supporting or harboring terrorists would be considered hostile to the United States. He repeated this position in his September 20 speech to a joint session of Congress, and Bob Woodward reports that in late November 2001, the president asked Secretary of Defense Donald Rumsfeld to begin considering plans for the invasion of Iraq (ibid., 1).

The world watched as American leaders moved to eliminate the hostile government in Iraq. The essential problem facing the Bush administration in this effort was not the question of success, for that outcome was never in doubt. The difficult issue was how to justify an invasion, and here the administration fumbled about in a fashion that was painful to witness.

Foreign Policy lists the results of a survey by Devon Largio in which he examined statements by ten major foreign policy players. He catalogues a total of twenty-one different reasons for the invasion; however, the administration eventually seemed to settle on four or five prime rationales for preemptive action (2004, 18). Throughout the planning and policy debates leading up to the actual invasion of Iraq, differences within the administration surfaced and were often leaked to the media. To some extent, these leaks account for the variety of rationales listed by Largio. There seems little doubt, however, that President Bush made up his mind in the fall of 2001 that the Hussein regime had to go. Certainly, the president's public position on that point never wavered.

Bush reinforced his concern about Iraq in his State of the Union speech of January 29, 2002, in which he identified the Axis of Evil as North Korea, Iran, and Iraq. He again made it plain that the United States would not tolerate hostile regimes that possessed or were developing WMD or nuclear weapons. By the summer of 2002, he had accepted the possibility—perhaps the necessity—of preemptive action against such regimes. In his strongly worded speech to the cadets at West Point on June 2, he declared that protection of American liberty might require preemptive military action. He further pledged that America would never again allow its military predominance in the world to be challenged.

Bush's aggressive stance began to open cracks within his foreign policy team. Vice President Cheney remained intensely committed to the overthrow of Hussein, and he argued that military action was really the only option in this respect. However, Secretary of State Colin Powell, the sole top-level foreign policy adviser ever to have experienced combat, worried about the repercussions of preemptive action and the problems posed by a postwar Iraq. Occasionally, these differences spilled over into the media.

Largely as a result of Powell's pleading, the president addressed the United Nations in September 2002. In this speech Bush challenged that body to act to enforce its resolutions against Iraq. He concluded his speech by declaring, "We must stand up for our security, and for the permanent rights and hopes of mankind . . . [T]he United States of America will make that stand. Delegates to the United Nations, you have the power to make that stand as well" (White House 2002). With these words Bush was widely interpreted as saying that with or without the United Nations, the United States would act. At the same time he suggested that another U.N. resolution might bring Iraq around to obeying its previous agreements with the United Nations. On November 8, the U.N. Security Council responded unanimously with Resolution 1441, which ordered new weapons inspections in Iraq and warned of serious consequences if that nation failed to comply.

In the meantime the administration was working assiduously to persuade members of Congress to grant formal support for military action against Iraq. This effort relied on a variety of intelligence sources, few of which could be called highly reliable. Nonetheless, the administration's suspicions about WMD in Iraq and about that nation's potential for developing nuclear weapons convinced majorities in both the House and the Senate to authorize military action. On October 8 the House voted 296–133 to support such action, and the Senate followed on October 11 with a 77–23 vote. In retrospect members of Congress offered a variety of rationales for their affirmative votes, and the failure to discover either WMD or facilities for producing nuclear weapons in Iraq later led to vigorous investigations of U.S. intelligence shortcomings.

Despite U.N. Resolution 1441, which insisted that weapons inspectors be allowed back into Iraq and that they have complete authority to investigate potential locations of WMD, Hussein played a cat-and-mouse game with the United Nations for months, raising suspicions that Iraq did indeed have such weapons. From Hussein's viewpoint, however, his maneuvering projected an appearance of cunning and represented a position of leadership against western forces. The United States, once again, prepared to request U.N. support, and on February 5, 2003, Secretary of State Powell, who was generally perceived as less hawkish on the Iraq question, presented a lengthy brief for acting aggressively against that nation. However, Powell's case was undercut by the February 14 report of Hans Blix, the chief U.N. inspector in Iraq. Blix reported that Iraq's cooperation remained reluctant but that no serious violations of U.N. weapons mandates had been found. Subsequent efforts by the United States and Great Britain to obtain the necessary nine votes needed for Security Council approval of military action against Iraq proved fruitless, and the United States withdrew its proposed resolution to that effect without bringing it to a vote.

President Bush continued to maintain that Iraq was violating U.N. mandates (Woodward, op.cit., 333), and the United States prepared for war. On March 17, the president gave Saddam Hussein forty-eight hours to leave the country or face attack. On March 19, the United States launched attacks against Iraq.

Bush based his case against Iraq on a number of claims. First, as noted, he argued that Iraq had consistently failed to honor commitments that it had made to the United Nations. He also offered a humanitarian basis for action, noting that the Iraqi leadership had killed many of its own people. The contention that seemed to have the most impact with the media and the public was the president's argument that Iraq was developing weapons of mass destruction—namely, biological, chemical, and nuclear weapons. Iraq, of course, had given credibility to such claims by refusing to allow weapons inspectors into the country. With somewhat less emphasis Bush indicated that the intelligence services saw Iraq as protecting and encouraging terrorist organizations, although the linkage to al-Qaeda remained tenuous. These claims continued to form the major thrust of the Bush administration's justification for the invasion of Iraq, even though the failure to obtain sufficient votes for Security Council support of preemptive action indicated that many nations had serious reservations about those claims.

In retrospect, what appears to have been the pivotal issue for the Bush people was summarized by the president's statement that "our principles and our security are challenged today by outlaw groups and regimes that accept no law of morality and have no limit to their violent ambitions" (White House, ibid.). The problem facing the Bush administration and the people of America, as brought to the fore by the September 11 attacks, was whether the United States in the future could allow hostile, renegade nations to exist. Have those attacks confirmed that terrorist organizations and training bases cannot be allowed to exist anywhere in the world? And must the United States now act against such a possibility wherever it appears? Obviously, to state the problem so baldly would raise serious concerns among Americans and certainly among other nations. In an essay examining future American foreign policy, John Lewis Gaddis concludes that "[t]he American claim of a broadly conceived right to pre-empt danger is not going to disappear, because no other nation or international organization will be prepared anytime soon to assume that responsibility" (Gaddis 2005, 6). Gaddis argues that to stabilize the international situation and to improve its standing therein, the United States must approach terrorism from a stance of cooperation with other nations. America must convince other nations that preemptive action, properly legitimized, protects everyone from terrorism.

Yet can the United States afford to wait until attacks are again launched across the nation's porous borders? Or must other justifications for action, such as the need for humanitarian intervention or the possibility of the existence of weapons of mass destruction, have to be linked with the cold-hearted calculation of self-interest and self-preservation? Have the dangers posed by terrorist use of modern technology become so great that they constitute a threat unlike any the world has previously known and thus justify new kinds of measures by the United States?

Of final concern for the student of American foreign policy must be President Bush's enthusiasm for spreading democracy throughout the world. In the case of Iraq, this goal took the form of regime change. The president had stated clearly the importance of promoting freedom, democracy, and capitalism worldwide. Obviously, Iraq's hostility to the United States—demonstrated in one instance by a failed attempt to assassinate President Bush's father—made the military approach to regime change more palatable. It may be America's place to do everything possible to protect the world against terrorism, but how has it been invested with the obligation to spread democracy to populations that have never before experienced such a system of government and politics?

Ethical Analysis of the Case

America's position as the world's only superpower does not release the United States from its obligation to obey the law. Though defense of vital interests remains our chief justification for our use of force abroad, America continues to recognize that its power is enmeshed in a system of international law. We do not make the claim that might makes right.

Did the United States act in accordance with international law when it decided to use force in Iraq? The invasion was undertaken under the doctrine of preemptive strike. Is this a tenable position in international law?

Traditionally, under international law all states enjoy the right to self-defense, even if this means preemptive action. The most widely accepted standard for such action was stated in the nineteenth century by Secretary of State Daniel Webster in the *Caroline* affair. This involved secret American aid to Canadian rebels in retaliation for a raid on the American vessel *Caroline*. Webster held that the action must be a necessity, that the threat must be "instant, overwhelming, and leaving no choice of means and no moment for deliberation" (quoted in Welsh 2003). The response also must be proportionate to the threat.

In addition to the tradition of international law, there is also Article 51 of the U.N. Charter, which guarantees the right of self-defense to states. Many international law experts believe that Israel's preemptive strike in its 1967 war with Arab states was compatible with Article 51. Should it also properly apply to the invasion of Iraq in 2003?

Ruth Wedgwood, a professor at Yale Law School and at the Johns Hopkins School of Advanced International Studies, has argued that "[n]ine-eleven showed that any actor, state or nonstate, can undertake asymmetric attacks of which we will have no warning whatsoever" (quoted in Murdoch 2003). Does this doctrine justify the Iraq invasion? When terrorists and rogue states possess WMD, does this fact constitute an imminent threat? Some critics would distinguish rogue states from terrorists, arguing that the behavior of rogue states can be predicted. These critics also argue that rogue states can be deterred, which would make the action of the Bush administration an act of prevention rather than preemption. Preventive war is not a legitimate recourse. It focuses on a state's capacity rather than its intent (ibid.). Other experts cannot see the difference between preemption and prevention. Still others argue that adopting the doctrine of preemption is dangerous for the world's political stability, since it creates a precedent that other states may be only too eager to imitate.

Edwin Williamson, another legal expert, believes that the United States did not need to invoke a right to preemptive strike. It could simply have called its invasion an enforcement action. The Iraqis were manifestly in violation of the cease-fire agreement which ended the Gulf War, and Security Council resolution 678 of 1990 authorized U.N. member states to use "all necessary means . . . to restore international peace and security in the area" (ibid.).

But what is the legal significance of the action of the United Nations at the time of the invasion, when the Security Council had called for a longer waiting period to give time for the U.N. inspectors to complete their work? President Bush received authority from the Congress, but not from our principal allies, to proceed with the use of force in Iraq. Though he claimed to be acting under authority of a U.N. resolution, the dominant voice in the United Nations was to hold off for yet a while longer.

There are other prudential considerations to take account of. Henry Kissinger claimed that our invasion of Iraq caused a revolution of the international order by making regime change the object of our invasion (Galston 2002). We took it upon ourselves to remold the order of the state system. Were we putting ourselves above the law by doing so? Also, was the move politically wise, with reference to our disposable power? How would we adequately meet new threats from other quarters?

Utilitarians evaluating our move into Iraq would cast the problem as a cost-benefit analysis. They would first list all the foreseeable benefits of the move and then the costs of it. But what would utilitarians use as a measure to compare the two lists? What they took to be a quantifiable problem would turn out not to be one. There is no way in which one would be able to state costs of life in dollar terms, though courts have done this in compensation cases. How would one go about setting a dollar value on the life of a 20-year-old marine in comparison with that of a 50-year-old Iraqi civilian killed incidentally in a car-bomb explosion? Even if it were possible to do this—and some analysts might try—how would someone state the costs in international prestige in dollar terms? Or how would one deal with the problem of reduced resources to meet threats elsewhere while our troops are pinned down in Iraq? How would one develop a stable estimate of the costs of rebuilding the Iraqi economy?

A deontologist attempting to judge whether the American invasion of Iraq was justified as a preemptive war would probably want to universalize the principle. What if we imagined the maxim behind the decision to invade were made a principle that every state might act upon? We would have to imagine a situation in which all states, fearing an imminent attack by another, launched preemptive strikes. Since the criteria for striking are in each case based on private judgment rather than on a commonly accepted one, each state would be trying to get in a successful blow before every other one. But if we imagine all states striking at the same time, then none would in effect get in the first blow. When universalized, preemption thus becomes impossible, and the intention of the act is nullified all around. Could a deontologist argue instead that nations have equal rights to be free from invasion by those stronger than they? Has this not been an accepted principle of international relations?

Lastly, we must ask how prudent pragmatists would go about making a judgment in this case. Their starting point would no doubt be similar to that of the utilitarian—evaluating the presumed costs and benefits of a preemptive strike. Pragmatists would not, however, attempt to fit dollar values to the various items in the lists, but rather weigh and balance one against another in light of the circumstances as they develop. Would success in taking out Hussein's WMD and overthrowing his regime be worth the loss of leadership of the world community and the accusation of imperialism? Would the short- and long-term economic costs incurred be balanced by the momentary security gained by the invasion? Would the diminished ability to meet other threats from other rogue states such as Iran and North Korea be outweighed by the security obtained by doing away with Saddam's WMD? (We cannot here figure in the fact that the invasion revealed that there were no such weapons, but we must rather accept the circumstances as assessed prior to the invasion. But it would be appropriate to make an appraisal of the probable adequacy and accuracy of the intelligence that was on hand before the decision to invade was made. This would require an examination of the adequacy of our intelligence that was rather more stringent than the one that was actually made.)

TREATMENT OF ENEMY PRISONERS IN WARTIME: *JUS IN BELLO*

What rights are accorded to enemy prisoners of war under international law? How well have these rights been observed by American forces in wartime over the years?

In premodern times prisoners of war had neither legal status nor rights of any kind. Defeated enemies were routinely killed or enslaved, including women and children. As late as 1625, the jurisprudent Hugo Grotius stated in his treatise *On the Laws of War and Peace* that victorious powers had the right to enslave their enemies. He recommended, however, that they be ransomed or exchanged instead.

With the 1648 Treaty of Westphalia, commonly understood as the foundation stone of the nation-state system, new principles began to take hold. The treaty provided for the release of prisoners without ransom, and it also established the principle that hostilities should aim only at the enemy's defeat and should avoid so far as possible the destruction of human life and property.

In the next century the humanitarian ideals of Enlightenment philosophy further supported this view. The flowering of the idea of the rights of man during the French Revolution and thereafter added still more impetus to the humane treatment of a defeated enemy. And by the mid-nineteenth century a set of international principles governing the treatment of prisoners of war came into being. Though not formalized as a treaty, these principles came to be incorporated in treaties of peace. A codification at last took place under the auspices of the Hague Peace Conferences of 1899 and 1907. Widespread destruction and the mistreatment of prisoners during World

War I brought a return to more humane attitudes after the end of the war, and this change led to the eventual enactment in 1929 of the Geneva Convention. This was revised in 1949, following World War II, and completed with an additional protocol in 1977. (See Fujita in Towle et al., eds 2000, 87–102; Flory 1942, 7–23.)

The Geneva Convention requires that prisoners of war at all times be treated humanely, and it states that they are entitled to respect for their persons, both physically and morally. The following acts are forbidden:

> Any unlawful act or omission causing death or seriously endangering . . . health . . . . , not to mention physical mutilations, medical or scientific experiments which are not justified by the patient's treatment, removal of tissue or organs for transplantation; acts of violence on the part of civilians or military persons; prolonged questioning, whether or not accompanied by acts of brutality with the aim of extracting information; continual harassment; omission of medical care to the wounded or sick . . . . Humiliating and degrading treatment is . . . .banned. (Pilloud, in UNESCO 1988: 169–70)

American Practice in the Treatment of Prisoners of War

American experience in the treatment of prisoners of war in the nineteenth century is mixed. During the American Civil War of 1861–1865, conditions in prisoner of war camps were deplorable on both sides. The most notorious of them was the Confederate detainment camp at Andersonville, Georgia, where ten thousand Northern prisoners died within a period of seven months. But conditions at federal camps, such as the one at Elmira, were "only a little less miserable" (Leckie 1981, 504). During the Vicksburg campaign it has been noted, however, that General Grant treated Confederate prisoners "with compassionate understanding" (ibid., 461).

The United States entered World War I late, and few issues arose regarding the treatment of enemy prisoners. There was mistreatment, however, on both sides of the struggle, which led to the Geneva Convention in 1929.

In World War II there were over half a million German prisoners of war alone, who were detained in over 500 camps around the United States. Many of the soldiers were employed near the camps by local businesses or worked on nearby farms. Officers were not required to work, and they were even allowed to wander outside the camps up to a distance of fifty miles.

Their treatment in the camps appears to have been good, though there were untoward incidents. One such was a guard going berserk and machine-gunning eight prisoners in their sleep. He had been courtmartialed for various delicts and had served time at hard labor. He obviously should not have been allowed to serve as a guard (Riconda 2003, 190). Escapees were punished simply by the imposition of extra work requirements. The prisoners received good food and were also allowed to enroll in educational programs (ibid.). There was also an extensive program of political reeducation, due to the ideological nature of the war and the intense propaganda to which German soldiers had been submitted at home. Technically, this might be considered a violation of the Geneva Convention against denationalization. But it was considered an important objective in bringing the war to a successful conclusion all around. (See Gansberg 1977.)

The most problematical time for a war captive is in the first hours after surrender, and there were numerous accounts of atrocities by both Allied and German forces. There is also evidence of brutality in the interrogation of prisoners for tactical information, both immediately after capture and in camps in the United States later on. (See ibid., 14–16.)

One injustice to detainees during World War II does stand out. This was the internment of the entire Japanese American population of the West Coast for fear of subversion. Altogether, 112,000 men, women, and children were sent to relocation centers in 1942, 73 percent of them being citizens born in America. There was no allegation of physical abuse, but the uprooting and detention were, of course, a major mistreatment in themselves. Though the act received the blessings of the Supreme Court during the war, this judgment was later overridden, and a determination was made that the people had been deprived of their constitutional rights. (See Riconda, op. cit., 229–30.)

The Korean War produced the new phenomenon of unwillingness on the part of some North Korean captives to be repatriated. Many had been dragooned into service in the north and uprooted from their lives as farmers, and anticommunism was widespread in the prison camps. The Vietnam War was notable for the brutality of the Vietnamese toward their American captives, rather than the reverse, although atrocities occurred on both sides close to the front. Noteworthy was the massacre at My Lai by Lt. Calley and others.

Treatment of Prisoners During the Second Iraq War

The experience of 9/11 has radically altered the character of warfare for the first part of the twenty-first century. The principal enemy of the United States is no longer a state with uniformed armies deployed in a line of battle, with a visible leadership headquartered in a capital city and directing operations across frontiers marked with symbols of national authority. It consists instead of shadowy conspiracies, operating stealthily, both inside and outside our borders, to mount guerilla operations and sudden terrorist attacks against a variety of unannounced targets, both human and nonhuman. The distinction between combatants and noncombatants has been entirely lost. The targets are sometimes located in states within our sphere of influence (such as Afghanistan and Iraq) sometimes within the United States itself, sometimes almost at random in places where Americans are traveling or working. Principal among these conspiracies is a decentralized terrorist organization named al-Qaeda, whose exact structure and command system is unknown.

The hiddenness of this new enemy—together with the utter unpredictability of when and where it will strike—and the ruthlessness and barbarism of its methods have given rise to a new kind of fear. This enemy's methods have also created a sense of urgent need for intelligence about its plans and intentions. With this need has developed a willingness to relax restraints in the treatment of prisoners who might be able to satisfy this need. In the words of Cofer Black, State Department counterterrorism coordinator, "After 9/11 the gloves came off" (quoted in Parry in Levinson 2004, 145).

In law, both that of the United States and of the world community, the torture of prisoners is "unequivocally and absolutely forbidden" (Levinson 2004, 23). The United Nations Convention Against Torture and Other Cruel, Inhuman or Degrading Treatment of prisoners, which came into force in 1987, enshrines the principle that torture should be universally condemned. Article 2 (2) of this document reads, "No exceptional circumstances whatsoever, whether a state of war or a threat of war, internal political instability or any other public emergency, may be invoked as a justification for torture" (in Levinson 2004, 40). One hundred thirty nations, including the United States, have ratified the Convention. Nevertheless, torture is practiced even by the signatory states. And a debate is currently underway among legal scholars and philosophers as to whether torture can in some way be legitimated or justified even in the face of such a flat prohibition.

A Philosophical Discussion

Positions on the torture question have been developed within the three major philosophical traditions with which we have been working. The utilitarian view is the easiest and least complicated to state. As usual, the utilitarian criterion of good is whatever constitutes the greatest good of society. Moral rules and prohibitions are simply guidelines, which summarize what has been found most useful in the past. But these guidelines may be overridden on a showing that they do not work well in a new case. It is simply a matter of calculation, and if it can be shown that torture is required to maximize the good in a given instance, then it is to be allowed (summarized in Walzer in Levinson 2004, 61, 67).

Some utilitarians, however, believe that the social costs of permitting torture would always outweigh the benefits of the practice. "A correctly calibrated cost-benefit analysis must always lead to the same conclusion, namely, that torture should not be allowed regardless of any specific context" (Gross in Levinson, 2004, 230). But clearly, there is not available a system of quantification that could do this to everyone's satisfaction. Some consequentialists would call for a cost-benefit analysis on a case-by-case basis. But again we are faced with the problem of a universally agreed-upon measure of social good. Oren Gross has pointed out that people who engage in such calculations have been accused of a bias toward immediate results while discounting long-term consequences (ibid., 230). Another utilitarian approach to the evaluation of torture holds that its costs should be assumed to outweigh its benefits "unless the magnitude of the threat to society . . . . is of a particularly large scale" (ibid., 231).

A purist version of the deontological position, one that Kant himself might have taken, would place an absolute prohibition on torture because it is incompatible with the Categorical Imperative. This position would be taken by a person who is willing to abstain from extraordinary methods of interrogation even in the case of questioning someone who knows where a bomb is hidden, which at an appointed hour will blow ten thousand innocent people to smithereens. *Fiat Justitia pereat mundus!* However, it should be recognized that an absolute ban on torture has important symbolic value. As Oren Gross has pointed out, this ban upholds the idea of "human dignity and the inviolability of the human body." It has, therefore, an important educational value. Easy acceptance of the legitimacy of torture eats away our humanity and degrades the moral character of a society (ibid., 234, 235).

An important derivative of the deontological view, but one which accepts the necessity of torture in particular cases, has been stated by the well-known Harvard professor, Michael Walzer. It is appropriately thought of as a tragic position, since it holds that torture can never be moral but that it may sometimes be necessary for the common good. In developing his theory, Walzer several times invokes the name of Machiavelli, who taught that a ruler must learn how "not to be good" in order adequately to serve the legitimate needs of his or her society. While doing evil did not disturb Machiavelli, it will disturb a good person who believes that torture is absolutely wrong—but, nevertheless, grants that it may sometimes be required. This is a true moral dilemma, which is commonly referred to as the problem of "dirty hands."

Walzer actually frames the problem of "dirty hands" as a conflict between deontological and utilitarian ethics. "A particular act of government," he writes, "may be exactly the right thing to do in utilitarian terms and yet leave the man who does it guilty of a moral wrong. . . . The notion of dirty hands derives from an effort to refuse 'absolutism' without denying the reality of the moral dilemma" (Walzer in Levinson 2004, 62). Walzer believes that the dirty hands problem extends beyond the torture dilemma to embrace political activity in general. He writes, "No one succeeds in politics without getting his hands dirty. This is conventional wisdom . . . . sometimes it is right to try to succeed, and then it must be wrong to get one's hands dirty. But one's hands get dirty from doing what it is wrong to do. And how can it be wrong to do what is right? Or, how can we get our hands dirty by doing what we ought to do?" (ibid., 63).

I have called Walzer's position essentially deontological, since he believes that fundamental moral principles are general and absolute rules that admit no exceptions. But there is another school of ethics that denies this—casuistry, or in the language we have adopted in this book, prudent pragmatism. Walzer simply refuses to recognize this approach, which he calls "an attractive description of moral decision-making, but . . . also a very improbable one" (ibid., 66). A casuist view of torture is presented, however, in the same collection of essays that contains Walzer's essay. It is by Jean Bethke Elshtain, a professor of social ethics at the University of Chicago, who was brought up in the tradition of Catholic ethical reasoning.

Elshtain notes the salience of 9/11 for her thinking on torture. Before the attack on the World Trade Center, she had placed torture "in the category of 'never.' " But with that event her attitude changed. She began to understand the question now from the standpoint of Christian responsibility for one's neighbor rather than as a question of ethical rules. In her view it is a choice between "rule mania . . . . and the route of concrete responsibility" (Elshtain in Levinson 2004, 83). To whom would her first responsibility be owed in a hypothethical case—to "school-children who cannot defend themselves or [to] a prisoner who cannot defend himself either?" (ibid., 79) In light of the circumstances—especially insofar as the prisoner in question belongs to a group that does not itself hesitate to practice torture and to engage in barbaric bombings and beheadings of noncombatants—and "aware of the stakes and the possible deaths of hundreds of children," she opts for torture (ibid., 83). She also notes that the word *torture* covers a very broad range of actions—every thing from coercive pressure to maiming and the severance of body parts—although the Geneva Convention simply forbids the practice of torture without defining it. She implies that in many cases what is really at stake is a question of coercion rather than torture in its extreme forms—what has been termed *torture lite*. "Far greater moral guilt falls on a person in authority who permits the deaths of hundreds of innocents rather than choosing to 'torture' one guilty or complicit person." (ibid., 87).

In Chapter 3 of this book, we observed that in expounding his theory of moral descriptions, a version of casuistry, Julius Kovesi argues that words carry notions of good and evil in their very names. Thus *murder* is always evil, though not all killing is murder. Similarly, *torture*, as a name, means an intrinsically evil act. In a like vein, Elshtain argues that for an interrogation that involves harsh treatment but not extreme maiming acts, "we surely need a different name, like coercive interrogation" (ibid., 87). She is not willing ever to excuse extreme violence to prisoners.

In her concluding statement Elshtain departs from the casuist tradition to adopt an aspect of Walzer's dirty hands theory. The person who engages in coercive interrogation does not receive legal or moral immunity for his or her actions. "The norm remains; it may have to be broken; the one who broke it for a strong reason must nevertheless make amends in some way . . . . the interrogator must . . . be prepared to defend what he or she has done and, depending on context, to pay a penalty" (ibid.).

The Problem of Accountability: Moral and Legal Responsibility

The issues that we have discussed thus far in this book have all concerned policy choices. In the case of torture, there are also questions of individual and institutional responsibility and accountability to be considered. As we have seen, both international law in specific covenants, such as the Geneva Convention, and the domestic law of numerous states explicitly condemn the practice of torture of prisoners of war. Yet the practice continues to be widespread as a tacit policy of state, especially in the period since 9/11. Alan Dershowtiz, a noted legal scholar and a civil libertarian who is especially well-known for his defense of individual rights, has written that "nonlethal torture is currently being used by the United States in an effort to secure information deemed necessary to prevent acts of terrorism. It is being done below the radar screen, without political accountability, and indeed with plausible deniability." This also "encourages hypocritical posturing" (Dershowitz in Levinson 2004, 257).

Dershowitz cites at length the experience of Israel in its attempts to resolve the accountability problem. Traveling to Israel in the late 1980s, he found there "a pervasive *system* of coercive interrogation" produced by the threat to Israeli security posed by intermittent Palestinian *intifadas*, or insurgencies. Recognizing the danger to the maintenance of the rule of law in the Israeli state when agents of that state were continually operating outside the law, the government established the Landau Commission to investigate the situation and to recommend a solution. The procedure recommended by the commission, which was subsequently enacted, was to incorporate existing practice into the law. The Israeli "law of necessity" provides that "a person may be exempted from criminal responsibility for any act or omission if he can show that it was done or made in order to avoid consequences which could not otherwise be avoided. . . . Provided that he did no more than was reasonably necessary for that purpose and that the harm caused by him was not disproportionate to the harm avoided" (cited in ibid., 260–61).

The law was an effort to provide a legal rule for state-of-nature behavior within a legal system, which may be a logical impossibility. The classic theorist of the "state of nature," Thomas Hobbes, defines that condition as one in which no law operates and in which every person attempts to protect him- or herself by any and all means at his or her disposal. In the words of the commission, the recommended law provided "full exemption from criminal responsibility" (ibid., 261). But the law did not work, and in 1999 the Israeli Supreme Court specifically outlawed even the nonlethal techniques typically employed today by democratic states in combating terrorism. It did, however, leave one loophole for the interrogators. A member of the security services who honestly believed that he had to employ torture as the only means available to save lives in imminent danger could invoke the defense of necessity if accused in a court of law.

Dershowitz found this solution problematical because it "leaves each individual member of the security services in the position of having to guess how a court would ultimately resolve his case" (ibid., 263). His own remedy for the problem of accountability is the idea of a judicial warrant issued by a judge to the interrogator—a "torture warrant." Dershowitz believes this warrant will significantly reduce the incidence of torture and will at the same time create public accountability for its use. He sees it "not as a compromise with civil liberties but rather as an effort to maximize civil liberties in the face of a realistic likelihood that torture would, in fact, take place below the radar screen of accountability" (ibid., 259). He suggested this expedient to the Israeli government at the time the Landau Commission was doing its research, but it was rejected. The government apparently thought it inappropriate for judges of the law to give permission to break the law before the fact. Ethicists have also reacted negatively to Dershowitz's proposal. Jean Elshtain, for example, calls it "a stunningly bad idea" (Elshtain, op. cit., 83). It is repugnant to her to give the color of law to an act of necessity or to place it in the category of the routine.

Oren Gross, a legal scholar, agrees with Elshtain's view of this matter and opts instead for "*official disobedience* in circumstances amounting to a catastrophic case" (op cit., 240). In his view, going completely beyond the law preserves the rule of law better than "bending the law to accommodate for catastrophe" (ibid.). Implicitly, therefore, he would also reject the Dershowitz notion of torture warrants. "Recognizing the possibility of ex post ratification is not the same as authorizing the use of preventive interrogational torture ex ante" (ibid., 247). Richard A. Posner, another noted legal scholar also accepts this position. "Better to leave in place the customary legal prohibitions," he writes, "but with the understanding that of couse they will not be enforced in extreme circumstances" (Posner in Levinson 2004, 296). Whether this leaves hanging the question of accountability with which Dershowitz is centrally concerned, however, remains unresolved.

Dennis Thompson, a political theorist at Harvard University, some years ago published an insightful treatise on the problem of accountability, or responsibility, in a hierarchical system (Thompson 1980). It does not focus on the question of unauthorized torture in military investigations; but it is intended as a general analysis of moral responsibility in organizations. The author's point of departure in the essay is to observe that it is often difficult, when studying political decision making, to identify who is morally responsible for policy outcomes, which he dubs the "problem of many hands." He then goes on to criticize the two commonest methods of ascribing responsibility—the hierarchical and the collective models.

Both are inadequate. The hierarchical model fails because it refers responsibility to the top, but in doing so, it violates the basic principle of moral responsibility—that one should be blamed only if he or she could have acted differently. It would be unfair to hold top officials responsible for events they could not possibly have controlled completely; subordinates in practice always enjoy some discretion. But more especially this model produces no actual responsibility. When the person at the top "assumes full responsibility" for something that goes wrong, no one is punished. The act becomes a mere ritual, and it has no negative effect on the leader. More often than not, it actually strengthens the hand of the so-called courageous person that accepts the "buck." Also, Thompson writes, "the ritual often quells public debate about a controversial decision or policy and blocks effective inquiry into the actual moral responsibility of those involved" (ibid., 907).

The great problem of the collective model of responsibility is that assigning responsibility to the collectivity for things that go wrong results in exculpating all the individuals involved. No one is blamed. The group structure is made responsible, but the structure is not a moral person. This method of attributing responsibility may lead to ferreting out organizational defects that need correction. But it does not help when trying to assign moral responsibility for evil actions.

Thompson concludes that only personal responsibility can serve as an adequate model to ensure that a system of democratic accountability is maintained. Only this model "can accommodate many of the complexities of a political process in which many different officials contribute to policies and decisions" (ibid., 908). In this model, an individual is morally responsible for an event if his or her actions are a cause of an outcome and also if the culpable actions are not done out of ignorance or under compulsion. *Cause* here is not to be interpreted as the sole cause or the most important cause. A number of individuals may contribute to the cause of a blameworthy action. The volitional criterion simply requires that a person was free to have done otherwise.

Thompson then goes on to refine the model by discussing the excuses an individual may appropriately adduce to exculpate him- or herself when accused. One is the excuse from alternative cause—if the accused did not do it, someone else would have. Thompson finds this sometimes acceptable in the following form: "If I had not done it, someone worse would have, with much worse results." He cites the example of an SS officer in World War II, who pleaded that he stayed in his post to prevent even worse things from happening. There is also the excuse "from null cause," in which an official states that it was not his or her job to intervene to prevent something from happening. "One cannot be culpable for all the policies on which one could have had an influence." This, Thompson believes, may be an excuse that at least reduces an individual's culpability. But the closer one is to the evil result, the less this is so. In this regard the author comments on the claim that advisers are not responsible for evil flowing from advice they give, since it can be rejected. Thompson disagrees. He states, "If an official adopts a proposal mostly because he trusts the adviser personally . . . . we might want to say that the adviser should accept equal responsibility for the decision, or in some cases even more responsibility than the official who makes the decision" (ibid., 912). We shall have occasion to refer to this excuse in our later analysis of the case study of the incidents at Abu Ghraib prison.

Thompson also comments on volitional excuses. In a hierarchical system, must one always intend a result in order to be held responsible for it? Certainly not in the case of common patterns of fault; a competent official will know what to anticipate and will take preventive action.

Also, "when a superior puts great pressure on subordinates to produce results and gives the impression that questionable practices to achieve those results will be condoned . . . . then the blame falls at least equally on the superior. Ignorance ceases even to mitigate responsibility" (ibid., 913). Similarly, when there is a tacit understanding about what needs to be done to achieve a given result, "the superior can no more escape responsibility for the subordinates' actions than they can" (ibid.).

Thompson concludes by remarking that excuses mitigate responsibility not only on the basis of general principles of causality and volition, but also because of a variety of surrounding circumstances. He has, therefore, not attempted to present any general theory of responsibility, but rather a "casuistic analysis of a range of exemplary cases." In the following case study we shall also confine ourselves to a casuistic method in commenting on the scandalous incidents that took place in Abu Ghraib prison during 2003.

INTERROGATIONS IN ABU GHRAIB PRISON: A CASE STUDY

In the fall of 2003 Coalition Forces experienced a sudden spike in insurgent activity in Iraq—the so-called Ramadan Offensive. Especially worrisome was an increase in suicide bombings. In the city of Falluja, the headquarters of the International Red Cross together with four police stations were destroyed in less than one hour by suicide bombers. There was also a doubling of daily attacks by insurgents against coalition troops (Danner 2004, 1).

The response of the coalition to this activity was a program of massive arrests in the areas of insurgency, a program that used a "cordon and capture" method. Areas in which it was suspected that insurgents were hiding were blanketed with troops and cordoned off. Houses were then searched roughly and thoroughly. The arresting troops often descended on the suspect area after dark, breaking down doors, waking the residents up with shouting and yelling, and herding family members into a single room while the rest of the building was searched. Suspects had their hands tied behind them with flexi-cuffs, were hooded, and were led away. Little attempt was made to segregate the most likely offenders from others. At times all adult males were arrested, including the sick, infirm, and aged. They were roughed up, punched, kicked, struck with rifles, and insulted. The arresting troops usually failed to identify themselves and to explain why the arrests were being made. Rarely were arrestees or their families told where they were being taken or for how long they would be held. They simply disappeared (International Red Cross Report, cited in ibid., 2).

The International Red Cross also reported that it was told by coalition intelligence officers that between 70 and 90 percent of these arrests were by mistake (ibid.). The Fay/Jones Report (2004) later observed that between 85 and 90 percent of the detainees were of no intelligence value (31).

The manner of treatment of Iraqi war prisoners came to public attention because of reports of extraordinary abuse of the detainees at Abu Ghraib prison, the Baghdad Central Confinement Facility. In January 2004, Specialist Joseph M. Darby handed over to the Army's Criminal Investigation Command a number of CDs that contained several hundred images of prisoner abuse. On the last day of the month, an investigation of the 800th Military Policy [MP] Brigade was begun under the direction of Major General Antonio M. Taguba, who submitted his findings to his superiors in March. Seymour M. Hersh reported on the investigation in an article in *The New Yorker* on May 1, and the photographs were released to the public at about the same time (cited in 2004, 277).

Detainees were hooded in order to disorient them and to prevent them from breathing freely. The *Taguba Report* (2004) listed the abuses of the Iraqi detainees with which the military police were charged. They included punching, slapping, kicking, and jumping on their naked feet. The police had also arranged prisoners in sexually explicit positions to be photographed, and guards had forced some of the men to masturbate while being photographed and videotaped, with female members of the police looking on and gesturing at them. The guards had arranged male detainees in a pile and jumped on them. The police had forced male prisoners to wear women's underwear. In several cases detainees were stripped of their clothes and kept naked for a number of days at a time. Military working dogs, unmuzzled, were used to intimidate detainees; in one case a dog had bitten and severely injured a prisoner. These and similar abuses were documented with photographs, written confessions, statements by the detainees, and statements by witnesses.

The general's report went on to list several other acts described by the detainees, which he found credible because of the clarity of the prisoners' statements and because witnesses had supplied supporting evidence. These acts included breaking chemical lights and pouring the phosphorescent liquid on the prisoners, pouring cold water on naked prisoners, beating them with a broom handle and a chair, sodomizing a detainee with a chemical light, and threatening male detainees with rape (*Taguba Report*, 292, 293). In addition to pressure caused by pain, fatigue, and psychic stress, the practices were designed to be especially humiliating to Muslim male prisoners.

Several of the enlisted men and women among the military police involved in the activities described here have since been indicted on criminal charges, and at the time of this writing three of them have been convicted and sentenced. In their defense the accused claimed that they had been told by military intelligence personnel that it was their job to soften up the prisoners so that they would talk. In his report General Taguba found that "interrogators actively requested that MP guards set physical and mental conditions for favorable interrogation of witnesses" (ibid., 294). In explaining an incident in which a detainee was stood on a box and in which wires were attached to his toes, fingers, and penis, SPC Sabrina Harman testified that it was her job to keep prisoners awake. According to General Taguba's report she said, "MI wanted to get them to talk. It is Grainer [sic] and Frederick's job to do things for MI and OGA to get these people to talk." Another police officer testified that Graner said he had been asked to do things by "Agents and MI [Military Intelligence] soldiers" but that he complained that "nothing was ever in writing." Sergeant Jarval Davis is quoted in the report as claiming that MI had said to Graner and Frederick, "Loosen this guy up for us . . . Make sure he has a bad night . . . Make sure he gets the treatment." Davis also claimed that Graner received compliments on his work from military intelligence personnel, with statements like "Good job, they're breaking down real fast. They answer every question. They're giving out good information. . . . Keep up the good work" (ibid., 294, 295).

Sergeant Davis told Taguba's investigators that he had "witnessed prisoners in the MI hold section . . . . being made to do various things that [he] would question morally." But when asked why he did not report these things to superiors, he replied that he assumed "that if they were doing things out of the ordinary or outside the guidelines, someone would have said something" (ibid., 294). This was not universally believed among the military police on duty, however. Specialist Joseph Darby, who turned over the incriminating photographs to the Army's Criminal Investigation Command, was a military policeman there. Master-at-Arms First Class William J. Kimbro, a Navy dog handler, was commended in General Taguba's report for refusing "to participate in improper interrogations despite significant pressure from the MI personnel at Abu Ghraib"(ibid., 325).

The abuses at Abu Ghraib were made the subject of four separate investigations. One was conducted by the International Red Cross, which confined itself to a description of the arrest and treatment of the prisoners. A second was set up under the direction of Major General Antonio Taguba to examine the conduct of the 800th Military Police Brigade, at the instance of Lieutenant General Ricardo S. Sanchez, Commander of Combined Joint Task Force Seven. A third was appointed to investigate the conduct of the military intelligence units involved in the Abu Ghraib interrogations. This was headed up by Major General George R. Fay, who was succeeded by Lieutenant General Anthony R. Jones. Last, an independent panel under the direction of James R. Schlesinger was created by Secretary of Defense Donald Rumsfeld to review the conduct and findings of the two army investigations.

Our description above of the abuses at Abu Ghraib was drawn from the Red Cross and Taguba reports. The Taguba and Fay/Jones reports explain the occurrence of the abuses only in part as the work of a few sadistic soldiers. They also report, as major causes, weak leadership, poor command relationships, unclear and contradictory interrogation policies, inadequate doctrine and procedures governing interrogations, lack of training, insufficient personnel, inadequate equipment, and overcrowded and inadequate internment facilities. Responsibility was widely diffused and fell on many shoulders, from the bottom to the top of the military hierarchy. In Thompson's language, it was a classic failure of "many hands."

The *Toguba Report* states flatly that the 800th MP Brigade was not adequately trained for its mission of operating a penal institution at the Abu Ghraib complex. "Soldiers were poorly prepared and untrained to conduct I/R operations prior to deployment, at the mobilization site, upon arrival in theater, and throughout their mission." The *Schlesinger Report* (2004) concurs (in Danner, op. cit., 286, 300, 312, 357). Heavy reliance was placed on people who had worked as corrections officers in civilian life. Sergeant Graner was one of these people. In addition, "there was no clear delineation of responsibility between commands, little coordination at the command level, and no integration of the two functions. Coordination occurred at the lowest possible levels with little oversight by commanders" (ibid., 313). The MP units that performed guard duty were also understrength (ibid., 287). In the *Taguba Report* we also read that "[t]here is a general lack of knowledge, implementation, and emphasis of basic legal, regulatory, doctrinal, and command requirements within the 800th MP Brigade"(ibid., 298). "Doctrine is lacking to address the screening and interrogation of large numbers of detainees whose status (combatants, criminals, or innocents) is not easily ascertainable" (ibid., 368). "The lack of relevant doctrine meant the design and operation of division, battalion, and company collection points were improvised on an ad hoc basis" (ibid., 361). The *Schlesinger Report* adds that "commanding officers and their staffs at various levels failed in their duties and that such failures contributed directly or indirectly to detainee abuse" (351). "The unclear command structure at Abu Ghraib was further exacerbated by the confused command relationship up the chain" (ibid., 353). One commander is quoted in the *Schlesinger Report* as saying that "[a]nything that could go wrong went wrong" (ibid., 358).

The *Fay/Jones Report* summarizes the multiple failures as follows: "The primary causes are misconduct (ranging from inhumane to sadistic) by a small group of morally corrupt soldiers and civilians, a lack of discipline on the part of the leaders and soldiers. . . . and a failure or lack of leadership by multiple echelons within CJTF-7. Contributing factors can be traced to issues affecting Command and Control, Doctrine, Training, and the experience of the Soldiers we asked to perform this vital mission" (ibid., 405).

Brigadier General Janis Karpinski, Commander of the MP Brigade, was disciplined by removal from her command and by the issuance of a reprimand. Somewhat later, she was also demoted to the rank of colonel, which to all practical purposes put an end to her military career. Subordinate officers within her chain of command were similarly disciplined for their weak and incompetent leadership.

The *Fay/Jones Report*, which focused on failures within the 205th Military Intelligence Brigade, does not cite culpable individuals within the military intelligence group, as does the *Taguba Report* on the MP unit. Nor have any military intelligence officers or private contractors working for MI been indicted for criminal behavior as of this writing. The *Fay/Jones Report* does observe, however, that "twenty-seven 205 MI BDE Personnel allegedly requested, encouraged, condoned or solicited Military Police (MP) personnel to abuse detainees and/or participated in detainee abuse" (406). And like the *Taguba Report*, the *Fay/Jones Report* points to a number of procedural and systemic failures within the 205 MI BDE: "failure to effectively screen, certify, and then integrate contractor interrogators/analysts/linguists; lack of a clear understanding of MP and MI roles and responsibilities . . . ; Dysfunctional command relationships" (ibid., 414). In one place the report announces very broadly that "the intelligence structure was undermanned, under-equipped, and inappropriately organized for counterinsurgency operations," but the report goes on to say that some reforms were made under the leadership of MG Barbara Fast (ibid., 418).

A central theme of the *Fay/Jones Report* is that no governmental or military policy was responsible for the violent abuses. It states, "No policy, directive or doctrine directly or indirectly caused violent or sexual abuse . . . . Soldiers knew they were violating the approved techniques and procedures" (ibid., 406). In several places, however, the report speaks of nonviolent and nonsexual abuses caused by a misinterpretation of policy and of confusion among the police and interrogators about what techniques were condoned. The acts in question included removal of clothing, sleep deprivation, isolation, and the use of dogs. One source of the confusion was "policy memoranda promulgated by the CJTF-7 Commander," General Sanchez. Other sources were "the proliferation of guidance and information from other theaters of operation [Afghanistan, Guantanamo Bay]; individual interrogator experience in other theaters; and, the failure to distinguish between interrogation operations in other theaters and Iraq" (ibid., 413). The *Schlesinger Report* notes that "[p]olicies approved for use on al-Qaeda and Taliban detainees, who were not afforded the protection of the Geneva Conventions, now applied to detainees who did fall under the Geneva Convention protections." It concludes, "This clearly led to confusion on what practices were acceptable" (ibid., 337).

Another factor in the situation at Abu Ghraib was pressure on the interrogators from persons at various points in the chain of command. The *Schlesinger Report* observes that "[w]ith lives at stake, senior leaders expressed, forcibly at times, their need for better intelligence" (ibid., 365). High-level officials visited the Abu Ghraib site to underline this need in August/September 2003. These visitors included the Commander of CJTF-7 and his chief intelligence officer. The latter expressly recommended the use of dogs in policing detainees, although the report denies that he ever recommended their use in interrogations. Nor were dogs used in interrogations by

MI; rather MPs employed them in "setting the conditions" for interrogation. In November 2003 Abu Ghraib received a visit from a senior member of the National Security Council (NSC), which led to speculation that even the White House was interested in intelligence from that facility. The *Schlesinger Report* includes a recommendation that the meaning of guidance terms such as *setting the conditions* needed to be defined with precision (ibid., 379).

The *Schlesinger Report* contains a brief Appendix H, entitled "Ethical Issues." This section states that countries with value systems like ours find detention and interrogation practices ethically challenging, since they involve deceit, seduction, incitement, and coercion in ways normally not acceptable in our society. Military necessity produces "moral uncertainty" so that it is especially important for American troops to have strong ethical foundations in order to face this situation adequately. The next paragraph presents a rationale for coercive action in interrogations based on the liberal democratic principle of consent as the basis of moral obligation. Insurgents and terrorists, analogously to criminals, by disrespecting others' rights, have consented in advance to capture, detention, interrogation, and even death (ibid., 400). Implied consent thus justifies what the interrogators have to do.

The report goes on to give the "ticking bomb" story as a model for an approach to the dilemma. The interrogator in such a situation would recognize that violating moral norms was "understandable but not necessarily correct." He would then have to "offer his actions up for review and judgment by a competent authority" (ibid., 401). This is a dirty hands approach that is very similar to the one propounded and recommended by Michael Walzer. In opting for such a solution to his problem, a prospective interrogator would use a "minimum harm" rule of thumb to guide his or her decision making. But the tension between our national values and military necessity cannot be removed. The appendix ends with a recommendation that there be more adequate professional ethics education for the military.

Ethical Analysis of the Case

The Abu Ghraib case poses two kinds of problems. First is the assessment of responsibility. Second, is the policy question. What kind of national policy is ethical for a liberal democracy to adopt in a time when it is pursued by a ruthless enemy who is willing to suspend all rules of humane and civilized action?

How adequate for evaluating what happened in this case are the models of hierarchical or collective responsibility? Unlike the Bay of Pigs fiasco, for which President Kennedy took responsibility, or the Watergate scandal, for which Mr. Nixon took responsibility and paid the price, no one in the top leadership of the country has suggested that the president be the scapegoat for the scandals at Abu Ghraib. Perhaps this was because there was no avowed national policy for the torture of detainees, even though Attorney

General Gonzales wrote a memo to him justifying torture in some instances. There were also a number of treaty commitments that required U.S. soldiers to avoid the kind of thing that went on at the prison. President Bush insisted that the entire blame belonged to the "few bad apples" at the bottom of the barrel—the enlisted men and women among the military police who participated in the well-documented abuse.

At this writing three of the police guards at Abu Ghraib have been tried, convicted, and sentenced for their roles. Staff Sergeant Ivan Fredericks in October 2004 pleaded guilty to conspiracy, dereliction of duty, maltreatment of detainees, assault, and committing an indecent act. He was sentenced to eight years in prison, reduced to the rank of private, ordered to forfeit his pay, and dishonorably discharged. In January 2005 Army Specialist Charles Graner was given a term of ten years in prison, reduced in rank and dishonorably discharged. In May, SPC Sabrina Harman received a prison term of six months. Fredericks' attorney called his sentence excessive. He thought it should have been mitigated because the soldier had not been trained. Would you agree? Was this a valid excuse to offer in this case? Similarly, Graner's plea was ignored; the court rejected the claim that he had been urged to abuse the prisoners by intelligence personnel and praised by them as well for helping to "break" the detainees involved. Were these excuses that should have in whole or in part exculpated him? Should action also be taken against the MI personnel who urged the MPs to "soften up" the detainees?

Brigadier General Karpinski was removed from her command and issued a reprimand for her failure to correct a whole string of organizational faults in her command. She was later demoted to the rank of colonel. In April 2005, four top officers, including Lt. General Ricardo Sanchez, senior commander in Iraq at the time of the scandal, were cleared of all wrongdoing, despite the fact that they were responsible for detention and interrogation policy. Should they not have been punished for their failure to prevent the torture incidents? Janice Karpinski claims that the severe punishment meted out to her made her a scapegoat in a matter for which other higher-ups should have been punished. Do you agree? Should civilian actors in the drama, such as Secretary of Defense Donald Rumsfeld, also have been penalized? The story of Abu Ghraib shows that the military was entirely unprepared for the insurgency that followed an early victory in the field, and it had mounted an entirely inadequate system of intelligence. Who should be held responsible for these things, and what kind of punishment should be meted out to those who are found guilty?

The journalist Seymour Hersh, in commenting on the *Taguba Report*, tells us that it "amounts to an unsparing study of collective wrongdoing and the failure of Army leadership at the highest levels" (ibid., 8). But how do we effectively assess and punish collective wrongdoing? Is there a way to convert this judgment into an effective series of judgments against individuals?

Now consider the matter of policy. Appendix H of the *Schlesinger Report*, which we discussed in part earlier, seems to suggest that the United

States does not have and should not have a policy permitting torture under certain circumstances. Its author would not think well of Professor Dershowitz's suggestion about warrants to torture. In keeping with the Walzer dirty hands concept, it places full responsibility on the interrogating officer to decide when to act coercively and to accept blame from higher authority under review. In effect, it would substitute ethics training for military intelligence personnel rather than a torture policy. How do you evaluate this idea? Should we keep coercive action, one involving the breaking or suspension of basic rules of humane and moral treatment of individuals, in the category of extraordinary action to be judged only post hoc under the category of national necessity? Should such actions always and everywhere be considered beyond the moral pale?

There is possibly a dangerous reverse side to the policy of having no official policy on the torture of detainees—that is, that the military will develop one covertly as an operational matter that is never published. Arthur McCoy, professor of history at the University of Wisconsin-Madison, claims that during the 1950s and 1960s the CIA conducted secret research on coercion and human consciousness, with a budget of about $1 billion a year. The research, according to McCoy, explored practices from electrical shock to the administration of LSD to unsuspecting subjects and to sensory deprivation. According to a report on McCoy's work in *The National Catholic Reporter*, "[t]he basic techniques—the use of stress positions, sensory deprivation and sexual humiliation—are aimed at making victims feel responsible for their own pain and suffering" (Hodge and Cooper 2004, 12). McCoy told the NCR reporters that the results of the CIA experimentation were codified in 1963 in a secret manual that provided a model for interrogations carried out by American-trained counterintelligence teams in Honduras and Nicaragua. They also provided material for manuals employed by the U.S. Army's School of the Americas, which trains Latin American forces in counterinsurgency techniques. There is evidence in the Fay/Jones and Schlesinger reports that CIA trainers had some influence on the interrogation pratices at Abu Ghraib. The authors of the article write that "[a]n examination of CIA interrogation manuals shows that they date back before the Vietnam War, supporting charges by human rights advocates that Abu Ghraib is no aberration. What is new is that photographic evidence became public" (ibid.).

The policy implied by Appendix H would probably fit most easily into the category of deontological reasoning: a "tragic" deontology. A utilitarian, whose sole moral rule is to maximize the social good, would likely disagree with this approach. But what kind of measure should he or she employ? In a utilitarian calculation, a comparison would have to be made of the comparative benefits and risks involved in an announced acceptance of a torture policy—namely, the benefits of information extorted versus the risks of imperiling one's own troops in a war of insurgency. Is torture effective . . . will people say anything to avoid pain? There would also have to be a comparison made between the risks of a frank torture policy abroad feeding back into callousness at home, the neglect of citizens' rights, and the benefits of the policy in gains in the field. In addition, would a torture policy put Americans at risk?

A casuist or prudent pragmatist would want to avoid calling coercive action against detainees by the name of *torture*, which connotes something evil in itself. Would an ethicist working in this tradition press for a definitional refinement in the matter of torture? What sort of concepts would be potentially useful from this point of view? Would it be better to have no overall policy—and leave judgment to the individual interrogator—or to have a narrow definition of acceptable coercion and a clear statement of the kinds of behavior that would be tolerated under no circumstances?

REFERENCES

Bacevich, Andrew J. *American Empire.* Cambridge, MA: Harvard University Press, 2002.

———. *The New American Militarism.* New York: Oxford University Press, 2005.

Clark, Ian. *Waging War,* 2nd ed. Oxford, England: Clarendon Press, 1990.

Danner, Mark. *Torture and Truth: America, Abu Ghraib, and the War on Terror.* New York: New York Review of Books, 2004.

Dershowitz, Alan. "Tortured Reasoning." In *Torture: A Collection,* ed. Sanford Levinson, 257–80. New York: Oxford University Press, 2004.

Elshtain, Jean B. "Reflection on the Problem of 'Dirty Hands,' " In *Torture: A Collection,* ed. Sanford Levinson, 77–92. New York: Oxford University Press, 2004.

Fay/Jones Report. AR 15-6. "Investigation of the Abu Ghraib Prison and 205th Military Intelligence Brigade," In Mark Danner, *Torture and Truth: America, Abu Ghraib, and the War on Terror,* 403–579. New York: NY Review of Books, 2004.

Ferguson, Niall. "A World without Power." *Foreign Policy* (July/August 2004): 32–39.

Flory, William E.E. *Prisoners of War: A Study in the Development of International Law.* Washington, DC: American Council on Public Affairs, 1942.

Fujita, Itisakazu. "POWs and International Law." In *Japanese Prisoners of War,* ed. P. Towle et al., 87–102. New York: Hambledon and Condon, 2000.

Gaddis, John Lewis. "Grand Strategy in the Second Term." *Foreign Affairs* (January/February 2005), 2–15.

Galston, William. "Perils of Preemptive War." *The American Prospect* (September 23, 2002), at http://www.Prospect.org/print/V13/17/galston_w.html (accessed 4/28/2005).

Gansberg, Judith M. *Stalag: USA: The Remarkable Story of German POWs in America.* New York: Crowell, 1977.

Gross, Oren. "The Prohibition on Torture and the Limits of Law." In *Torture: A Collection,* ed. Sanford Levinson, 229–56. New York: Oxford University Press, 2004.

Grotius, Hugo. *On the Laws of War and Peace.* Trans. William Whewell. Cambridge, England: Cambridge University Press, 1853.

Halberstam, David. *War in a Time of Peace.* New York: Scribner, 2001.

Hersh, Seymour M. "Torture at Abu Ghraib." *New Yorker: Annals of National Security* (2004), at www.newyorker.com/fact/contact/?040510fa_fact (accessed 01/04/2005).

Hodge, James, and Linda Cooper. "Roots of Abu Ghraib in CIA Techniques." *National Catholic Reporter* (November 5, 2004), 11–14.

Huntington, Samuel P. *The Clash of Civilizations and the Remaking of the World Order.* New York: Simon & Schuster, 1996.

Kennan, George F. "The Sources of Soviet Conduct." *Foreign Affairs* (July 1947): 566–82.

Largio, Devan. "21 Rationales of War." *Foreign Policy* (September/October 2004): 18.

Leckie, Robert. *Wars of America.* New York: Harper-Collins, 1981.

Levinson, Sanford. "Contemplating Torture: An Introduction." In *Torture: A Collection,* ed. Sanford Levinson, 23–46. New York: Oxford University Press, 2004.

Mearsheimer, John J. *The Tragedy of Great Power Politics.* New York: W.W. Norton, 2003.

Mueller, John. *The Remnants of War.* Ithaca, NY: Cornell University Press, 2004.

Murdoch, Stephen. "Preemptive War: Is it Legal?" *DC Bar* (January 2003), at http://www.dcbar.org/for lawyers/washington-lawyer/January 2003/war.cfm (accessed 4/28/2005).

Parry, John T. "Escalation and Necessity: Defining Torture at Home and Abroad." In *Torture: A Collection,* ed. Sanford Levinson, 145–64. New York: Oxford University Press, 2004.

Pilloud, Claude. "Protection of the Victims of Armed Conflicts: II. Prisoners of War." In UNESCO, *International Dimensions of Humanitarian Law*, 167–85. Boston and London: Martinus Nijhoff, Publishers, 1988.

Posner, Richard. "Torture, Terrorism, and Interrogation." In *Torture: A Collection,* ed. Sanford Levinson, 291–98. New York: Oxford University Press, 2004.

Project for a New American Century. "The Statement of Principles," at http://www.newamericancentury.org/statementofprinciples.htm (accessed 04/05/2006).

Red Cross Report, "Report of the International Committee of the Red Cross (ICRC) on the Treatment by the Coalition Forces of Prisoners of War and Other Protected Persons by the Geneva Conventions in Iraq During Arrest, Internment and Interrogation," In *Torture and Truth: America, Abu Ghraib, and the War on Terror*, ed. Mark Danner, 255–75. New York: New York Review of Books, 2004.

Riconda, Harry P. *Prisoners of War in American Conflicts.* Lanham, MD: Scarecrow Press, 2003.

Schlesinger Report. "Final Report of the Independent Panel to Review DOD Detention Operations." In *Torture and Truth: America, Abu Ghraib, and the War on Terror*, ed. Mark Danner, 329–402. New York: NY Review of Books, 2004.

Taguba Report. AR 15-6. "Investigation of the 800th Military Police Brigade." In Mark Danner, *Torture and Truth: America, Abu Ghraib, and the War on Terror*, 279–328. New York: NY Review of Books, 2004.

Thompson, Dennis F. "Moral Responsibility of Public Officials: The Problem of Many Hands." *The American Political Science Review* 74 (December 1980): 908–16.

Walzer, Michael. *Just and Unjust Wars.* New York: Basic Books, 1977.

———. "Political Action: The Problem of Dirty Hands." In *Torture: A Collection,* ed. Sanford Levinson, 61–76. New York: Oxford University Press, 2004.

———. *Arguing about War.* New Haven, CT: Yale University Press, 2004.

Welsh, Steven, S.C. "Preemptive War and International Law." *International Security Law Project* (December 5, 2003), at http://www.cdi.org/news/law/preemptive-war.cfm (accessed 4/28/05).

White House. "The President's Remarks at the United Nations General Assembly" (September 12, 2002), at http://www.whitehouse.gov/news/releases/2002/09/20020912.html (accessed 04/04/2006).

Woodward, Bob. *Plan of Attack*. New York: Simon & Schuster, 2004.

CHAPTER 12

Conclusion

We have canvassed a number of the ethical issues that confront American public policy today. This has been done from several different ethical standpoints—that of the utilitarian, the deontologist, and the prudent pragmatist. And we have attempted to show that, by and large, prudent pragmatism presents the most adequate framework of the three for reasoning about ethical dilemmas. In a sense, it embraces and incorporates the leading values of the other two schools, fusing them together into a different sort of instrument. It avoids abstract judgment and argues from facts to principles and values, rather than the other way round, thus situating problems in their actual context, rather than in an ideal world. We have also tried to show that ethical reasoning is not like mathematics. Its conclusions do not flow with logical necessity from clearly defined assumptions. These conclusions are nuanced, often tentative, and they are subject to revision in the light of new evidence. In addition to mental capacity, ethical reasoning requires virtue and experience on the part of its practitioners.

The ethical analysis we have presented with each case is in outline only to indicate the lines on which each kind of evaluation should proceed. We expect the reader to carry the analysis forward to completion. This might well be done in a class discussion of the cases. The prudent pragmatic analyses in particular can be enriched by the adducement of relevant circumstances and values that we have neglected to supply. The exercise in case analysis is designed to be Socratic. In no case should one expect it to constitute the final word on the matter. There is no single "correct" analysis.

We submit that the ethical problems we have not mentioned may also be best handled with a prudent pragmatist method—the rightness of the death penalty, the acceptability of human cloning, environmental problems of all kinds (from deforestation to global warming), social security reform, education policy, the role of international institutions in American foreign policy, and a host of other questions that are prominent on the national agenda.

In urging the superiority of prudent pragmatism to other methods of ethical analysis, we have stressed the importance of weighing principles in the light of circumstances in contrast to the slide-rule approach of utilitarianism and deontology. The latter schools encourage the analyst to judge on the basis of an ideological position, in an abstract manner, rather than on the basis of the particular merits of a case. Deontological methods usually subsume an egalitarian viewpoint, and they tend to give individual rights a privileged position in an argument, ignoring other values inherent in a case. Furthermore, they tend to accord to the chosen values an absolute status, which may not be compromised. Utilitarian analysis, by contrast, emphasizes efficiency and majoritarian concerns to the detriment of other values, leaving absolute norms out. Prudent pragmatism requires that the analyst, when approaching a policy dilemma, consider all the American values inherent in a situation, recognizing their often conflicting and damaging character, and stressing the need prudently to weigh and balance them against one another in the light of the special circumstances of the moment. One is forced out of a subjective approach to the subject and into a dispassionate regard for all the facts of the matter.

Thus, in coming to judgment about whether individual rights need to give place to general security in a time of terrorism, one must weigh in the balance national defense capabilities, the reliability of security forces, the reliability of the intelligence on hand, the political motives of the administration, the likelihood and character of terrorist strikes of various kinds, the extent of damage to national security already done, and many other factors before making a decision. One will not stand on abstract principle alone, ignoring the special character of the situation. True, different persons will come up with different judgments using this approach. For those who possess the virtues of prudence and objectivity, this approach will not mean using the analysis to rationalize one's own pet values. The detailed examination of the facts, the conscious weighing of all values, not only those that one prizes most highly, should, rather, force one's mind away from an ideological stance and into an effort at dispassionate judgment. Deontology and utilitarianism, by contrast, place the case in a procrustean bed, which too easily cuts the judgment to fit a preordained conclusion.

Prudent pragmatism also emphasizes the time-bound character of ethical analysis. What may be judged right today may well be bad policy tomorrow if significant circumstances of the national life have changed. Ethical judgment thus involves constant reevaluation, a constant updating of the facts and a continuing reappraisal of needs and capabilities. Policymaking is unavoidably a loop. For example, analysis of the new Medicare prescription drug program might conclude in its favor. But if we add to the description the extraordinary financial burden on the government caused by hurricanes Katrina and Rita, this new fact might tip the balance of judgment in the other direction. We must ask whether the strain on national solvency produced by the drug program is worth the value achieved by the program. Rebuilding New Orleans physically and helping the suffering people of that city to rebuild their lives are unavoidable expenditures. Does this new necessity move the prescription drug plan to a lower priority? As the calendar changes from day to day, new circumstances will have to be added to each of the case studies, additions that may or may not radically alter the ethical analyses of the cases.

The complexity of ethical choice also militates against the idea of producing an unproblematical judgment. A decision may always be challenged, especially when it can be shown that an important value or significant fact has been ignored. This is why prudent pragmatism can only be exercised in a political system whose citizens strive to embody in its processes continuing and widespread discussion and debate—that is, one that strives to embody the ideals of discursive democracy. As we tried to show in Chapter 5, the two are intimately interlinked.

At the present time there is a growing division in our political culture about the place of religion in public life, the reverse side of which is the question of freedom of lifestyle. Both on the conservative religious and liberal sides, there seems to be an increasing adamancy of opinion, which is not healthy for a pluralistic culture. Some liberals seem intent on removing any reference to a creator from public life—in the form of prayers at public events, such as football games between high school teams, or in symbolic displays such as Christmas crèches. On the conservative side there is a movement afoot to have intelligent design textbooks at least paired with, if not supplant Darwinian evolution texts in public schoolrooms.

We submit that if carried far enough, this growing cultural cleft could destroy the consensual political culture which makes a common ethical analysis of public policy questions a possibility. Pressed to the extreme, it could reduce ethical debate to political warfare of the most rancorous kind. We think that embracing the method of prudent pragmatism in these circumstances might mitigate this cultural cleavage by stressing in every issue the particulars of circumstance rather than general principles in policy decision. It should help sustain the consensus on which our liberal democratic practice depends.

We have taken as given the leading values of American political culture, values that are actually at work in our daily policy deliberations—in particular, liberty and equality in their many definitions and shades of public meaning. In view of this bold acceptance of what is given by the culture as the substance of good, we may well be open to the charge of provincialism. Do our analyses have meaning and relevance beyond the national borders if they are based only on national values? Doesn't the ethical signify that which is right as such, that which is good in itself, not biased by the assumptions of a particular culture?

In order to answer this question, we need to examine the values that are actually pursued in the world beyond our borders. Since ethical problems are resolved within institutional frameworks, perhaps it would be best to do this examination within an institutional setting. And there is one available for our frame of reference—the United Nations, of which the United States is a leading member. As grounding documents of this international order, we have available the U.N. Charter and also the Universal Declaration of Human Rights. In the latter, we have embodied, in large letters, the central values of our own Bill of Rights and Declaration of Independence—liberty and equality for individuals, and for the states of which they are citizens, together with mutual contracts of support and help. In making these observations, we come to the recognition that we talk the same moral language as the rest of the world and that the moral aspirations we share are universal.

To understand the reality of this view, we note that there is under construction a world public opinion within the world society that the United Nations incorporates. This is signaled by the initiation in 1999, under the leadership of Secretary General Kofi Annan, of a U.N. Global Compact that respects human rights, that favors legislation eliminating all kinds of forced or juvenile labor, and that attempts to deal with threats to the integrity of the environment worldwide. Testifying to the importance of economic organization in realizing moral values on a world scale is the fact that 700 corporations worldwide have pledged support for the Compact (Lefevere 2004).

A similar ethical reality is found in the world of formal religion. Meeting in Chicago in 1993, a Parliament of the World's Religions was presented with a draft of a Global Ethic, one prepared by the liberal Catholic theologian Hans Küng. Dr. Küng formulated the document after a comparative study of the Jewish Torah, the Islamic Qur'ān, the Hindu Bhagavad-Gita, and the Christian Sermon on the Mount, together with the sayings of Buddha and Confucius. He found that all these religions shared the idea of equality as a basic value and that they all revered the virtues of compassion, love, and honesty. In addition all the creeds believe in the humane treatment of all persons and in the Golden Rule. From these things can be derived, according to Küng, a series of principles and rules for ethical behavior:

> Not to murder, torture, torment or wound, but to commit
>   Oneself to a culture of nonviolence and reverence for life.
> Not to lie, deceive, forge, manipulate, but to speak truthfully, and
>   Act tolerantly;
> Not to steal, exploit, bribe or corrupt but to work toward a culture
>   Of fairness and a just economic order;
> Not to abuse sexuality [sic], cheat, humiliate or dishonor, but to
>   Commit to a culture of partnership and equal dignity for
>   Men and women. (ibid.)

In a time of economic globalization, there is an emerging world culture that more and more informs world society, one which is also incorporated in a world political order, albeit one that is still highly decentralized. It is also the case that the ethical substance of this world society and polity shares much in common with our own liberal democratic political culture. Our values under these circumstances turn out to be universal, not parochial. We do not need to change them or go beyond them, but to live them more fully.

One might respond to this analysis with a question—how can there be a world liberal democratic political culture developing with globalization when we find daily news about culture wars of extreme violence? At the time of this writing, there are daily car bombings and mass executions by insurgents in Iraq. In Afghanistan there are still outbreaks of violence by the Taliban, who angrily deny the equality of women with men and who wish to suppress modern secular learning in the name of supreme religious texts. These people wage Jihad, a holy war against not only Christians and Jews, but also against Muslims who embrace interpretations of Islam different from their own. How are these things compatible with the idea of a single universal moral culture?

There is evidence that the zealots who embrace the violent creeds we have mentioned do so out of an alienation and revanche that stem from their own suppression and degradation by the globalizing world. They are a product of disrespect and of political and economic subjection by the forces of modernization. (See Pape 2005.) Theirs is a culture of hostility and anger born of this experience. They do not represent the Muslim world as such, many of whose values are compatible with those of the liberal democratic culture of the globalizing world, but rather a distortion of Islamic culture. It is a great irony that they are best understood as a product of the modernizing world's failure to live up to its own core values. Only as the free world of the United Nations is able to encourage its adherents to a consistent allegiance to the values of liberal democratic culture, which will bring with it a spread of the material and psychological goods that are the rightful due of all persons and peoples, will the anger and frustrations that flow from repression disappear.

Bringing the globalizing world to a recognition of its duty to live up to its inherent norms of liberty, equality, respect, and good living for every person will not occur by itself. We believe that teaching prudent pragmatic reasoning to citizens, policy analysts, and decision makers will help to accomplish this goal as we confront the world's policy agenda. We also believe that the ability of people to learn this lesson is itself dependent on other learning processes—those we have described here as the procedures of deliberative democracy. The fostering of institutions that inculcate the norms and facilitate the practice of deliberation is vital for the future of liberal democracy. And as the world, as a communications network, grows more interdependent and as the division of labor becomes more and more complex, this goal becomes ever more difficult to accomplish—simply from the sheer magnitude of the work. We need not only more national deliberation days—but also international deliberation days as well. We also need more regard paid by decision makers to grass-roots opinion. It is too easy to look for shortcuts to success by centralizing authority and power in elite centers cut off from grass-roots influence. Particularly in the economic world, efficiency seems to demand more and more consolidation and centralization, a tendency that must be ever balanced with a counterpoint of decentralization. The hierarchy of command structures needs at every point to be matched by the stimulating autonomy of individual units. The free movement of the market must be combined with the free interchange of opinions about what it is best to do. What should be the public policy of an integrating world?

REFERENCES

Lefevere, Patricia, "Hopeful Realist Hans Küng Points Pathway to Global Ethics," *National Catholic Reporter*, September 3, 2004, 8, 9.

Pape, Robert A., *Dying to Win: The Strategic Logic of Suicide Terror*, NY: Random House, 2005.

INDEX